The Diversity Paradox

The Diversity Paradox

Immigration and the Color Line
in Twenty-First Century America

Jennifer Lee and Frank D. Bean

Russell Sage Foundation
New York

The Russell Sage Foundation

The Russell Sage Foundation, one of the oldest of America's general purpose foundations, was established in 1907 by Mrs. Margaret Olivia Sage for "the improvement of social and living conditions in the United States." The Foundation seeks to fulfill this mandate by fostering the development and dissemination of knowledge about the country's political, social, and economic problems. While the Foundation endeavors to assure the accuracy and objectivity of each book it publishes, the conclusions and interpretations in Russell Sage Foundation publications are those of the authors and not of the Foundation, its Trustees, or its staff. Publication by Russell Sage, therefore, does not imply Foundation endorsement.

Library of Congress Cataloging-in-Publication Data

Lee, Jennifer, 1968-
  The diversity paradox : immigration and the color line in 21st century America / Jennifer Lee and Frank D. Bean.
      p. cm.
  Includes bibliographical references and index.
  ISBN 978-0-87154-041-6 (alk. paper)
  1. United States—Emigration and immigration—Social aspects. 2. Immigrants—United States—History. 3. United States—Race relations. I. Bean, Frank D. II. Title.
  JV6475.L38 2010
  304.8'730089—dc22

                                                                      2010003237

The paper used in this publication meets the minimum requirements of American National Standard for Information Sciences—Permanence of Paper for Printed Library Materials. ANSI Z39.48-1992.

Text design by Genna Patacsil.

RUSSELL SAGE FOUNDATION
112 East 64th Street, New York, New York 10065
10 9 8 7 6 5 4 3 2 1

To Our Families—
Sangrin, Wonja, and Jeena Stephanie Lee
and
Frank D. Bean Sr., Alta Scott Bean, Carolyn P. Boyd, and
Alan, Deborah, Peter, and Michael Bean

~ Contents ~

~ About the Authors ~

JENNIFER LEE is associate professor of sociology at the University of California, Irvine.

FRANK D. BEAN is Chancellor's Professor of Sociology and Economics and director of the Center for Research on Immigration, Population, and Public Policy at the University of California, Irvine.

JAMES D. BACHMEIER is post-doctoral research associate in the Center for Research on Immigration, Population, and Public Policy at the University of California, Irvine.

ZOYA GUBERNSKAYA is Ph.D. candidate in the department of sociology at the University of California, Irvine.

~ Acknowledgments ~

This book reflects longstanding theoretical and empirical interests, and like all projects that take years to complete, this one owes manifold debts. We conceived of this book when the Russell Sage Foundation invited proposals for research projects that sought to understand how contemporary immigration affects racial and ethnic relations in the United States. As scholars with long-standing interests in the intersection of immigration and race/ethnicity, we took advantage of the opportunity offered by the Russell Sage Foundation to develop a multi-method study that merged our complementary intellectual, empirical, and methodological interests. We think working together on this project resulted in a book that is greater than the sum of our individual parts, thus providing an example of the productive potential of scholarly collaboration.

For giving us the opportunity to pursue this research, we would first like to thank Eric Wanner, President, and Aixa Cintrón-Vélez, Senior Program Officer, at RSF. They saw merit in our proposal and provided enthusiastic support along the way. We thank our editor at RSF, Suzanne Nichols, for her guidance and encouragement as we embarked on writing the manuscript, for keeping us accountable to the deadlines we set, and for being endlessly patient when we missed them. We also thank April Rondeau, who mined through the editorial changes and shepherded the manuscript through the final stages of production, and, finally, David Haproff for ardently supporting the "mediagenic" authors. At the University of California, Irvine, we thank the superb support staff and, in particular, Carolynn Bramlett, who went above and beyond her call of duty and managed to keep us organized at every stage of the manuscript's development.

This book was also made possible by the aid of some very capable graduate research assistants who helped with the data collection and analyses, including Jody Agius Vallejo, James Bachmeier, Jeanne Batalova, Zoya Gubernskaya, Mark Leach, and Sabeen Sandhu. Most of these students have since graduated and secured academic and policy positions, and we feel fortunate to have had the chance to work with them during their brief tenure at UC Irvine. We are also fortunate to have colleagues who provided insightful comments on various drafts of the manuscript. Nancy Foner and John Skrentny read the manuscript in its entirety, and proved to be incisive, balanced critics whose suggestions are reflected throughout the manuscript, resulting in a significantly stronger, more focused book. Other colleagues whose comments also helped strengthen the manuscript include Susan K. Brown, Prudence Carter, Philip Cohen, Leo Chavez, Michael Dawson, Troy Duster, Cynthia Feliciano, Patricia Fernandez-Kelly, Herbert J. Gans, Tomas Jimenez, Eric Oliver, Jen'nan Read, Belinda Robnett, Ruben Rumbaut, Mario Small, Edward Telles, Jennifer Van Hook, Roger Waldinger, and Min Zhou.

Not only did we profit from the comments we received from our colleagues, but we also richly benefited from the feedback we received when we presented our research to colloquia participants at the Center for Advanced Study at Stanford, Cornell, Harvard, Japan Women's University, Nanzan University, MIT, Northwestern, Princeton, the Russell Sage Foundation, UCLA, UCSD, University of Chicago, University of Iowa, University of Pennsylvania, and the Woodrow Wilson Center. Of course, not all of the colloquia participants and critics agreed with us, but we learned a great deal from our disagreements, and take full responsibility for mistakes that remain.

Not only did we receive generous research support from the Russell Sage Foundation, but we also received fellowship support that provided much-needed time to undertake the data collection and analyses, to develop our arguments, and finally, to write the manuscript. Frank D. Bean was awarded a Guggenheim Fellowship, a Visiting Scholarship from the Russell Sage Foundation, and a Distinguished Visiting Senior Scholar from the Center for Comparative Immigration Studies and the Center for U.S.-Mexico Relations at UCSD. Jennifer Lee was awarded fellowships from the Center for Advanced Study at Stanford and the Center for the Study of Race, Politics, and Culture at the University of Chicago, as well as a Fulbright Scholarship to Japan. In a time of diminishing grant and fellowship assistance for social science research, we are very grateful for these sources of support.

There would be no book to write, however, had we not succeeded in finding people willing to answer our many and often inconvenient questions. We are truly thankful to the interracial couples and multiracial adults who gave so freely of their time and indulged us whenever we had follow-up questions to their responses. We promised not to reveal their real names or the names of their children, but we hope that they feel that we painted an accurate portrait of their experiences.

Last, but certainly not least, we are indebted to our families for providing immeasurable support, unwavering enthusiasm, and boundless patience. Our families help to put everything into perspective, and help us achieve a balanced, happy life. To our families who provide unconditional love, encouragement, and support, we dedicate this book to them as our best, if barely adequate, form of gratitude.

~ PART I ~

Historical Background,
Theoretical Framework,
and Sociodemographic Context

~ Chapter 1 ~

Introduction: Immigration
and the Color Line in America

On November 4, 2008, the United States elected Barack Obama president, elevating an African American to the country's highest office for the first time. Because Obama's rise illustrates how far the United States has come from the days when blacks were denied the right to vote, when schools and water fountains were segregated, when it was illegal for blacks and whites to marry, and when racial classification was reduced to an absolutist dichotomy of black and white, it is fitting to ask: Does Barack Obama's election signify substantial erosion in the country's long-standing black-white color line? Many scholars and pundits assert that his victory indicates that the country has finally moved beyond race and that the color line long dividing blacks and whites has largely disappeared. For example, Abigail and Stephan Thernstrom, in an op-ed piece titled "Is Race Out of the Race?" (*Los Angeles Times,* March 2, 2008), argued that Obama's enormous appeal among white voters reflects a dramatically changed political climate in the United States and that Americans no longer struggle under the burden of race. Other observers proclaimed, in a similar vein, that the Civil War had finally ended and that the United States has become a "postracial" society, no longer bound by racial strictures (see Michael Eric Dyson, "Race, Post Race," *Los Angeles Times,* November 5, 2008, "Opinion"; Thomas L. Friedman, "Finishing Our Work," *New York Times,* November 5, 2008, op-ed; Adam Nagourney, "Obama Elected President as Racial Barrier Falls," *New York Times,* November 5, 2008, op-ed).

Undoubtedly, Obama's ascendance to the presidency is a historic event of great importance, one that has broken through barriers many thought would never be breached. In light of W. E. B. Du Bois's famous and pessimistic prophecy over a century ago, "The problem of the twentieth-century will be the problem of the color line—the relation of the darker to the lighter races of men" (1903/1997, 45), few probably would have thought that shortly after the end of the twentieth century, the son of a white mother and a black father would become the nation's forty-fourth president. Rather, many would have expected Du Bois's racial realism to cause him to anticipate the drop in President Obama's public-opinion ratings that occurred by Labor Day of his first year in office (see Adam Nagourney, "Looking for Tea Leaves in Obama's Sliding Numbers," *New York Times,* November 23, 2009). What, then, are we to make of Obama's presidency? What does it signify? Does his election suggest that the color line in the United States is well on its way to being eradicated? Does the decline in Obama's poll ratings hint merely that an exceptionally talented and appealing individual—one who just happens to be black and who had the good fortune to follow one of the most unpopular occupants of the White House in history—ran a great campaign and was elected president of the United States but is now being judged on his performance according to the standards applied to any president?

Given the crushing burden the black-white divide has imposed on African Americans throughout American history, questions about the persistence and disappearance of the color line inspire considerable scholarly interest and carry enormous policy significance. These questions about the color line are hugely important, too, because of the tectonic shift that took place in immigration in the latter half of the twentieth century and the first decade of the twenty-first that has brought millions of newcomers to the country (counting both the foreign-born and their children) who are neither black nor white (Foner and Fredrickson 2004; Bean and Stevens 2003). Almost sixty million such people, largely Latinos and Asians, currently reside here (Bean et al. 2009). On which side of the black-white color line do these new nonwhites fall? If there were convincing reasons that the old black-white divide has largely disappeared, then the question of where the new immigrant groups fall would be largely moot, and the forces driving the color line's dissolution would also probably work to enhance the sociocultural and economic incorporation of the new immigrant groups. Their successful integration would not constitute a significant societal or public-policy challenge resulting from substantial discrimination against them. If, on the other hand, the historic black-white color line continues to exist, then the question of which side of the divide Latino and Asian immigrants fall on matters a great deal.

In this volume we examine today's color lines through the intermarriage and multiracial experiences of both blacks and the major, new immigrant groups. We look at these phenomena from a number of different angles. If our inquiries lead us to conclude that Asian and Latino newcomers are positioned on the black side of the line, then it is likely that their sizable numbers over the past thirty years, together with their continuing high rates of current entry, are probably exacerbating long-standing problems in U.S. race relations (Bean et al. 2009). But if Asians and Hispanics (we use the terms *Hispanic* and *Latino* interchangeably here) are falling largely on the white side of the line, it would imply that successful incorporation among the new immigrants is not only possible but probably also actually occurring. Given this case, important questions arise as to how the nonwhite diversity brought about by immigration is contributing to the weakening of boundaries between the new immigrants and native whites, and whether Latinos and Asians are involved in these processes in similar ways and to the same degree. Even more important, if growing diversity seems to be loosening the ethnoracial boundaries that have previously constrained the life chances of new immigrants, is this diversity, along with rising familiarity among native-born Americans of an ever more multicultural country, beginning also to erode the black-white divide?

In seeking answers to these questions, we pull together in this book four different kinds of information about the United States' contemporary ethnoracial situation. First, we rely on previous research and on comparative and historical evidence to develop hypotheses about comparative differences in intermarriage and multiracial identification within major U.S. ethnoracial groups examined across time and place. In this regard we seek to follow the tradition of comparative scholarship on immigration and race exemplified by George Fredrickson (2000) and Nancy Foner (2005). Second, we present descriptive current statistics from the 2000 U.S. census and the ongoing annual American Community Survey (ACS) for the years 2007 and 2008 combined (which we subsequently refer to as data for 2008)[1] about recent trends in immigration, racial and ethnic self-identification, intermarriage, and ethnoracial diversity. In the process, we illustrate what the important features of the ethnoracial composition of the country are, how they have changed over time, and how and where the greatest diversity is emerging. Third, we present extensive, new in-depth qualitative data on both intermarried couples with children and multiracial adults in California derived from personal, face-to-face interviews. These provide rich and detailed insights about the experiences and meaning of intermarriage and multiracial identification and the perceptions of racial boundaries among persons living in the region of the country with the greatest ethnoracial diversity. Finally, we carry out quantitative analyses of a large volume of representative 2000 census data and recent ACS data on states and cities to gauge not only the extent to which recent immigration, intermarriage, and multiracial reporting weaken ethnoracial divides but also the extent to which diversity itself erodes those boundaries still further (Foner 2005; Perlmann and Waters 2004).

Adopting a multimethod research approach, we conducted analyses at both the cultural and structural levels that used both qualitative and quantitative data. This allowed us to achieve sharper focus and take better advantage of the strengths of each level of analysis and kind of data to overcome weaknesses in the other, and vice versa. For example, our main analytical lenses for examining today's color lines and the ways immigration and diversity are shaping them are intermarriage and multiracial identification. These experiences represent boundary-crossing phenomena, at least in the context of the United States (Telles and Sue 2009; Bailey 2008, 2009), so they are both sociologically revealing and challenging to understand. Relying on both qualitative and quantitative evidence to study these experiences helps avoid the shortcomings inherent in using either approach alone. After drawing on existing research and comparative and historical work to place our study in context, we began by comparing major ethnoracial groups, using large-scale census and survey data. These data portray national-level structural changes in intermarriage and multiracial identification across groups and show which parts of the country exhibit the greatest prevalence of such boundary-crossing phenomena.

But such results do not necessarily reflect the cultural dynamics behind or the subjective meanings involved in intermarriage and multiraciality, especially in private as opposed to public spheres, where perceptions and expectations about racial boundaries are often most forcefully embraced (Patterson 2009). Consequently, we also conducted in-depth qualitative interviews with multiracial individuals and interracial married couples with children in California, the most populous and diverse state in the country, to obtain deeper insight into the personal perceptions of the key pathbreaking phenomena we wanted to examine. Doing so, however, involved "sampling on the dependent variable." That is, by delving into these phenomena only in the most diverse state in the country, the information gathered provided only a limited basis for inferring connections that exist generally between diversity and ethnoracial boundary dissolution. Nor did such qualitative data provide adequate grounds for assessing the structural origins of cross-group differences in perceptions of and expectations about intermarriage and multiracial identification. Thus, to close our investigative circle, we concluded our inquiry with quantitative analyses that estimate the strength of relationships among variables measuring immigration, diversity, intermarriage, and multiracial identification across a representative range of places to provide a firmer foundation for drawing inferences about the implications of the country's growing diversity for color lines, including the black-white fault line.

The Comparative and Historical Context

When W. E. B. Du Bois predicted in 1903 that the problem of the twentieth century would be that of the color line, the United States was in the midst of its rise to become the world's leading industrial power. More than other analysts, Du Bois recognized that U.S. economic development would expose the social fissures stemming from a rigid black-white fault line and make them increasingly hard to ignore, especially as the country's growing economic prosperity spread to a wider swath of whites but not to blacks. In his poignant statement, "The problem of the twentieth-century will be the problem of the color line," he foresaw that slavery's contradictions would become ever more conspicuous and that its legacy—painfully apparent in the stain of Jim Crow racial discrimination, rationalizations, and continuing stereotypes put forth to justify resulting inequities—would long continue to plague the country (Berlin 2003; Du Bois 1935). As penetrating as Du Bois's insights were, he failed to account for another—and more often emphasized—defining theme in American history: the opportunity and prosperity promised by immigration and symbolized in nineteenth-century America by the Statue of Liberty and Ellis Island (Handlin 1951/1973). If slavery represented the scar of race on America and the country's failure, immigration exemplified hope and the prospect of success. Such dreams turned into reality for many of America's nineteenth-century immigrant settlers, who fueled the expansion of the westward frontier. In this they were aided by the Land Act of 1820 and the Morrill Act of 1858, which provided land and technical assistance for America's new arrivals, though not for ex-slaves and their descendents (Nevins 1962).

As the western frontier began to close at the end of the nineteenth century (Turner 1893, 1920; Klein 1997), the United States increasingly became an industrial society in the early twentieth century, and it still saw itself in need of newcomers, now to fulfill a growing demand for laborers to work in the burgeoning factories of its mushrooming cities. Immigrants once again provided a solution. The new arrivals, like their predecessors in earlier waves, seized the opportunity to construct, or (re)construct, themselves anew through geographic mobility, eagerly participating in the American tradition of seeking opportunity and identity through starting over, rather than remaining in Europe where they and their governments faced the challenge of trying to knit together peoples torn apart by internecine conflict (Zolberg 2006). Nation building in America, at least outside the South, involved new immigrant settlements and work opportunities, guided by dreams that encouraged newcomers to embrace the idea that they were part of a "nation of immigrants."

By World War I, American immigration had thus served multiple purposes: the early waves provided the country with settlers eager to begin new lives in a land of opportunity; later waves, including those of Du Bois's era, provided sorely needed muscle power for the country's workforce. But whereas American immigration represented the optimistic side of the country's past and future, slavery and its aftermath tainted the fabric of national memory—a blot many sought to eradicate through denial and romanticization (Blight 2001). Indeed, the desire to overlook the lingering contradictions of slavery's legacy became a reason to reinforce the country's frequent emphasis on its immigrant origins.

Immigration and race thus played strangely symbiotic roles in shaping the founding mythology of America, evident in the fact that the two phenomena were often divorced from each other in treatments of the country's history (Glazer 1997). Well after the end of the Civil War, the country coped with the inconsistent and seemingly irreconcilable motifs arising from immigration and slavery (and, by extension, race) by compartmentalizing depictions of the immigrant and slave experiences, especially at an intellectual level. Many historians tended to embed discussions of immigration in narratives about the frontier and industrialization, and others confined treatments of slavery only to the history of the South (Davis 1998). Race might have been a historical problem, but scholars often seemed to view the issue as a regional matter confined to the southern states, not one that afflicted the country as a whole.

But in the early twentieth century the changing national origins of immigrants began to undermine such convenient compartmentalizations. With the arrival of America's third wave of newcomers from 1900 to 1914, from eastern and southern Europe, agitated natives started to advocate the "Americanization" of groups they viewed as non-Nordic and thus hopelessly unassimilable (Gerstle 1999; Ignatiev 1995; Jacobson 1998; Roediger 1991). The new arrivals scarcely resembled the western and northern European immigrants of the country's past. Moreover, they were Catholic, not Protestant, and they largely settled in industrial cities outside the South. Thus, the tendency in this period for foreigners to be viewed in reductionist terms that conflated national origin and race (Zolberg 2006; Nightingale 2008) resulted in many non-Southerners having to confront and cope with persons of "races" different from their own, a dilemma previously faced to a lesser degree in the case of the Irish. The attendant tensions contributed to the rise of nativism and the passage of restrictive national-origins immigration legislation in 1921 (Higham 1963; Brown, Bean, and Bachmeier 2009). But denials that racism existed and that racial relations involving blacks were less than exemplary continued as national problems through the Great Depression and World War II. It was not until the 1960s that substantial change finally began to occur (Bean and Bell-Rose 1999; Fredrickson 2002). This period saw the emergence of geostrategic exigencies from the Cold War that emphasized more equitable treatment of Asian-origin groups, as well as claims for equal opportunity emanating from post–World War II black veterans; both were developments that dramatized the contradictions created in American society by racial discrimination and generated calls for change that were not easily denied (Morris 1984).

Such shifts led to the passage by the U.S. Congress of two landmark pieces of legislation: the Civil Rights Act in 1964, making discrimination against blacks illegal, and the Hart-Celler Act in 1965, abolishing national-origin quotas as the bases for immigrant admissions (Bean and Stevens 2003; Reimers 1985/1992; Skrentny 2002). Scholars such as Nathan Glazer (1997) thought the former would quickly lead to the full incorporation of blacks into American society. Supporters of the Hart-Celler Act generally did not expect it to generate much new immigration; rather, they thought it simply would remove the embarrassment of the country's prior discriminatory admissions policies (Reimers 1998). The two laws thus both contributed to the prospect of improved racial and ethnic relations in the United States. However, neither turned out as anticipated. Blacks did not quickly become economically incorporated, and millions of new Asian and Latino immigrants unexpectedly began to arrive to the country (Alba and Nee 2003; Bean et al. 2009; Foner 2000; Lee 2002; Skrentny 2001a). Many of them were considered nonwhite.

Now, nearly half a century after the passage of these watershed pieces of legislation, we are addressing two broad and interrelated questions: To what extent has the country's contemporary immigration redefined race in America? Conversely, to what extent has the country's prior experience with race influenced its perception of today's nonwhite immigrants? To be sure, the United States is more racially and ethnically diverse now than at any other time since the early 1920s, and overt racial discrimination is now illegal, but to what degree have racial and ethnic relations, especially black-white relations, improved? If race is declining in significance, as many have claimed, is it declining equally for all nonwhite groups? Or is the cancer of racial discrimination that is the legacy of slavery so potent that it has metastasized to include America's nonwhite immigrant newcomers?

Scholars line up on both sides of the issue. Some believe that the problem of race is beginning to fade and contend that even the gulf between blacks and whites is contracting. For example, Abigail and Stephan Thernstrom (1997), emphasizing the progress that has occurred over the past four decades, have suggested that the pernicious black-white color line is disappearing. In fact, in an op-ed piece in the *Los Angeles Times,* the Thernstroms, referring to Barack Obama's unprecedented popularity across racial lines, posed the provocative question, "Is race out of the race?" Other observers and analysts point to structural reasons for optimism about the country's potential to absorb both ethnoracial minorities and newcomers over the next few decades, noting trends that portend the loss of the ethnoracial divide's negative grip on the nation. Richard Alba (2009) and Dowell Myers (2007), for example, think the looming retirement of postwar baby boomers (the unusually large cohorts of Americans born during the two decades after World War II) will create enormous new job and housing possibilities for blacks and immigrants, opportunities owing to the much smaller cohorts of whites coming behind the baby boomers not being large enough to replace them. As a result, Alba and Myers argue, any vestiges of ethnoracial discrimination directed against nonwhites will fade away.

But other analysts remain more pessimistic as to whether much change— or any change—is taking place in ethnoracial divides, particularly in the black-white divide. They point especially to persistent glaring disparities between blacks and whites in educational attainment, income, wealth, and residential segregation (Bobo 1997, 1999; Carter 2005; Charles 2001; Conley 1999; Hacker 1992/1995; Massey and Denton 1993; Oliver and Shapiro 1995). These social scientists underscore the enduring and consequential effects of a color line that, they conclude, continues to separate whites and blacks in the United States. Others take the argument further, suggesting that the black-white chasm is deep and wide enough to apply also to the new nonwhite immigrant groups, especially Mexicans, Puerto Ricans, and other Latino groups (Itzigsohn 2009; Massey 2007). Still others note that the end of the twentieth and the beginning of the twenty-first centuries have coincided with widening and deepening economic inequalities that threaten the undoing of any progress resulting from cultural and demographic change (Katz and Stern 2006).

The Present Focus and Approach

Apart from propounding conjectures like those just described, social scientists have only begun to analyze the role the new immigration has played in shaping contemporary ethnoracial issues. Unanswered questions abound. On which side of the color line do the new immigrant groups fall? In the case of Mexican immigrants, is their experience more like that of immigrant ethnic groups or more like that of racial minority groups (Bean and Stevens 2003; Skerry 1993; Telles and Ortiz 2008)? Stated differently, do the incorporation experiences of the mainly Asian and Latino new immigrants more closely parallel those of earlier-arriving immigrant groups, such as Italians—who were rather completely incorporated by the end of the 1960s (Alba 1990, 2009)—or of African Americans, who are still substantially poorly incorporated (Bean and Bell-Rose 1999)? Is immigration loosening ethnoracial boundaries by increasing diversity, which in turn helps to foster mechanisms generating greater tolerance for all ethnoracial minority groups? Or has the rapid growth of nonwhite groups through immigration generally increased perceptions among majority whites that their superordinate position is threatened, leading to intensification of white efforts to maintain the divide between themselves and other groups?

We seek to answer such questions with considerable caution and humility for two reasons. First, perhaps no topic in American social science has commanded more attention—or at least more fervent attention—than the country's ethnoracial issues. We realize that many of the arguments we introduce here as possible answers to such questions have previously been advanced by others, often in terms that are both eloquent and profound (see, for example, Alba and Nee 2003; Cornell and Hartmann 1998; Foner and Fredrickson 2004; Foner 2006; Gans 1999; Gerstle 2001; Itzigsohn 2009; Jaynes 2000; Kasinitz, Mollenkopf, and Waters 2002; Kasinitz et al. 2008; Lieberson 1980; Massey 2007; Portes and Rumbaut 2001; Telles and Ortiz 2008; Waldinger 1996; Waters 1999b). Here we draw and build on this rich body of work, seeking to synthesize previous findings and to organize and present in one place several new and relevant kinds of evidence. This offers the possibility of developing new insights by scrutinizing boundary-breaking behaviors and experiences, allowing us to discern the existence and strength of ethnoracial divides involving multiple, not just two, ethnoracial groups in early-twenty-first-century America. It also helps clarify the roles that immigration and diversity are playing in dissolving or maintaining such divides.

The second reason is that the concept of race itself is very problematical. As the distinguished historian Barbara Fields (1990, 2001, 2003) has so powerfully reminded us, using the term "race" connotes a reality that does not exist and encourages the reification of the idea of race. This presumption of concreteness appears to warrant attention on its own, quite apart from the power dynamics and racism that perpetuate specific observed differences emerging from comparisons across official racial categories. Needless to say, we wish to emphasize here that we do not view the concept of race in such reified terms. We neither wish to convey the impression that we underestimate the negative consequences that such usage can cause nor to say somewhat simply and ritualistically that we view race as a "social construction." Rather, we agree with Carl H. Nightingale (2008), who puts the matter as follows: "A vast consensus has emerged among scholars in many disciplines that color and race categories are continually reinvented within the context of social and political contestation, and that they have no all-embracing meaning outside those contexts" (50). Thus, in this book we avoid using the term "race" if possible, in an effort not to reinforce a perceived but misleading concreteness regarding the concept. Instead we use the adjectival form of the term, as in the phrase "racial status," in an attempt to connote the social, historical, and contextual contingency of racial categories. In some instances, however, in writing about the way other individuals or organizations use the term, we employ the single word "race," as when we note the U.S. Census Bureau's own discussions of its methods for measuring "race."

Our overarching research purpose, then, is to seek indications of the change and persistence of ethnoracial divides in early-twenty-first-century America and of the structural and cultural factors that bring about shifts or maintain the status quo. We do so by scrutinizing patterns of difference and change in both quantitative and qualitative data, often examined across official racial categories. We recognize the irony of this endeavor and its potential traps: namely, that we are undertaking a search for evidence of increased or diminished ethnoracial significance in data organized by putative, rather essentialist racial categories. Thus, when we argue that increased multiracial reporting indicates that the power of absolutist racial status (as exemplified in black-white categories) has declined and ethnoracial boundaries loosened, we remain aware that were the salience of racial status to vanish altogether, it would not even be possible to think and speak in multiracial terms. To state the matter succinctly, there would be no mixed racial status without the existence of racial status (Goldberg 1997; Telles and Sue 2009). For the moment we postpone further discussion of such matters and their complexity, but we return to them in the final chapter.

Racial Status and Immigration: Beyond Black and White

As previously noted, many questions about racial status in the United States have traditionally revolved around the axis of the black-white color line. Reflecting this is the tendency for pundits and scholars to speak of one color line: "*the* color line." But today the country has moved far beyond this nexus, at least partly as a result of contemporary immigration (see Foner and Fredrickson 2004). As we have noted, the arrival of large numbers of new immigrants who have been classified in the U.S. racial-categorization scheme as nonwhite raises several questions, two of which are initially important: Where do such persons fall in regard to the black-white color line? Do such persons fall on neither the black nor the white side of the traditional color line, but somewhere different altogether?

The flood of new immigrants to the United States became possible with the passage, in 1965, of the Hart-Celler Act, which eliminated national-origin quotas. Unlike earlier immigrants, the recent waves of immigrants originated from non-European countries. During the 1980s and 1990s, over 80 percent of immigrants came from Latin America, Asia, or the Caribbean, and only about 14 percent hailed from Europe or Canada (U.S. Immigration and Naturalization Service 2002). The shift in national origins of immigrants to the United States from Europe to Latin America, Asia, and the Caribbean is the single most distinctive aspect of the "new immigration" in the United States (Bean and Bell-Rose 1999; Waldinger and Lee 2001; Zhou and Lee 2007). Today's immigrant newcomers have since made an indelible imprint on the nation's racial-ethnic landscape, transforming it from a largely black-white society at the end of World War II to one now consisting of multiple, new nonwhite ethnic groups (Alba and Nee 2003; Bean and Stevens 2003; Sears et al. 2003). In 1970, Latinos and Asians made up only 5 percent and 1 percent, respectively, of the nation's population, but by 2008 these percentages had risen to over 15 percent and 5 percent (according to 2007 and 2008 American Community Survey data [Ruggles et al. 2009]). America's Latino and Asian populations are continuing to grow, and according to the U.S. Census Bureau projections, by the year 2050, they are likely to constitute about 30 percent and 9 percent of the U.S. population, respectively (Sam Roberts, "Minorities Often a Majority of the Population Under 20," *New York Times,* August 7, 2008, A15).

Like the declining significance of race, the topic of immigration sparks considerable debate. Whereas European immigrants of America's past have come to symbolize the search for opportunity and hope, today's non-European immigrants seem to generate anxiety in the minds of many Americans. At the core of the concern is the question of difference—the degree to which nonwhite immigrants and their descendants are becoming incorporated into the host society. Some native-born white Americans seem to assume the "unassimilability" of today's nonwhite newcomers—over 30 percent of whom arrive from Mexico—pointing to their non-European origins, their low education and job skills, and their alleged unwillingness to assimilate and adopt mainstream cultural values (Borjas 2001; Camarota and McArdle 2003; Huntington 2004). Others remain apprehensive that a restructured economy has reduced economic opportunities, which, together with national-origin and racial-ethnic distinctiveness among the new immigrants, might make complete incorporation difficult, if not impossible for today's newcomers (Portes, Fernández-Kelly, and

Haller 2005; Telles and Ortiz 2008). Yet other observers adopt an entirely different view and point to the remarkable progress that America's new non-white newcomers have made since their recent arrival. They maintain that immigrants and their children not only are successfully incorporating economically, linguistically, and socioculturally but also are achieving rates of mobility comparable to, if not better than, those of the earlier European arrivals (Alba and Nee 2003; Bean and Stevens 2003; Kasinitz et al. 2008; Lee 2005; Smith 2003, 2006).

The difference in the two perspectives stems in part from divergent conceptualizations of racial status and dissimilar ideas about how racial boundaries affect today's newest nonwhite groups. Those who raise concerns alleging the "unassimilability" of contemporary immigrants often point to their non-European origins, suggesting that the experiences of today's newcomers with racial status and incorporation are more similar to those of blacks than to those of earlier European immigrants (López 2009). Given that black-white relations have arguably constituted the most intractable domestic difficulty in the country (Jaynes and Williams 1989; Smelser, Wilson, and Mitchell 2001), scholars who take a pessimistic view often conclude that a growing nonwhite population and increasing racial and ethnic diversity can only lead to more problems that will persist long into the future. By contrast, those who point to positive signs of incorporation underscore that ethnoracial status may not be as consequential for today's Asian and Latino immigrants as it still is for African Americans. Such scholars emphasize that racial boundaries have stretched in the past to comprise European immigrants previously considered nonwhite, such as the Irish, and are now being redrawn to include Asians and Latinos. More important, they contend, treating all nonwhite groups as disadvantaged racialized minorities conflates the dissimilar experiences of African Americans, whose ancestors were slaves and involuntary migrants to the country, with those of contemporary immigrants, who have come voluntarily and often bring with them high levels of human and social capital (Fields 2003).

The difference also reflects alternative, although often complementary, theoretical perspectives about racial and ethnic relations. According to the first perspective noted earlier (which derives from a black-white model of racial relations), throughout U.S. history, power relations have played an overwhelmingly strong role in influencing other relations between the two groups (Bonilla-Silva 2004a, 2004b; Omi and Winant 1994; Takaki 1979). This perspective thus tends to perpetuate, or at least not explicitly undermine, essentialist views of racial status (Telles and Sue 2009). It also often assumes that power relations apply more or less equally to relations between whites and other groups today and thus reinforces ideas that racial status is a given and is static. Furthermore it implies that structural differences are relatively immutable because they can change only as a result of profound shifts in power factors. It thus neglects the roles that cohort and compositional dynamics, not to mention cultural dynamics, can play in social change.

In contrast with this immutability, a more boundary-oriented perspective is increasingly used by other scholars who point to the potentially fluid, porous, and ever-evolving nature of group boundaries (Alba 2009; Barth 1969; Cornell and Hartmann 2006; Foner 2000; Lamont and Molnár 2002; Lee and Bean 2004; Telles and Sue 2009; Waters 1990; Wimmer 2008). In this volume we seek to a certain extent to adjudicate between the two views, the more static power-relations framework in which racial status is seen as immutable and the more flexible boundary-shifting paradigm. We strive to ascertain which perspective seems better to apply to racial-ethnic relations and color lines generally in the twenty-first-century United States (which has seen high volumes of recent immigrants), and which view is a better fit for certain subgroups.

Racial and Ethnic Diversity in the United States in the Twenty-First Century

The incorporation of today's nonwhite immigrants is occurring in a context where contemporary immigration is not the only factor contributing to the texture of today's ethnoracial diversity. The number of intermarriages—cross-group marriages among whites, Latinos, Asians, Pacific Islanders, Native Americans, and African Americans—has soared more than twentyfold over a forty-year period, from 150,000 marriages in 1960 to 3.1 million in 2000 (Jacoby 2001; Lee and Edmonston 2005). Whereas less than 1 percent of married Americans were intermarried in 1960 (Jacoby 2001), nearly a half century later, in 2008, about 7.0 percent of married Americans had spouses of different races (Ruggles et al. 2009). This increase actually is the opposite of what one would expect if the only factor affecting intermarriage were the size of the minority group. That is, the increases in the size of these nonwhite populations would lead one to predict less intermarriage as the structural probability of finding by chance alone a spouse from within one's own racial-ethnic group rises (Kalmijn 1998). Even marriage between black and white Americans, the most historically stigmatized of interracial unions, has steadily increased over the past four and a half decades, from less than 2 percent of either black husbands or black wives having white spouses in 1970 to over 7 percent of black married women having white husbands and nearly 15 percent of black married men having white wives in 2007 (Farley 2009).

We have also witnessed a resulting rise in the numbers of persons with multiracial backgrounds who willingly identify themselves as such, another trend that is signifying that the United States is moving beyond the absolutist black-white demarcations of the past. The multiracial population became especially visible when the 2000 census allowed Americans to mark more than one race as a way to identify themselves in official census terms. In 2008, about 2.2 percent of Americans, or one in forty-five, listed themselves as multiracial (Ruggles et al. 2009). Some analysts have suggested that by the year 2050, the percentage could rise to as much as 20 percent, and by 2100, to as much as

33 percent, or one in three (Farley 2004; Lee and Edmonston 2005; Smith and Edmonston 1997). Some even suggest that we are in the midst of a multi-racial baby boom and are witnessing the hybridization of the American population. Some refer to this process as the United States becoming "mestizo" (Gerstle 1999; Nash 1995). These tendencies touch ever more Americans, as shown by the multiracial kin networks of American families; even as early as 1990, one fifth of all Americans indicated that they had a close relative of a different racial or ethnic background (Goldstein 1999).

Each of these phenomena—the new immigration, the rise in intermarriage, and the growing multiracial population—reflects the increasing racial and ethnic diversity in the United States. At first glance, such trends seem to portend improving race relations in the country; not only do relatively more mixed-race marital unions occur now than in the past, but also the offspring of such unions are now able to acknowledge officially their multiracial backgrounds if they choose. Old strictures appear to be melting away, foreshadowing the possible birth of a new era of tolerance and universalism, or what David Hollinger (1995) refers to as a "postethnic America"—one in which racial and ethnic boundaries are more porous and the color line is disappearing altogether. Viewed against this backdrop, Obama's election would seem to confirm that we have become a "postracial" society in which racial ascription and ethnic heritage are no longer barriers to mobility in America's opportunity structure.

However, before accepting this conclusion we need to examine evidence carefully and comparatively across whites, Asians, Latinos, and African Americans to see whether intermarriage and multiraciality carry similar significance for the members of different racial and ethnic groups. Both intermarriage and multiraciality are important indicators of the breakdown of the social and cultural boundaries separating whites and nonwhite groups such as Asians, Latinos, and blacks. It is most important to ascertain whether the Asian-white and Latino-white boundaries are similar in nature and intensity to the black-white boundary. If not, what does this suggest about claims concerning recent improvements in race relations? Because Asians and Latinos are neither black nor white, the black-white historical model in the United States may not be a useful guide to predict their incorporation outcomes. Hence, it remains to be seen whether today's newest immigrant groups are closely tracking the footsteps of their European immigrant predecessors, or whether Asians and Latinos are becoming racialized minorities whose experiences are more akin to those of African Americans.

Central Question, Evidence, and Argument

If the problem of the twentieth century was that of the black-white divide, the question of the twenty-first century is whether color lines still exist and which groups fall on which side of any such divides. We tackle this question comparatively by reviewing the prior work of others and by introducing two kinds of new data:

1. Population information from official government sources, including changes in the approach of the U.S. census to issues of race, and responses to census questions concerning racial and ethnic categories

2. In-depth subjective interview data from our own studies of the ways Californians experience and view racial status and divides, including perceptions of intermarriage and multiracial identification

In the first category is information that is demographic-compositional and enables us to examine, across places and time, population-based measures of diversity and the prevalence of events such as intermarriage and multiracial identification. The second type of information is cultural-perceptual and enables us to assess experiences with and subjective views about these phenomena.

Both kinds of evidence are important. While indications of difference or change in demographic composition may reflect both social-structural behavioral and subjective-perceptual cultural change, compositional differences or change alone may not necessarily reflect or induce more deep-seated and underlying sociocultural shifts. This point is illustrated later by an example involving intermarriage. Moreover, compositional and sociocultural forces may often reflect changes that operate in opposing directions and thus offset each other to varying degrees. If one is greater than the other, first-order empirical observations may lead to the inference that the one associated with the stronger force is the only one at work, since evidence of the operation of the weaker force becomes masked under such conditions.

Intermarriage provides a good example of this sort of dilemma. Sociologists often proclaim that intermarriage is the litmus test of assimilation, its existence providing particular indication of strong acculturation (Gilbertson, Fitzpatrick, and Yang 1996; Gordon 1964; Kalmijn 1993, 1998; Lee and Bean 2004; Lee and Fernandez 1998; Lieberson and Waters 1988; Moran 2001; Perlmann and Waters 2004; Qian and Lichter 2007; Rosenfeld 2002). However, if a minority group is growing in numbers enough to increase its relative group size (a compositional change), the probability of exogamy for an individual in the group decreases (that is, the probability of in-group marriage increases) by dint of this factor alone. This can happen even when broad acceptance of intermarriage (a cultural shift) and actual intermarriage (a social-structural shift) are rising at the same time. This may be the situation prevailing today with contemporary inter-ethnoracial marriage. Among Asians and Latinos, immigration has so rapidly added numbers to their overall population sizes that the probability of endogamy for individuals in these groups has increased considerably just because of gains in the sizes of the groups. Thus, examination of population-based trends does not necessarily indicate whether cultural attitudes toward intermarriage are becoming more favorable, as we might expect if substantial sociocultural change were occurring. This is one reason why intermarriage can sometimes constitute a misleading indicator of integration (Song 2009). As a result, the research strategy we adopt here in the cases of both intermarriage and multiracial identification is to conduct both population-based and sociocultural analyses and to rely on evidence from both quantitative and qualitative research approaches.

Both kinds of data provide necessary and complementary information for addressing the central question at hand. Studying one without the other risks obtaining an incomplete or inaccurate portrait of how and why color lines may be different now than what they were a century ago. By joining the two approaches, we can better gauge whether today's black-white color line is disappearing altogether, shifting into some alternative form such as a white-nonwhite or black-nonblack divide, or possibly becoming transformed into a more complex tri-racial divide. To ascertain the placement of color lines at the quantitative level, we examine information on group differences in trends in immigration, diversity, intermarriage, and multiracial identification. To gauge color-line placements at the qualitative level, we provide in-depth portraits of experiences and the subjective meanings and significance of racial status, racial divides, intermarriage, and multiracial identification. Of particular value is the qualitative data in regard to intermarriage, because several of the immigrant groups under consideration are growing in relative size, a change that tends to move their own group rates of intermarriage in the opposite direction from any loosening of cultural boundaries between ethnoracial groups.

We focus on intermarriage because it signals declining racial and ethnic prejudice and fading group boundaries and is one of the final stages of a minority group's incorporation into a majority group's host culture; we study multiracial identification because seeing and identifying oneself in multiracial terms reflects a jettisoning of the exclusive and absolutist bases of racial categorization that have long marked racial identification in the United States. Both interracial marriage and multiracial identification thus speak volumes about the current meaning of racial status in American society; in particular, they signal where racial-group boundaries are fading most rapidly and where they continue to endure. Therefore, examining the trends and patterns in both the quantitative and qualitative data will help determine where the color line is being drawn in the twenty-first century.

We also focus on whether and to what degree ethnoracial diversity in general relates to indicators of ethnoracial boundary loosening, such as intermarriage and multiracial reporting. Robert D. Putnam (2007) has recently argued that such diversity seems to exert a negative effect on social capital and thus, by extension, on trust and social cohesion as well. He conjectures that neighborhood ethnoracial diversity results in people's "hunkering down" in their homes, a tendency that, if it does exist, would imply that greater diversity strengthens rather than weakens ethnoracial boundaries. In contrast, Robert J. Sampson (2009) generally finds positive effects of immigration-related diversity on neighbor-hood social life. The research findings we present later in this book suggest that ethnoracial diversity leads to more intermarriage and more multiracial report-ing, thus potentially encouraging less discrimination against minorities and more opening up of opportunities for them, a result more consistent with the findings of Sampson's research. Of course, larger ethnoracial groups may simply mean more persons are available for intermarriage. This can occur even as the probability of endogamy declines due to rising relative minority-group size. In other words, larger absolute numbers of intermarriages can occur even though the rate of marriages for a given group may decline. This could then lead to larger numbers of children with multiracial backgrounds, which could increase multiracial reporting. However, beyond this, we present results that also suggest that diversity per se exerts positive effects on boundary loosening that go beyond just its compositional impacts.

David Hollinger (1995) claims that multiracial Americans are performing a historic role at the moment by helping to move the United States in a "postethnic" direction, and Herbert Gans (1999) views multiracial identifica-tion as a harbinger of progress in race relations because it reflects the dimin-ishing significance of the current racial categorical regime. Gans predicts, further, that today's racial labels may become increasingly less relevant in each gener-ation until they disappear into obscurity. Richard Alba and Victor Nee (2003) also recognize the salience of intermarriage and multiracial identification and posit that the disappearance of "racial distinctions" between Asians and Latinos and whites will depend largely on how the children of Asian and Latino intermarriages view themselves and are viewed by others in such terms, as well as on the opening up of opportunities for upward social mobility for these groups (Alba 2009). Taken together, trends in intermarriage, patterns of multiracial identification, and the ways the members of various groups feel about these phenomena reflect the permeability and rigidity of racial and eth-nic boundaries. Hence, intermarriage and multiracial identification become the analytical lenses through which we observe the strength and placement of changes in America's color line.

The findings from our analyses of both quantitative and qualitative data suggest that group boundaries are fading more rapidly for Latinos and even more rapidly for Asians than for blacks, signaling that today's new nonwhite immigrants are not incorporating as racialized minorities whose experiences and situations are more akin to those of blacks than of whites. Our research suggests that Asians and perhaps to a lesser degree Latinos are more closely fol-lowing the pattern of European immigrants, which places them closer to whites at this point in time than to blacks. Thus, a new black-nonblack color line appears to be emerging that places the new nonwhite immigrants on the nonblack side of the line and continues to separate African Americans from all other groups. Hence, although the color line may be fading and becoming more flexible in certain respects, the new color line continues to relegate many blacks to positions of disadvantage, just like the traditional black-white line, pointing to the persistence of a pattern of black exceptionalism in the United States. Paradoxically, the new diversity blurs some color lines more than others, leaving the old line more repositioned than eradicated.

Acknowledging the existence of a contemporary color line dividing black and nonblack Americans does not mean we suggest that "nonblack" is a homogeneous category synonymous with "white." In fact, we propose that there are many shades of nonblack, making this category more nuanced and complex than the category often defined as white. Perhaps because whiteness as a category has expanded in the past to incorporate new immigrant groups, some may presume that it now is stretching again to envelop many Asians and Latinos. Some observers seeing the patterns of interracial marriage and multiracial identification might argue that Asians and Latinos are indeed the next in line to become "white," with multiracial Asian-whites and Latino-whites at the head of the queue. However, such an interpretation fails to consider that "whiteness" may no longer retain its previous meaning and significance. Hence, although Asians and Latinos may be nonblack, this does not necessarily mean that they are becoming white. This suggests that the old black-white divide will not reemerge but that a new category, nonblack, is emerging.

The Structure of This Book

This book is divided into three parts. In part I we outline four alternative theoretical perspectives concerning the origins and nature of today's color line(s); review the history of the various ways the U.S. government, through its major population statistical agency, the Census Bureau, has sought to determine the racial status of the population in order to fulfill its constitutional and legal mandates to provide data for political apportionment and other official government functions; and draw on 1990 and 2000 census data and on 2007 and 2008 American Community Survey data (Ruggles et al. 2009) to describe national and place-based trends in immigration, nonwhite population growth, diversity, intermarriage, and multiracial reporting. We also document the shifts in the ethnoracial demography of the United States in recent decades, especially the arrival after 1965 of a new wave of immigrants from non-European countries that has dramatically altered the ethnoracial landscape of the country and ushered in a new era of diversity.

Modifications in census definitions, increases in immigration, and group differences in population trends provide clear indications of change in this respect, but such shifts do not provide a complete picture of the cultural and attitudinal changes that may have accompanied them. Hence, in part II, in four largely qualitative chapters, we present data on more deeply rooted subjective and perceptual accounts of the ways persons experience and view intermarriage and multiracial identification. In part III we examine large representative data sets for places (cities and states) in order to develop assessments of the strength of relationships among size of minority group, ethnoracial diversity, inter-marriage, and multiracial identification. We conclude by discussing what all of the results imply about the placement of today's color line(s).

We here present the contents of each chapter in greater detail. In chapter 2 we note that reaching more definitive conclusions about the placement of and factors contributing to shifting color lines requires additional evidence that taps historical changes in legal strictures regarding racial status and cultural differences in subjective feelings and orientations about intermarriage and multiraciality. This is made necessary by the fact that certain structural changes may not always reflect greater tolerance toward racial-ethnic minori-ties, as one might initially think. As a guide for interpreting such data, we introduce four theoretical models of where contemporary U.S. color lines might now be drawn.

Chapter 3 describes in detail how the U.S. census has measured race since its first inception in 1790 to its latest and perhaps most path-breaking shift in matters of racial identity, whereby Americans may identify themselves by marking more than one racial category. This decision is epochal because the option to "mark one or more races" gives official status and recognition to Americans who see themselves as persons of mixed-race backgrounds—an acknowledgement that speaks volumes about how far the country has come since the days when the "one-drop rule" of hypodescent (whereby a person with "one drop" of African American blood was considered black) carried the force of legal legitimacy. Because census practices have often mirrored the cen-trality of racial status in the country, by examining how the census has mea-sured race throughout its history we gain an enlightened perspective about the changing nature of America's color line.

In chapter 4, we use analyses of census data to chart the recent growth of racial and ethnic groups in the United States and to assess the extent to which recent changes are due to contemporary immigration. Looking at trends in immigration, we show how newcomers from Latin America and Asia are changing the racial and ethnic terrain of the country, making some cities and states extraordinarily diverse. By more "diverse" we mean areas where larger and greater numbers of racial and ethnic minority groups come to constitute larger proportions of state or metropolitan-area populations. We illustrate which parts of the country have been most affected by the rapidly expanding new racial and ethnic diversity, and also show how this diversity represents a departure from the traditional diversity of black and white.

In chapter 5 we attempt to assess cultural shifts by documenting recent trends in intermarriage and examining their significance by means of in-depth interview data from interracial couples. More specifically, we examine how inter-racial couples construct definitions of racial status, how their understanding of racial categories affects whom they consider suitable marriage partners, and whether they believe that intermarriage facilitates incorporation. Although social scientists agree that intermarriage is an indicator of incorporation, they have not fully examined whether the incorporative power of intermarriage works similarly across groups.

In chapter 6 we examine how interracial couples choose to identify their children and how their choices in turn affect patterns of incorporation. Historically, the legacy of the "one-drop rule" of hypodescent has determined the racial identification of children born to black-white unions. It is unclear whether the children born to Asian-white and Latino-white unions are subject to the same constraining principle. In part this is because the racial identification of multiracial Asian and Latino children did not become salient until fairly recently, and in part it is because Asians and Latinos are neither white nor black, and so the children of Asian-white and Latino-white unions lack a historical precedent that governs their identification. It is not yet apparent whether their identities will be closely circumscribed, as has historically been the case for multiracial black children, or whether their identities will be more flexible, fluid, and even largely chosen for symbolic reasons, by which we mean selected on a discretionary and volitional basis, like those of European white ethnics, as opposed to endured because they are ascribed by others, like those of African Americans.

In chapter 7 we continue the line of inquiry about cultural differences by raising the question of who is multiracial—or, more specifically, who chooses to claim a multiracial identification? We first unpack interesting patterns that emerge from the 2000 census and more recent ACS data, and then delve into the mechanisms and processes that lead some groups to report higher rates of multiracial identification than others. Given that the one-drop rule of hypodescent is no longer legally enforced and that all Americans may now officially claim a multiracial background, we investigate why some groups are less likely to report multiracial identifications than others. In other words, in lieu of the legal invocation of the one-drop rule, we examine what cultural and institutional mechanisms may now be in place that keep the rate of multiracial reporting lower in some groups than others. The findings underscore the critical point that the incorporative power of racial mixing differs by group, with members of some groups feeling less able to freely claim a multiracial identification.

In chapter 8 we assess what the patterns of intermarriage and multiracial identification indicate about group boundaries more generally. Boundary work has been a fundamental part of the immigrant incorporation experience (Alba 1985, 1990; Gans 1999; Gerstle 1999; Ignatiev 1995; Jacobson 1998; Lamont 2000; Perlmann and Waldinger 1997; Waters 1990). Previously, nonwhite European ethnics achieved "whiteness" by crossing over the color line, leading to the eventual shift in the boundary separating whites and nonwhites. Today, so complete is their incorporation that the boundaries among white ethnics are no longer regarded as racial differences but rather as ethnic differences that are symbolic, situational, and optional. Whereas white Americans may enjoy "ethnic" options, nonwhites often carry the burden of their racial labels, but it is unclear where multiracial Americans fit along the continuum of volitional and ascribed identities. Are their identities more symbolic and situational, as they are for white ethnics, or are they more constrained and consequential, as they are for racialized minorities such as African Americans? We close the chapter by assessing what the empirical patterns we observe suggest about the fluidity of boundaries for America's nonwhite groups more generally.

In chapter 9 we analyze how racial and ethnic diversity is geographically linked in the aggregate to patterns of multiracial identification across places, and we analyze how the size of specific minority racial and ethnic groups in certain places directly relates to multiracial reporting in those areas, and indirectly relates to such reporting through diversity and through intermarriage. Given the historical specificity of black-white relations in the United States, larger black populations may affect intergroup relations differently than do larger Asian and Latino populations. We conclude by discussing what such differences suggest about intergroup relations and changing color lines from such a quantitative perspective.

In chapter 10 we offer a synthesis of our findings and draw out implications of our research for the future of race and ethnic relations. We also suggest what we believe are some fruitful directions for further research.

~ Chapter 2 ~

Theoretical Perspectives on
Color Lines in the United States

At the beginning of the twentieth century, when W. E. B. Du Bois famously proclaimed that "the problem of the twentieth-century [will be] the problem of the color line," (1903/1997, 45), there was little ambiguity about the state of U.S. race relations. So rigid and powerful was the black-white color line that it affected all spheres of life—economic, political, social, and legal—and accurately reflected America's racial reality. More than one hundred years later, the United States is composed of a kaleidoscope of ethnicities, a rainbow largely created by immigration from non-European countries. Newcomers from Latin America and Asia have created a multihued cast of Americans and have helped boost Latin American and Asian populations to 15 percent and 5 percent, respectively, of the country's population. These fractions are projected to continue to grow so that by 2050, the Census Bureau estimates, Latinos will account for almost one third of the U.S. population, and Asians for nearly one tenth (Sam Roberts, "Minorities Often a Majority of the Population Under 20," *New York Times,* August 7, 2008, A15).

Given the country's new ethnoracial diversity, we can now ask whether, and how, W. E. B. Du Bois's statement about the color line is relevant in the twenty-first century. If the problem of the twentieth century was the existence of the color line, the question for the twenty-first is: Will the color line persist, and if so, where will it be redrawn? Where do Latinos and Asians fit along the traditional binary black-white divide, and are they closer to whites or to African Americans at this point in time? Further, does their racial status as neither white nor black help to catalyze the erosion of the color line, or does it further solidify it? The traditional black-white color line may no longer reflect the reality of America's new ethno-racial diversity, but it remains to be seen whether the old line is morphing into a different type of color line: a white-nonwhite divide, a black-nonblack divide, or a more complex tri-racial hierarchy—or perhaps all color lines are disappearing altogether. In this chapter, we discuss these four theoretical perspectives on the repositioning of America's color lines in the twenty-first century: a white-nonwhite line; a tri-racial divide; a black-nonblack line; a disappearing color line.

A White-Nonwhite Divide

Some observers believe that a white-nonwhite divide could now be emerging in the country as an evolution of the white-black color line that has been legally enforced throughout the history of the United States and well into the twentieth century. Along with blacks, Asians and Latinos are seen to be positioned on the nonwhite side of the divide. Blacks, Asians, and Latinos have all faced severe de jure and de facto discrimination in the United States in the form of enslavement, exclusion, incarceration, confinement, or deportation. For example, African Americans suffered two and a half centuries of slavery, followed by another century of de jure segregation under Jim Crow, and decades of de facto segregation in housing, education, and employment. Moreover, the Chinese were barred from immigrating to the United States for ten years, beginning in 1882, and 110,000 Japanese Americans, including American citizens, were interned in camps between 1941 and 1947 (Kashima 1997). Mexicans were apprehended and forcibly deported during Operation Wetback in 1954 because of the growing fear of the burgeoning Mexican immigrant population, often with little regard to legal status. As these examples poignantly illustrate, for much of U.S. history blacks, Asians, and Latinos have had more in common with one another in terms of their status than with whites, and all faced severe discrimination.

Indeed, they also were often likened to one another by the country's Anglo-Saxons—citizens of English ancestry. For example, nineteenth-century whites compared Chinese immigrants to blacks because of their perceived racial and cultural peculiarities. The Chinese, labeled "coolies," were described as "undesirable immigrants" and "marginal members of the human race," who were considered no better than slaves (Sayler 1995; Takaki 1979). The grossly inferior status of blacks and Chinese vis-à-vis whites was reflected in California's antimiscegenation laws, which prohibited marriages between "white persons" and "negroes or mulattoes" in 1850, and was amended in 1878 to prohibit marital unions between whites and Chinese. Because most white Americans believed that the Chinese were full of "filth and disease," they feared that interracial unions between these groups would result in a "hybrid of the most despicable, a mongrel of the most detestable that has ever afflicted the earth" (Volpp 2003, 86).

At the root of the racial and cultural arguments against Chinese immigrants was the question of assimilability or, more precisely, Chinese immigrants' putative inability and unwillingness to amalgamate with Americans. Their alleged refusal to assimilate struck fear into the minds of white Americans, who believed that Chinese immigrants would soon endanger American culture and civilization (Sayler 1995). These fears persisted despite the fact that in 1878, several Chinese immigrants petitioned the federal courts in San Francisco to be naturalized as U.S. citizens. But this privilege extended only to "whites" and to persons of "African nativity or descent." The attorneys who represented the Chinese immigrants argued that the category "white" did not exclude Chinese, but the court did not agree, ruling that a white person was defined as someone of the Caucasian race, and that the Chinese were of the "Mongolian race," and therefore not white; consequently, the Chinese were ineligible for citizenship. The fear of unassimilability, intertwined with Americans' growing concerns about Chinese economic progress, resulted in the 1882 Chinese Exclusion Act, which suspended Chinese immigration to the United States for ten years. This was the first time that the United States adopted a policy that barred immigrants on the basis of race and national origin.

The white-nonwhite divide was clarified further in the early twentieth century in the state of Virginia through the passage of the Racial Integrity Act of 1924, which created two distinct racial categories: "pure" white and all others. The raison d'être of the statute, which defined a "white" person as one with "no trace whatsoever of blood other than Caucasian," was to legally ban intermarriage between whites and members of other races. Blacks were clearly nonwhite under the legislation, but Asians and Latinos also fell on the nonwhite side of the binary divide. The statute reflected the Supreme Court rulings of *Takao Ozawa vs. United States* (1922) and *United States vs. Bhagat Singh Thind* (1923), in which persons of Asian origin were not only classified as nonwhite but also considered unassimilable.

Takao Ozawa, Japanese-born but raised and educated in the United States, filed for U.S. citizenship under the Naturalization Act of June 29, 1906, on the basis of his adherence to American ideals and the argument that the color of his skin made him a "white person." Rather than challenging the constitutionality of the racial restrictions to U.S. citizenship, Ozawa attempted to have Japanese persons classified as "white." Although the Supreme Court conceded that Ozawa was "well qualified by character and education for citizenship," it ruled that color was not a sufficient indicator of race, given the "overlapping of races and a gradual merging of one into the other, without any practical line of separation" (Daniels 1962, 98). The Court noted that only Caucasians were white, and because the Japanese were not of the Caucasian race, they were not white. In short, white skin by itself did not guarantee membership in the "white" Caucasian race and the rights that it conferred (Foley 1998).

Three months later, in *United States vs. Bhagat Singh Thind* (261 U.S. 204 1923), the Supreme Court handed down a similar ruling, denying citizenship to a "high class Hindu." Thind asserted that he was white because of his Aryan and Caucasian roots, arguing that Aryans of India are a "tall, long-headed race with distinct European features, and their color on average is not as dark as the Portuguese or the Spanish." Despite the fact that anthropologists had defined members of the Indian subcontinent as members of the Caucasian race, the Court dismissed anthropological evidence altogether in Thind's case. Although the Court did not dispute that Thind was a Caucasian, it ruled that not all Caucasians were white, as "used in common speech, to be interpreted in accordance with the understanding of the common man." The Court elaborated, "We venture to think that the average well-informed white American would learn with some degree of astonishment that the race to which he belongs is made up of such heterogeneous elements." Thus, Takao Ozawa was denied citizenship because he was not of the Caucasian race and therefore not white, whereas Bhagat Singh Thind was denied citizenship because, although the Court conceded that he was Caucasian, he still was not white according to the common understanding of whiteness. Both rulings reflected the idea that regardless of how committed to American ideals and customs they might be, persons of Asian origin were not only a distinct racial or color category from whites but also "permanently foreign" and "racially unassimilable" aliens who were unfit for citizenship (Foley 1998; Ngai 2005). In essence, the Court not only fixed the boundaries of racial status but also specified the privilege associated with whiteness relative to other racial categories (Haney-Lopez 1996). Because of the benefits associated with whiteness, attaining whiteness became the most important possession to which an immigrant could aspire (Jacobson 1998).

In the only naturalization case involving a Mexican, the Court ruled in favor in granting citizenship, but it based its decision not on race but on the terms of the Treaty of Guadalupe Hidalgo. In the case *Re Ricardo Rodríguez* (1897), Ricardo Rodríguez, a Mexican-born man who had lived in San Antonio for ten years, petitioned for U.S. citizenship in Bexar County, Texas, in order to exercise his right to vote. The county court denied his application because Rodríguez was not "a white person, nor an African, nor of African descent," but a Mexican, and therefore ineligible for citizenship. Rodríguez appealed this decision to the San Antonio Circuit Court. The federal district judge overturned the ruling on the basis of the Treaty of Guadalupe Hidalgo, which specified the terms of Mexico's defeat in the 1848 Mexican-American War (Rodriguez 2007). According to the treaty, all Mexicans in the ceded territory who neither declared their intention to remain Mexican citizens nor left the territory in one year would be "incorporated into the Union of the United States" with the "enjoyment of all rights of citizens."

As in the rulings handed down in the Ozawa and Thind cases, the district court ruled that Rodríguez was not white. The judge stated that according to the classification adopted by anthropologists, Rodríguez "would probably not be classed as white," but rather "classed with the copper-colored or red men. He has dark eyes, straight black hair, and high cheek bones" (Saldaña-Portillo 2008). What is notable in all three cases is that none of the plaintiffs attempted to classify themselves as of "African descent," even though, at the time, Chinese, Asian Indians, and Mexicans were treated more like blacks than like whites and those of African descent had a right to become naturalized. But accepting this classification would result in a drop in racial status. The Court, too, never considered classifying the plaintiffs as black, because doing so would have given them a route to citizenship.

The white-nonwhite divide—legally enforced throughout the nineteenth and early twentieth centuries—gained political momentum and legitimacy in the 1960s. For instance, in a report to President Truman's Committee on

Civil Rights, Asians and Latinos were officially designated as minority groups alongside blacks on the basis of their color and distinctive cultural characteristics. As groups who had "suffered enough" to be perceived as "analogous to black," civil rights administrators extended affirmative action benefits to Asians and Latinos in employment, including self-employment (Skrentny 2002). Latinos, in particular, have garnered a great deal of recognition as a disadvantaged minority (Hollinger 1995).

By conflating Asians and Latinos with African Americans, civil rights administrators of the 1960s assumed that the experiences with discrimination of members of these three groups were similar and stemmed from their nonwhite racial status (Hollinger 2008). An unintended consequence of these policies was that Latinos and Asians—who made up only 5 percent and 1 percent of the country's population at the time—were perceived and labeled as racialized minorities, or "people of color," whose "color and cultural characteristics" would continue to set them apart from whites and make them more akin to blacks. That the country's policymakers placed Latinos and Asians on the non-white side of the divide reflects the perception that these groups were racially unassimilable, unlike the European immigrants who came before them.

The question of immigrant assimilability has reared its head again in the late twentieth and early twenty-first centuries with a specific focus on newcomers from Latin America. Scholars such as Samuel P. Huntington (2004) and George Borjas (2007) point in particular to Mexican immigrants, many of whom who arrive with low levels of human capital and often as unauthorized migrants, as being unassimilable. Huntington and Borjas fear that Mexicans—who constitute nearly one third of the U.S. immigrant population—will become mired in the bottom rungs of America's economic structure, and form a new urban underclass. For example, 11 percent of foreign-born Mexican adults have no formal education, and another 60 percent have not completed high school. The comparable figures for the native-born U.S. adult population are 1 percent and 18 percent, respectively. Hence, foreign-born Mexicans are three times as likely not to have completed high school than native-born Americans. Compounding their low levels of human capital is their legal status. About half of all foreign-born Mexicans in the United States entered the country illegally, and among the estimated 12 million undocumented immigrants in the country, nearly three quarters are from Mexico (U.S. Immigration and Naturalization Service 2003).

Other immigration scholars, such as Alejandro Portes, Patricia Fernández-Kelly, and William Haller (2005, 1006), point to other disadvantages that today's immigrants and their children face, in particular, their racial and ethnic distinctiveness:

> Children of Asian, black, mulatto, and *mestizo* immigrants cannot escape their ethnicity and race, as defined by the mainstream. Their enduring physical differences from whites and the equally persistent strong effects of discrimination based on those differences, especially against black persons, throws a barrier in the path of occupational mobility and social acceptance.

According to Portes, Fernández-Kelly, and Haller (2005), "the enduring physical differences" between whites and the children of "Asian, black, mulatto, and mestizo immigrants" coupled with the discrimination that ensues from these racialized differences will make complete assimilation and social acceptance difficult for many of America's nonwhite immigrants and their children. Because they "cannot escape their ethnicity and race," they will be subject to similar levels of discrimination as blacks have been, and as a result, today's immigrants and their children will perceive themselves and will be perceived by others as racialized minorities who are closer to blacks than to whites. In a similar vein, Gary Y. Okihiro (1994) and Ronald T. Takaki (1989) contend that today's immigrants from Asia, Latin America, and the Caribbean will be unable to escape their racial categorization and the caste-like status that ensues because of their non-European origins. Hence, rather than following in the footsteps of earlier European immigrants, many of today's nonwhite immigrants may follow a path of assimilation as a member of a racialized minority. In light of these disadvantages, some immigration and race and ethnicity scholars point to the salience of a white-nonwhite divide, in which Asians and Latinos continue to fall on the nonwhite side of the color line, just as they have done throughout much of U.S. history.

A Tri-Racial Divide

Other social scientists offer an alternate possibility—a tri-racial stratification system similar to that of many Latin American and Caribbean countries. Eduardo Bonilla-Silva (2004a, 2004b) proposes that in the United States, a tri-racial divide would consist of whites, so-called honorary whites, and what he calls "collective blacks." Included in the "white" category would be whites, assimilated white Latinos, some multiracials, assimilated Native Americans, and a few Asian-origin people. "Honorary whites" would include light-skinned Latinos, Japanese, Koreans, Chinese, Asian Indians, Middle Eastern Americans, and most multiracial Americans. The "collective black" category would include blacks, Filipinos, Vietnamese, Hmong, Laotians, dark-skinned Latinos, West Indian and African immigrants, and reservation-bound Native Americans.

Bonilla-Silva argues that because many of today's new immigrants hail from Latin America and the Caribbean, leading to a "darkening" of the United States, a more complex tri-racial order may naturally emerge. A few new immigrants might fall into the "honorary white" stratum and may even eventually become "white," but the majority will become part of the "collective black" stratum. This will include most Latino immigrants, whom Bonilla-Silva labels "racial others" as he sees their experiences with race as similar to those of blacks. Thus the tri-racial model is distinguished from the white-nonwhite model by Bonilla-Silva's hypothesis that most Latinos are racialized in a manner similar to African Americans and therefore fall on the black side of the divide.

There has been some support for the "Latin Americanization" thesis—that the recent arrival of many Latin Americans has led to the creation of a third category in America's racial profile—but it has not gone unchallenged. Edward Murguia and Rogelio Saenz (2004) argue that a three-tier system predated substantial Latin American immigration to the United States. Other social scientists contest the characterization of Latinos as a monolithic group (Forman, Goar, and Lewis 2004; Murguia and Saenz 2004). Examining Latinos' social attitudes toward other racial and ethnic groups, Tyrone Forman, Carla Goar, and Amanda E. Lewis (2004) find that Latinos fall into different segments of the tri-racial hierarchy, depending on their national origin. Puerto Ricans differ from Mexicans in their expressed feelings toward blacks, demonstrating greater variation in their attitudes, which depend on each individual's own skin color. Darker-skinned Puerto Ricans tend to hold more favorable views of African Americans than lighter-skinned Puerto Ricans do (Forman, Goar, and Lewis 2004). Mexicans are much more uniform in their feelings toward blacks, expressing attitudes closer to those of non-Hispanic whites than to those of non-Hispanic blacks; namely, they view blacks as belonging to a separate race. This view of blacks as belonging to a separate race may result from the history of racial mixing in Mexico, which involved very few Africans, unlike in Puerto Rico (Forman, Goar, and Lewis 2004), where Africans were part of the racial mix. Regardless of their own skin color, however, Latinos express attitudes toward blacks that are closer to those of non-Hispanic whites than to those of non-Hispanic blacks. Such results suggest considerable variation in the racialization experiences of Latinos in the United States. It remains to be seen whether most Latinos, and especially Mexicans, will fall into the collective black category, as Bonilla-Silva posits in his theory regarding the formation of a tri-racial hierarchy in the United States.

A Black-Nonblack Divide

In the 1990s, social scientists began to notice the possible emergence of a new racial structure that differed from the black-white divide, the white-nonwhite divide, and the tri-racial hierarchy. What appeared to be forming was a new binary color line, a black-nonblack divide, reflecting the continuing and unique separation of blacks not only from whites but also from other nonwhite ethnoracial groups (Alba 1990; Gans 1999; Gitlin 1995; Glazer 1997; Hochschild 1996; Hollinger 2003; Perlmann 2000; Sanjek 1994; Waters 1999a; Yancey 2003). The concept of the black-nonblack divide surfaced in conjunction with a flurry of research that documented the processes by which previously "nonwhite" immigrant ethnic groups, such as the Irish, Italians, and eastern European Jews, came to be considered "white" (Alba 1985, 1990; Brodkin 1998; Gerstle 1999; Ignatiev 1995; Jacobson 1998; Roediger 1991). For example, the Irish were once considered an inferior "race" by American English immigrants and other "white" citizens, who regularly characterized nineteenth-century Irish immigrants as "savage," "low-browed," and "bestial." The Irish eventually clawed their way into whiteness (Roediger 1991).

Although the courts defined European immigrants as white and thus eligible for citizenship, scientists, reformers, and nativists challenged their racial fitness and questioned whether the Irish—whom many considered little better than "white Negroes"—could ever function as American citizens (Alba 2009; Gerstle 1999; Guglielmo 2003; Ignatiev 1995). Many Irish immigrants arrived as refugees from the famine in extremely poor health, in poverty, and unable to speak English. But the Irish eventually attained whiteness by shifting their political alliances, achieving economic mobility, and adopting deliberate and extreme measures to distance themselves from African Americans. Economic mobility in particular led to the decoupling of national-origin differences from differences perceived as "racial," contributing to the development of the idea that for Irish and other European immigrants, racial status was malleable rather than fixed. As economic and cultural differences diminished and eventually faded between white and nonwhite immigrant groups, the Irish, Italians, and eastern European Jews became racially reclassified as white. Whiteness became an achieved rather than an ascribed status (Alba 1990, 2009; Haney-Lopez 1996; Perlmann and Waldinger 1997; Waters 1990). Restrictions on immigration that were put into place from the 1920s to the 1960s and the internal migration of blacks from the South to northern cities were two phenomena that hastened the process of firmly establishing previously nonwhite European immigrants in the white category and sharpened the dividing line between nonblacks and blacks (Foner 2000, 2005; Jacobson 1998).

Research has shown that European immigrants are not the only groups to have changed their status from nonwhite to white. Asian ethnic immigrant groups, such as the Chinese and the Japanese, also managed to change their racial status from almost black to almost white. James Loewen (1971) documents how Chinese immigrants in the Mississippi Delta made concerted efforts to modify their lowly racial status through economic mobility, the emulation of the cultural practices and institutions of whites, and the intentional distancing of themselves from blacks. The Mississippi Chinese not only actively distanced themselves both physically and culturally from blacks but also rejected their fellow ethnics who married blacks, as well as any multiracial children they bore. By adopting the antiblack sentiment embraced by Mississippi whites and by closely following the region's moral codes, the Chinese accepted rather than challenged the existing racial hierarchy and essentially crossed over the black-white color line. As a consequence of such deliberate efforts, the racial status of the Chinese in the region changed from almost black to almost white.

The historian Paul R. Spickard (1989) notes a similar process of change among Japanese Americans, who at the beginning of the twentieth century were at the bottom of the racial hierarchy, along with blacks, and who were interned during World War II because of their foreign and alien status and image. Yet after 1965, with the arrival of a wave of highly skilled and highly educated immigrants from Asia, the position of Japanese and other Asian ethnic groups in the United States changed so dramatically that they now don the status of "honorary whites." In fact, so extreme is the shift in America's racial hierarchy and the perception of Asians that they have become America's "model minority" and represent the group against which other nonwhite minorities are often judged and compared. This is a far cry from the derisive designation "yellow horde" used to describe Asian immigrants at the turn of the twentieth century (Gans 2005; Lee and Zhou 2004; Zhou 2004).

The boundaries of whiteness have changed in the past and appear to be expanding yet again to incorporate new immigrant groups, such as Asians and Latinos, reflecting the inconstant and changing nature of racial categories for all groups, except perhaps blacks (Gallagher 2004; Gans 1999; Gerstle 1999; Haney-Lopez 1996; Warren and Twine 1997). Pointing to patterns of residential segregation, for example, scholars find that blacks are more likely to be segregated than other racial and ethnic groups, regardless of household income (Charles 2003; Massey and Denton 1993). Research also shows that Asians and Latinos are marrying whites at higher rates than blacks are marrying whites, thereby enhancing the possibility that the children of these unions will find it increasingly easy to adopt a nonblack identity (Gerstle 1999; Hollinger 2003; Perlmann 2000; Perlmann and Waldinger 1997). France Winddance Twine's (1996) research on multiracial identification reinforces this point; she finds that the children of black intermarriages with whites or members of other racial groups are usually perceived by others as monoracially black, whereas the children of Asian and Latino intermarriages are not similarly perceived as monoracially Asian or Latino (see also Hollinger 1995). Jonathan Warren and Twine (1997) posit that this is because Asians and Latinos appear to "blend" more easily with whites than do blacks, at least from the perspective of many Americans. These trends lead some scholars to hypothesize that Asians and Latinos are the next in line to become "white" (Gerstle 1999; Hollinger 2003; Perlmann 2000; Perlmann and Waldinger 1997).

Thus, a number of immigrant ethnic groups have changed their status from nonwhite to white or almost white, while black immigrants and African Americans so far have not been able to do this. West Indian immigrants attempt to change their status by distancing themselves from black Americans and do what they can to make sure they are not associated with them (Foner 2005; Waters 1999a). In fact, most West Indian immigrants feel superior to black Americans and do not want to share the identity of "black American" because this identity connotes downward mobility into a stigmatized status (Waters 1999a). After only one generation, however, U.S.-born West Indians find it increasingly difficult to distinguish themselves from black Americans, and more often than not they choose to identify as black Americans, both because they feel that their West Indian ethnicity is no longer salient and because others treat and identify them as such (Waters 1999a).

In a society that recognizes blackness—and little else—on sight, black immigrants and African Americans have not been able to change their racial status. Herbert Gans (2005, 19–20) refers to this as the pattern of African American exceptionalism, elaborating, "The only population whose racial features are not automatically perceived differently with [the achievement of] upward mobility are African Americans: Those who are affluent and well educated remain as visibly black to whites as before." Jonathan Warren and France Winddance Twine (1997, 208) argue that this is because the construction of "whiteness" depends on the perceived existence of "blackness":

> Because Blacks represent the "other" against which Whiteness is constructed, the backdoor to Whiteness is open to non-Blacks. Slipping through the opening is, then, a tactical matter for non-Blacks of conforming to White standards, of distancing themselves from *Blackness,* and of reproducing anti-Black ideas and sentiments.

They explain that throughout the history of the United States, blacks have served a critical role in the construction and expansion of whiteness as a category by serving as the definition of what white is not. Richard Alba and Victor Nee (2003) expand upon this idea and link it directly with questions about immigration and assimilation. They raise the question of whether social closure directed against African Americans is a necessary step in the process of assimilation for immigrant groups. In other words, they ask, is it essential for new immigrant groups to mark African Americans as the out-group and to distance themselves from blacks in order to enhance the racial bond with whites and eventually become white? Recognizing the centrality of this question, Alba and Nee posit, "Whether the existence of racial out-groups is essential to the process of assimilation is the most vexed question in the entire American literature on ethnicity and race" (120).

Group boundaries have expanded throughout history and may continue to change, yet the one group for whom this seems not to apply is blacks. Pointing to indicators such as residential segregation and intermarriage, scholars argue that the apartness of blacks is real, and that black racial identity and social status are fixed (Glazer 1997; Yancey 2003). Given the unique history of African Americans, who are the only group to have been brought here as slaves and the rigidity of the boundary surrounding blacks, some social scientists argue that a black-nonblack divide is emerging, in which Asians and Latinos fall on the non-black side of the divide. Hence, unlike the white-nonwhite divide, whose premise is the formation of a "people of color" grouping versus whites, the premise of a black-nonblack divide is a pattern of "black exceptionalism" in race and ethnic relations, such that blacks continue to stand apart from other nonwhite groups.

The Disappearance of Color Lines

Perhaps no other event in U.S. history marked the possibility that the color line may be disappearing altogether than Barack Obama's election in November 2008 as the country's president. During his campaign Obama presented a vision of a postracial America where racial status continues to decline in significance in a country that is strengthened rather than divided by its multiracial and multicultural diversity. Obama's message resonated so strongly with many Americans in part because Obama himself symbolizes change because of his multiracial and multicultural heritage and not only because of his progressive political agenda. Immediately after his election, journalists and pundits proclaimed that the color line had collapsed and that we are now a "postracial" society in which anything is possible (see Michael Eric Dyson, "Race, Post Race," *Los Angeles Times,* November 5, 2008, "Opinion"; Thomas L. Friedman, "Finishing Our Work," *New York Times,* November 5, 2008, op-ed; Adam Nagourney, "Obama Elected President as Racial Barrier Falls," *New York Times,* November 5, 2008, op-ed; Abigail Thernstrom and Stephan Thernstrom, "Is Race Out of the Race?," *Los Angeles Times,* March 2, 2008, op-ed).

David A. Hollinger sketched such a society in his influential and visionary book, *Postethnic America* (1995), in which he proposes the possibility that color lines may be altogether fading, and that the United States may be moving into a cosmopolitan, or "postethnic," era. In a postethnic America, racial and ethnic affiliations would be porous and voluntary, and identities could be multiple and symbolic so that individuals could "affiliate or disaffiliate with their own communities of descent to [the] extent that they choose, while affiliating with whatever nondescent communities are available and appealing to them" (116). In this scenario, racial and ethnic identification would take on a character similar to that of religious affiliation, in which individuals could not only choose their affiliation but also preserve the "right to exit" from that group. Essential to Hollinger's vision of a postethnic society is the element of choice in ethnoracial identification. Hollinger (2008) stipulates that postethnic is not anti-ethnic nor is it colorblind; rather, postethnic means that individuals could devote as much or as little of their energy to their community of descent as they choose. In short, descent is not destiny.

Hollinger (1995) claims that multiracial Americans are performing a historic role at the moment by helping to move the United States in a postethnic direction, since they are able to freely choose "how tightly or loosely they wish to affiliate with one or more communities of descent" (165). In a similar vein, Herbert Gans (1999) views multiracial identification as a harbinger of progress because it reflects the diminishing significance of the current racial scheme.

He further predicts that today's racial categories may become increasingly less relevant in each generation until they fade altogether. With the increasing hybridization of "American stock," we may be reconfiguring the country along nonracialist lines (Gerstle 1999; Nash 1995).

Given the trends in intermarriage and a small but rapidly expanding multi-racial population, the United States may be moving in a postethnic direction, where group boundaries no longer circumscribe ethnoracial identification and opportunity structures. That the United States has elected its first black president, who hails from multiracial and multicultural origins, appears to signal that we may indeed be moving in this direction. However, it remains to be seen which of these scenarios best characterizes the state of racial relations in twenty-first-century America, and it is to this vexing question that we turn our attention in the remainder of this book.

~ Chapter 3 ~

What Is This Person's Race?
The Census and the Construction
of Racial Categories

At its inception more than two centuries ago, in 1790, the decennial census began the process of counting the American population by race, setting the stage for the national institutionalization of racial status and the color line during the postindependence era of slavery, and race has remained a classification category in all subsequent U.S. censuses. But the way the census has measured it has remained far from consistent over time. Because census practices have often reflected the centrality of racial status as an organizing principle of the legal, political, social, and economic life in the United States, studying the changes in the census racial categories yields revealing information about the changing nature of America's color line over the past two centuries (Haney-Lopez 1996; Nobles 2000; Prewitt 2004). However, racial categories used in the census—like those used in civil rights legislation—do more than reflect the country's racial reality; they play a key role in the social and political construction of that reality (Kertzer and Arel 2002; Nobles 2002). The construction of racial categories impacts the way that we think, talk, and write about race and, ultimately, the way we see and identify ourselves in racial and ethnic terms (Bumiller 1988; Foner and Fredrickson 2004; Itzigsohn 2004; Nobles 2000, 2002; Padilla 1985; Prewitt 2004; Skrentny 2002).

In this chapter we examine how the U.S. census has measured race throughout its history, including the latest change, which allows Americans to mark more than one race to identify themselves. A number of factors have influenced these modifications, the two most important being the black-white color line and immigration. We also show how the creation of racial categories by the U.S. census and civil rights legislation can promote collective identities among groups with disparate national origins. Institutional forces not only reflect but also shape ethnoracial boundaries.

The U.S. Census and the Office of Management and Budget Directive Number 15

Article 1, section 2, of the U.S. Constitution mandates that the country's population be counted every ten years, for the purpose of congressional apportionment. Since its inception in 1790, the census has been used to determine a national system of taxation, the number of U.S. representatives from each state, and the boundaries of congressional districts. The census has always counted the U.S. population by gender, age, and race; the U.S. government has collected data on racial status for more than two centuries. (In 1790, color, not race, was the primary basis of classification.) The way that race has been conceptualized, and even the categories themselves, have undergone considerable change over time. Categories have been added, dropped, and altered throughout the history of the U.S. census, and only three categories—white, Chinese, and Japanese— have consistently appeared on the census enumeration forms in the twentieth century (Farley 2002).

In an effort to standardize the racial and ethnic categories used by the federal government, the Office of Management and Budget (OMB), part of the executive branch of the U.S. government, issued Statistical Policy Directive Number 15 in 1977. The OMB determines which racial and ethnic categories are employed by the federal government in its statistical systems. The purpose of the racial- and ethnic-classification scheme has been "to provide a common language for uniformity and comparability in the collection and use of data on race and ethnicity by federal agencies" (Anderson and Fienberg 1999, 170). Classifying the population by race and ethnicity allows for consistent reporting of federal data collection and record keeping, providing a basis for assessing compliance with civil rights directives and legislation by both the private and public sectors, including agencies at various levels of the U.S. government.

Thus, the main reason for classifying the U.S. population by race and ethnicity is not an interest in race per se, but rather stems from an effort to meet the requirements of the Constitution and to monitor discrimination and enforce civil rights legislation. In the 1970s, in the wake of the post–civil rights era, new agencies such as the Office of Federal Contract Compliance Programs in the Department of Labor, the Equal Employment Opportunity Commission, and the Office for Civil Rights in the Department of Education emerged to ensure that employers, schools, and public and private organizations reported the racial composition of their workforces, student bodies, and clients. Classifying the U.S. population by race allows the federal government to determine conditions that may result from discrimination or that may violate the civil rights of racial or ethnic minorities in arenas such as education, employment, small business, and housing (Harrison 2002). Having data available on hiring, firing, and promotion by census racial categories enables the U.S. government to ascertain whether employers hire and promote blacks in various occupational sectors, whether school and university systems enroll black students, and to what extent federal funds go to minority-owned small businesses (Farley 2004). Official statistical representation in the census is also important to racial and ethnic minority groups because it allows them to qualify for and participate in federal programs designed to assist disadvantaged minorities (Skrentny 2002).

Race and the Color Line

Since the first census, different racial and ethnic groups have been defined and counted differently in the census, and the terms used to define "racial" and "ethnic" have their own history within that of the census.

"Black"

In the era of slavery, the decennial census began the process of enumerating the U.S. population for the purposes of representation and taxation, yet the seemingly simple task of counting Americans set the stage for the institutionalization of America's color line. Before enumerating the U.S. population, Congress had to decide who should be counted and, in particular, whether slaves should be included as the equivalent of free persons for the purposes of taxation. Northerners thought that slaves should be the equivalent of free persons, but Southerners thought that each slave should be counted as only a fraction of a free person. In 1783, Congress decided on a compromise, approving a motion to multiply states' slave populations by three fifths, which reduced the official slave population by two fifths (Anderson 2002; Williams 2006).

This decision was enormously significant since counting a slave as a fraction of a free person marked the legitimization and institutionalization of a racial hierarchy and the black-white color line in government policy and practice. The prevailing view at the time was that counting a slave as the equivalent of a free white person would have diminished the worth and identity of free white persons in the United States (Nobles 2000). The decision also reflected the view that slaves constituted a "species of property" to be excluded from the possibility of political participation and property ownership (Anderson 2002). By agreeing to the three-fifths counting method, those who agreed to this early approach to enumeration lent validation, perhaps unintentionally, to the idea that slaves were intrinsically less worthy than and therefore unequal to free white persons, further legitimizing slavery itself. This practice of legitimating black inferiority and cementing the black-white color line in the census held for more than eight decades, until the passage of the Fourteenth Amendment in 1866, at which time slaves were finally fully counted as the equivalent of free white persons.

The enumeration of slaves as a fraction of free white persons was not the only way in which the census reinforced the black-white color line. In 1840, the census included categories that measured handicaps and mental illnesses, such as "deaf," "blind," "illiterate," "insane," and "feebleminded." Higher proportions of the black population, both slave and free, reported handicaps or mental illness, and this data provided proponents of slavery with a "scientific" reason to bolster their view of black inferiority and to justify enslavement. Such measures illustrate the ways in which categorization was used for the expressed purpose of advancing the racial theories of some scientists (Nobles 2002).

Other attempts to measure the black population throughout history reflect attempts to tightly control racial mixing and the black-white color line and also to test racial theories. For example, the category "mulatto," meaning part white and part black, was added to the census questionnaire in 1850, in order to assess whether black-white mixed-race people lived shorter lives than either blacks or whites. If this were the case, some scientists believed that it would support the hypothesis that blacks and whites were separate species and, therefore, unfit to mix (Nobles 2000). Over the next few decades, however, the mulatto population nearly tripled in size, from 11.2 percent of the black population in 1850 to 29.0 percent in 1910. Thus, by the early twentieth century nearly one-third of the population labeled black was actually racially mixed; although these figures seem high to us today, they are undoubtedly undercounts, since they are based on enumerators' reports of the visible white ancestry of blacks rather than on self-reports (Davis 1991/2001).

Census planners continued to change racial categories in an attempt to more accurately measure the extent of mixture within the black population, resulting in the addition of the categories "quadroon" (a person with one-quarter black ancestry) and "octoroon" (one-eighth black ancestry) in 1890. In fact, the directions of the 1890 census cautioned census enumerators to take care when distinguishing among these categories (Nobles 2002, 53).

> Be particularly careful to distinguish between blacks, mulattoes, quadroons, and octoroons. The word "black" should be used to describe those persons who have three-fourths or more black blood; "mulatto," those persons who have from three-eighths to five-eighths black blood; "quadroon," those persons who have one-fourth black blood; and "octoroons," those persons who have one-eighth or any trace of black blood.

The government's decision to collect such data illustrates its fixation with tracking racial mixing and the black-white color line. The most famous case involving an octoroon was *Plessy v. Ferguson*, in 1896. The plaintiff, Homer Plessy, challenged not only the constitutionality of racial segregation but also the state's right to assign racial identities to individuals without their consent (Kennedy 2003b). Despite the fact that Plessy was an octoroon, one-eighth black and seven-eighths white, the Supreme Court ruled that Plessy was "colored" and upheld the law of segregation (DaCosta 2007).

By 1900, the categories of "quadroon" and "octoroon" had been eliminated because of difficulties that census takers experienced in accurately measuring mixed populations and because the "data" on such mixtures proved to be of little use to the Census Bureau. The inclusion of such categories in the census throughout the Reconstruction years, however, reveals the extent of concern among whites about racial mixing at the time and, specifically, the depth of apprehension that property and other wealth holdings might be passed down to the offspring of white fathers and black mothers. Tracking the black population according to even rough degrees of racial mixture was quite inconsistent as indicated by the Census Bureau estimation that by 1918 at least three fourths of all blacks in the United States were ancestrally mixed (Davis 1991/2001), implying a rate of growth in the mixed population that bordered on the implausible.

Given presumed increases in the country's mulatto population and the difficulty in gauging it precisely, southern states, such as Tennessee and Louisiana, took measures into their own hands by formally legalizing the rule of hypodescent in 1910, and other states soon followed suit. Henceforth, a person with any trace of black ancestry would be legally defined as black and as a result have no rights to inherit property and other wealth holdings from their white fathers. By 1925, nearly every state in the country had codified the practice as law.

By 1930, the Census Bureau made a decision that had a fateful and enduring impact on the way that Americans define who is black. Census enumerators were instructed to classify all mixed-race black-white individuals as "Negro." The directions read: "A person of mixed white and Negro blood should be returned as Negro, no matter how small the percentage of Negro blood. Both black and mulatto persons are to be returned as Negroes, without distinction" (Nobles 2000, 72). Partly because mulattoes were so numerous, and partly because they were not necessarily physically distinguishable from the black population, the Census Bureau dropped the mulatto category altogether and eliminated the divide between pure black and the racially mixed, calling them all blacks and thereby treating blackness as an all-encompassing monolithic category, without gradation. The sheer paradox of the one-drop rule is self-evident: it is not a two-way street. One can have mostly "white blood" (and even be seven-eighths white, like Homer Plessy) and not be white, but any "black blood" and one is black (Funderburg 1994).

The laws of much of the country during the first three decades of the twentieth century had come to adopt and institutionalize the "one-drop rule" of hypodescent, by which all persons with any trace of black ancestry were labeled racially black, as a criterion by which to attempt to delineate race and the racial divide (Nash 1995). The census followed suit in 1930. The elimination of the "mulatto" category brought the census categories in sync with the *Plessy v. Ferguson* ruling of 1896. Thus, the census provided another legal venue through which the rights and wealth holdings of whites could be preserved and the status of blacks could simultaneously be thwarted (DaCosta 2007). Not until *Loving v. Virginia,* in 1967, when the U.S. Supreme Court overturned the final ban on interracial marriage, did the one-drop rule also lose its legal legitimacy. American blacks are the only group to which the one-drop rule has applied, and consequently they are the only group for which the membership has been so tightly controlled (for examples of how racial mixture is conceived outside the United States, see Bailey 2008; Foner 2005; Kertzer and Arel 2002; Loveman and Muniz 2007; Nobles 2000; Schwartzman 2007; and Telles 2004).

Throughout the history of the U.S. census, not only the terms for racial mixture among the black population but also the labels for the category "black" have changed. In 1900 and 1910, the census used the category label "black." But this changed in 1920, when the word "Negro" replaced "black," and this remained in place for the next four decennial censuses: 1930, 1940, 1950, and 1960. In 1970, "Negro or black" appeared as an option and remained until 1990. In the year 2000 the census expanded the category to include "black, African American, or Negro" as a single racial category with multiple descriptors (Farley 2002).

In 1990 the census also added a brief addendum to the "other race" category that effectively racialized persons of West Indian and African origins as black. The instructions state: "The Black or Negro category also includes persons who identify as African-American, Afro-American, Haitian, Jamaican, West Indian, Nigerian, and so on." Hence, the census encouraged immigrants and the descendents of immigrants from Caribbean and African countries to adopt a black racial identity by instructing them to identify themselves as black rather than suggesting that they mark "other race" or another racial category. In this regard, the census created and imposed a collective black identity on members of disparate national-origin groups, who may have chosen to identify otherwise if given an option. This illustrates yet one more way that the census provided the locus of the country's color line.

"Mexican"

Other ethnoracial categories have similarly changed over the history of the census. In 1930—and only in 1930—"Mexican" was listed as a possible response to the "color or race" question, and enumerators were instructed to place any person of Mexican descent "who is definitely not white" into the "Mexican" category (Foley 1998). However, Mexican Americans, particularly elites, strongly objected to this, since they did not consider themselves a separate racial group from whites. In fact, the premier civil rights group for Mexican Americans at the time, the League of United Latin American Citizens (LULAC), founded in 1929 in Corpus Christi, Texas, decided against forging ties with the National Association for the Advancement of Colored People (NAACP) because LULAC members considered it "an insult" to be associated with blacks or with other "colored" races, such as Chinese and Indians (Foley 1998). LULAC restricted membership to U.S. citizens and attempted to construct a new identity for Mexican Americans as "Latin Americans," emphasizing English-language skills and loyalty to the U.S. Constitution.

Making the claim that Mexican Americans are "white" rather than "colored," LULAC vigorously argued that there was no need for a distinct "color or race" category for Mexicans. In the next decennial census, 1940, and in subsequent censuses, "Mexican" was dropped as a color or race category. Most Mexican Americans of the time may not have enjoyed the same social, economic, or political privileges as whites, but at least they were legally classified as white by the census and the U.S. government. This was a significant coup; LULAC members saw clearly that racial status—more specifically, being legally defined as white—was what mattered most with respect to opportunity and privilege.

To reinforce the status of Mexican Americans as whites, LULAC stressed the importance of maintaining a color line between their members and blacks, urging members to dissociate themselves from blacks and, in fact, expelling one member for having "married a Negress" (Foley 1998). Even though Mexicans may not have been socially considered white, it was clear that they were not black. The addition of "Mexican" as a color or race category in the 1930 census and its immediate removal in 1940 reflect the view that the group boundaries surrounding Mexicans were far more malleable and porous than those surrounding blacks at the time.

"Asian"

Census categories have done more than indicate the outlines of the color line in America; they have also reflected the changing racial and ethnic composition of the United States that occurred as a result of the arrival of new immigrants from Asian countries in the latter half of the nineteenth century. For example, in 1870, the census introduced "Chinese" as a "color" category, and in 1890 it added "Japanese" as an option. A relatively small Asian immigrant stream to the United States in the early twentieth century prompted the 1920 census preparers to add the categories "Filipino," "Hindu," and "Korean" in an effort to quantify the different racial groups in the country. In the early twentieth century, Asian-origin groups not only were considered a separate "color" but were also ineligible for U.S. citizenship under the Naturalization Act of 1906. In the case of Asian-origin groups, the census questions tracked the public sentiment that Asians were both foreign and of separate races.

The cases *Takao Ozawa v. United States,* in 1922, and *United States v. Bhagat Singh Thind,* in 1923, reflected the conviction that Asians were not white and therefore were ineligible for citizenship. In *Takao Ozawa v. United States,* the court denied Takao Ozawa the right to citizenship on the basis that Japanese were not Caucasians and therefore not white, so they were ineligible for citizenship because only whites and American blacks could be naturalized. In *United States v. Bhagat Singh Thind,* the court ruled that Bhagat Singh Thind, a Hindu, was ineligible for citizenship because according to the common man's understanding of whiteness, Hindus are not white, even though Thind may be Caucasian according to anthropological evidence.

The Naturalization Act of June 29, 1906, extended the right of naturalization to "whites and persons of African descent or nativity." Consequently, the Court, while ruling that neither Ozawa nor Thind was white, did not consider classifying them as black or, more precisely, "of African descent," because doing so would have made Ozawa and Thind eligible for citizenship. Perhaps just as important, neither plaintiff considered petitioning for naturalization as a black, since this would have meant accepting a racially inferior status. Throughout U.S. history, Asian ethnic groups have been classified as neither white nor black; whereas some Asians have attempted to be classified as white, none has attempted to be defined as black. The nonwhite and nonblack status of Asians has had the consequence of making them ineligible for citizenship for decades, until Congress, near the end of the 1940s, eventually abolished all restrictions on Asians acquiring U.S. citizenship.

However, "Asian" (or rather, "Oriental") was not recognized as an official government category until 1966, when President Johnson's administration, on the heels of the landmark civil rights legislation passed in 1964, sought to measure the levels of the hiring of minority groups by government contractors. At the time, for the purposes of carrying out the equal-employment mandate, Orientals were lumped together with other minority groups, including Negroes, Spanish Americans, and American Indians (Skrentny 2002), under the rubric "minority." In 1977, the OMB's Statistical Policy Directive Number 15 merged the disparate Asian-origin groups under the umbrella term "Asian Pacific Islander." However, fearing that Asians would be more likely to identify with their national origin rather than with the term "Asian," Representative Robert Matsui (D-California) insisted that specific national origins be listed on the census (Farley 2004), and in 1980, the Census Bureau added new ethnic categories, including Vietnamese, Asian Indian, Guamanian, Samoan, Eskimo, and Aleut, to reflect the growth in the Asian-origin population that was due to recent immigration. In 1990, the Census Bureau modified the racial categories once again so that the Asian Pacific Islander (API) category included those whose ethnic origins were Chinese, Filipino, Hawaiian, Korean, Vietnamese, Japanese, Asian Indian, Samoan, and Guamanian.

As the Census Bureau did with blacks, the 1990 addendum to the "other race" category racialized individuals of distinct Asian and southeast Asian national origins by specifying that they mark themselves under the API category. More specifically, the addendum stated: "The Other API category includes persons who identify as Burmese, Fijian, Hmong, Indonesian, Laotian, Bangladeshi, Pakistani, Tongan, Thai, Cambodian, Sri Lankan, and so on." By directing individuals with diverse national origins into the API category, the census reinforced a collective identity among people from a variety of east and southeast Asian ethnic backgrounds, thereby institutionalizing the racialization of these Asians as a single group (Anderson and Fienberg 1999; Espiritu 2004; Skrentny 2002).

"White"

Perhaps the most interesting aspect of the "white" category is that it has not changed at all since the first census was taken in 1790, unlike the categories relevant to blacks and Asians, whose nomenclatures and compositions have both changed. In fact, the census instructions did not offer any kind of guidance concerning who is white, but rather defined whiteness through a process of elimination—defining who is not white (Haney-Lopez 1996). Whiteness was the standard by which other racial groups were measured and compared. Again, the census mirrored the centrality of racial status and the way that whiteness was defined by law, under which only Caucasians with no trace of non-Caucasian blood were considered white.

The Shift to Self-Enumeration

In the late 1950s and 1960s, racial categories came under scrutiny once again, prompted in part by the civil rights movement and the new immigration. Special-interest groups asserted that the racial categories of the census should accurately reflect America's new demographic diversity and lobbied for new categories, the disaggregation of the "white" category, and the substitution of the term "ethnic" for "race." The most monumental shift came in 1970, when Americans argued for the right to identify themselves by marking their own racial status on the census form, rather than leaving this task to census enumerators. Heretofore the latter had had complete control over assigning a racial identification that was based on visual inspection alone. Taking into consideration both public sentiment and cost, the 1970 census—the first time the census was taken by mail—replaced enumerator identification with self-identification. This landmark change gave Americans complete freedom to choose the "color or race" category that best represented them.

One remarkable result of the shift to self-enumeration was that it had little effect on the size of the black population—an indication of just how strongly the one-drop rule had become ingrained in the consciousnesses of both black and white Americans (Davis 1991/2001). In other words, blacks with white ancestry did not suddenly choose to identify as white or as some other race when given the opportunity to do so. Likewise, Americans who had previously been identified by census enumerators as white or some other race did not suddenly choose to identify as black after the change to self-enumeration.

There was, however, an unexpected increase in the size of the American Indian population, which grew from 827,000 in 1970 to 1.42 million in 1980 to 1.96 million in 1990—far in excess of any plausible level of natural increase. Americans who had previously been identified as another race by census enumerators—primarily white—were now checking the "American Indian" box (Eschbach 1995; Eschbach, Supple, and Snipp 1998; Harris 1994). For many of these Americans, identifying themselves as American Indian was a choice, not a constraint imposed by outsiders' ascription. This signaled the symbolic nature of American Indian identity for those previously classified as white. The fact that self-enumeration did not result in an increase in the population self-identifying as black illustrates that the history of racial mixing and the resultant meaning of racial categories and boundaries are not similarly consequential for American Indians and blacks.

Hispanic Origin

The 1970 census contained a separate question concerning Hispanic origin, asking whether a person's "origin or descent" was Mexican, Puerto Rican, Cuban, Central or South American, Other Spanish, or none of the above. (This question preceded the question about "color or race" in the questionnaire.) The addition of the Hispanic-origin or Hispanic-descent question was the result of appeals on the part of the U.S. Interagency Committee on Mexican-American Affairs in the 1960s to better measure the growth of the Hispanic population due to the influx of new immigrants from Latin America, primarily Mexico. The Census Bureau decided to add a question about Hispanic origin in the 1970 census questionnaire, but because the short form of the 1970 census was already in production, the Hispanic-origin question was added only to the more detailed long form, which was administered to about one in five households.

What was novel and unique about the way the Census Bureau measured the Hispanic population was that it distinguished Hispanic "origin or descent" from "color or race," thus effectively treating Hispanic origin as a set of national origins rather than a racial status and not viewing these as equivalents. One could mark "yes" to the Hispanic-origin question, choose among the specific Hispanic origins listed, then choose among the racial categories. Those who considered themselves Hispanic could be of any race, including white, black, or "some other race." The separation of Hispanic origin from race was enormously significant, since it marked the first time that the measurement of this type of group identity was not racialized: although the Census Bureau classified Hispanics as a separate group, it did not categorize them as a distinct racial group (Choldin 1986; Skerry 2002). The vast majority of Hispanics identified as either "white" or "some other race"; only 6 percent choose "black" as their race.

The Hispanic-origin question was included on the short form of the 1980 census questionnaire so it went to all households. The change coincided with a 60 percent increase in the Hispanic population during the decade of the seventies. This substantial growth reflected not only the improvement in coverage of the Hispanic population (as indicated by the increased count of the Hispanic population) and the fact that Hispanics saw themselves as a distinct group but also the significant expansion of the Hispanic population resulting from new waves of immigration (Bean and Tienda 1987).

Although Hispanics are not counted as a separate racial category in the U.S. census, they are considered a minority category in civil rights legislation and were considered as such as early as 1966; they subsequently benefited from various affirmative action programs on the basis of their minority status (Skrentny 2002). There is also evidence that Hispanics tend to see themselves as a distinct group, apart from whites, blacks, and others. For example, a recent Census Bureau study of alternative ways of asking about race revealed that when "Hispanic" is not included among the race options, between 56 and 68 percent of Hispanics identify as white. But when the "Hispanic" category is included as a racial option, the percentage of Hispanics who identify as white drops sharply to 13.7 percent (Hirschman, Alba, and Farley 2000), indicating that many Hispanics see themselves as a group distinct from whites or, more specifically, Anglos (a term often used in the American Southwest to refer to persons descended from northern and western Europe, including England) and from blacks (Bailey 2001; Foner and Fredrickson 2004; Hitlin, Brown, and Elder 2007; Itzigsohn 2004, 2009). This explains in large part why many Mexicans (usually about half) choose the "some other race" option to indicate their racial status.

The "Some Other Race" Option

Americans also had the option of marking "some other race" on the census and writing in the racial designation of their choice, starting with the 1970 census. In both the 1980 and 1990 censuses, the fastest-growing racial category was "some other race." Almost ten million Americans checked "some other race" in the 1990 census, 97 percent of whom were Hispanic. Furthermore, 40 percent of Hispanics chose the "some other race" category, compared to only 1 percent of the non-Hispanic population (Anderson and Fienberg 1999). Census Bureau coding rules regarding the "some other race" population were partly responsible for this. If a person checked the "some other race" box and wrote Irish or German, the Census Bureau recoded him or her into the "white" category. But if the person wrote any phrase that denoted a Spanish origin, he or she remained in the "some other race" category.

Hispanics, however, are also more likely than any other group to choose the "some other race" option because Hispanics, with an interracial legacy that dates back to the mixing of Spaniards and the indigenous peoples of South and Central America, tend to see themselves as belonging to more than one race. This long-standing and widespread history of racial mixing has produced backgrounds that are characterized as "hybrid" or "mestizo" among many Hispanics (especially Mexicans) that involve mixtures of earlier racial groups (Martin, DeMaio, and Campanelli 1990; Rodriguez 2007). That Mexicans are more likely than any other Hispanic group to choose the "some other race" category also signifies that they do not fit neatly in the traditional, binary black-white framework that has long characterized racial status in the United States (Hitlin,

Brown, and Elder 2007). Other Americans—a quarter of a million—who marked the "some other race" option in 1990 were often those who reported multiracial designations such as "black-white," "Eurasian," or "Amerasian" (Edmonston, Goldstein, and Lott 1996).

The 2000 Census: "Mark One or More Races"

During the early 1990s, new advocacy groups arose that once again challenged the racial categories used by the Census Bureau or, more specifically, the way the Census Bureau measures race altogether. These groups criticized the Office of Management and Budget's Statistical Policy Directive Number 15 for not accurately measuring the diversity in the country brought about by increases in interracial marriage and the growth in the multiracial population. They strongly pressed for a reconsideration of the categories to be listed on the 2000 census; in particular they challenged the directive that forced Americans to choose only one racial option. Until 1990, persons who did not want to put themselves into only one racial category were forced to mark "other" as the only remaining option. The instructions read: "If you fill in the 'other' race circle, be sure to print the name of the race," and specified that a person should list only one. If a person wrote two or more races, the Census Bureau considered only the first one listed, which became the way the person was tabulated. Hence, if a person wrote in "white and black," he was counted as white, and if a person wrote "black and white," she was counted as black (Dalmage 2000).

In response to mounting pressure, in 1993 the OMB set out to assess the adequacy of the existing categories; it established a set of principles to govern any revisions in categories and solicited recommendations for changes. The following year the OMB established an interagency committee for the purpose of reviewing possible changes that drew its members from thirty federal agencies, including the Census Bureau, the Department of Justice, and the Department of Education (Williams 2006). Between its inception in 1993 and the completion of its work in July 1997, the federal review involved seven congressional subcommittee hearings, three national tests, and focus groups and workshops that aimed to assess the needs of those who relied on federal data on race and ethnicity. The review also considered oral testimony from ninety-four witnesses and the views of nearly eight hundred letter writers.

Most prominent among those who criticized Statistical Policy Directive Number 15 were Susan Graham from Project RACE (Reclassify All Children Equally) and Carlos Fernandez from the Association for Multi-Ethnic Americans (AMEA), who both argued that the OMB, in the interest of accuracy and fairness, should add a "multiracial" category to the racial options. They noted that the absence of this category undermined the accuracy of other racial data. Graham and Fernandez also asserted that it is an affront to impose a monoracial identity on multiracials or interracial parents with children by forcing them to choose only one race for themselves or members of their households. Not only was forced monoracial identification inaccurate, because it denied the existence of interracial marriages, but it was also ultimately discriminatory.

Project RACE also mounted its efforts for change at the state level, stressing that multiracial children suffered psychological damage when they are forced to identify with only one race. This argument persuaded legislatures in Ohio, Illinois, and Georgia to enact laws adding "multiracial" as a category in state-mandated data collecting. Working at the federal level, the AMEA organized the Loving Conference in June 1992. The event commemorated the twenty-five-year anniversary of the Supreme Court ruling *Loving v. Virginia* (1967), which overturned state laws prohibiting interracial marriage or sex. The Loving Conference caught the attention of Congressman Thomas Sawyer (Democrat of Ohio), who in 1993 held hearings and invited representatives from AMEA to speak, giving them a prominent platform from which to launch their appeals to add a multiracial category to the census. They proposed that "multiracial" should be a sixth category, and that the five existing categories could be sub-identifiers so that Americans could check both "multiracial" and also mark "all that apply" from the existing five racial categories. A year later, in 1994, the OMB declared that racial categories in Statistical Policy Directive Number 15 were of decreasing value, prompting a revision of the directive, which in turn produced three major Census Bureau surveys.

Not everyone, however, was in favor of adding a multiracial category or supported allowing Americans to mark more than one racial category on government forms. Certain civil rights groups—including the National Coalition for an Accurate Count of Asians and Pacific Islanders, the National Council of La Raza, the Mexican American Legal Defense Fund, the Urban League, the National Council of American Indians, and the NAACP—voiced concern about the prospect of adding a multiracial category. These groups feared that those who would otherwise be counted as Asian, Hispanic, black, or American Indian would now choose to identify as multiracial. Black advocacy groups in particular were extremely vocal critics of providing Americans with the proposed multiracial option because they feared that many blacks would become "racial defectors" who would exit out of the black category by choosing to identify with another race if given the opportunity (Perlmann 2000; Williams 2006).

The concern on the part of civil rights groups stemmed from their realization that identity politics is a numbers game—more precisely, a battle over minority-group sizes. Many organizations feared that a diminished count of their group's members would reduce their clout vis-à-vis other groups, which could then adversely affect the allocation of political and economic resources (Kertzer and Arel 2002). Civil rights groups expressed concern that the shift could have an adverse impact on enforcement of the Voting Rights Act, blur the categories undergirding antidiscrimination and affirmative action programs, and potentially undermine the size and the effectiveness of state and federal programs aimed at helping racial and ethnic minorities (Perlmann 2000). Civil rights groups were not the only contingent that opposed the addition of the "multi-racial" category on the 2000 census. Some social scientists, OMB and Census Bureau officials, and representatives from other federal agencies warned that statistical categories should be discrete, few in number, capable of generating consistent responses, and comparable with past categories.

Final hearings took place in July 1997, at which time the interagency com-mittee recommended to the OMB that the census allow Americans to select multiple responses from the race categories, but recommended against adding "multiracial" as a sixth category. OMB agreed that "multiracial" should not be a separate racial category because individuals who have multiracial heritages may have little in common with one another, given the numerous possibilities of different racial and ethnic mixtures. For instance, someone who identifies as multiracial and marks both black and white may have little or nothing in com-mon with someone who is multiracial and marks Chinese and white. Thus, a "multiracial" designation would not have added such valuable information, while possibly being misleading. Representatives from the AMEA accepted this recommendation, stating that the decision marked an improvement over forced monoracial identification, but members of Project RACE remained dissatisfied with it.

On October 30, 1997, the OMB announced its decision that starting with the 2000 census and extending to all federal data systems by the year 2003, all persons would have the option to identify with "one or more races." The racial options on the 2000 census included "white," "black," "Asian," "Native Hawaiian or other Pacific Islander," "American Indian and Alaska Native" (AIAN), and "other" and offered Americans the option to mark "one or more races" (see figure 3.1). Although "Latino" and "Hispanic" were not racial cate-gories on the 2000 census, the OMB mandated two distinct questions regard-ing a person's racial and ethnic background, one asking race and the other asking whether a person was "Spanish/Hispanic/Latino." Since someone who self-designated as "Spanish/Hispanic/Latino" could be of any race, the census asked both questions in order to accurately measure the Hispanic pop-ulation in the United States. The OMB also reviewed a proposal that would group Hispanics in one racial category, but they eventually decided against making Hispanics a separate race, since they concluded that this might result in fewer persons being classified in the Hispanic category and fewer whites being classified as white as well (Rodríguez 2000).

The OMB's decision to allow Americans to "mark one or more races" to identify themselves represents a landmark change in the way the U.S. Census Bureau collects data on race. Its significance derives from it giving official status and recognition to Americans who see their backgrounds as having involved racial mixing—an acknowledgement that speaks volumes about how far the country has come since the days when the one-drop rule of hypodescent held

Figure 3.1   *U.S. Census Questionnaire, Questions on Race (2000)*

→ NOTE: Please answer BOTH Questions 5 and 6.

5 Is this person Spanish/Hispanic/Latino? *Mark* ☒ *the **"No"** box if **not** Spanish/Hispanic/Latino.*

☐ **No**, not Spanish/Hispanic/Latino
☐ Yes, Mexican, Mexican Am., Chicano
☐ Yes, Puerto Rican
☐ Yes, Cuban
☐ Yes, other Spanish/Hispanic/Latino — *Print group.* ↘

6 What is this person's race? *Mark* ☒ *one or **more races** to indicate what this person considers himself/herself to be.*

☐ White
☐ Black, African Am., or Negro
☐ American Indian or Alaska Native — *Print name of enrolled or principal tribe.* ↘

☐ Asian Indian   ☐ Native Hawaiian
☐ Chinese   ☐ Guamanian or
☐ Filipino   Chamorro
☐ Japanese   ☐ Samoan
☐ Korean   ☐ Other Pacific
☐ Vietnamese   Islander —
☐ Other Asian — *Print race.* ↘ *Print race.* ↙

☐ Some other race — *Print race.* ↘

Source: U.S. Bureau of the Census (2001).

legal sway and admitted of only one "black" racial category, irrespective of any actual multiraciality. By allowing Americans to mark more than one race, the OMB rejected the premise of absolute mutual exclusivity in racial categorization in the United States. Another way of viewing this change is that the multiple-race option transforms what was once a single, categorical variable into a more continuous one with many racial hues (Prewitt 2004). Although some argue that there is no strong evidence that the multiracial movement has shifted the way people think about race (Farley 2004), we contend otherwise and posit that the movement itself and the subsequent change in the 2000 census has altered the way Americans talk and think about racial categorization (Nobles 2000, 2002; Prewitt 2002). The mere fact that some Americans have decided to mark more than one race when given the option to do so signals a shift in thinking. Acknowledging multiraciality means that the boundaries around racial categories are now less rigidly drawn than in the past and perhaps also suggests that the tenacious black-white racial divide may be fading.

Multiracial Results in 2000 and 2008

As noted earlier, in 2000 about 7.3 million Americans, roughly one in forty Americans or 2.6 percent of the population, marked more than one race to identify themselves or members of their households (Ruggles et al. 2009). In 2008, this number was 6.8 million, or 2.2 percent, according to ACS data (Ruggles et al. 2009).[1] At first glance the decline from 2000 to 2008 might appear to indicate that multiraciality has decreased and the tightening of racial boundaries has actually risen since 2000. But closer examination suggests that the decline resulted from two major nonsubstantive components of change that, when removed from the trend, reveal that an increase did in fact occur.

The first component appears to have been confusion and ambivalence about the "other" category. Almost three and a half million people (3.4 million) in 2000 marked "other" and at least one of the remaining race categories. According to ACS data, by 2008, two million fewer Americans reported multiracial identities involving "other" and one of the remaining racial categories, suggesting that these people seemed to have changed their minds about marking themselves as both "other" and another race (Ruggles et al. 2009). Among the six "multiracial" possibilities that include the category "other" plus something else—other-white, other-black, other-Asian, other-AIAN, other-PI (Pacific Islander), and other plus two or more races—the percentage declines ranged from 51.2 percent in 2000 to 76.1 percent, all substantial decreases (Ruggles et al. 2009).

By far the largest number of persons in 2000 who marked "other" and another race was the "other-white" group, the majority of whom (63.6 percent) were persons of Latino origin. In 2000 these persons may have been uncertain whether to list themselves as "white" or as "other" and therefore marked both. However, many of those who in 2000 had marked "other" and "white" (along with other multiracial identifiers designating the "other" category) apparently decided to identify in single race categories by 2008, especially those Hispanics listing themselves as "white." This is evident by the inordinately large growth in the white Hispanic single race category, which jumped 59.5 percent—a rate of increase far outstripping those for any of the other single-race groups. This rise is too large to attribute to a surge in the white Hispanic population, so it must have come about from Hispanics switching from "other" multiple-race identifications in 2000 to single-race white identifications in 2008.[2]

The second component of change lowering the 2008 rate of multiracial reporting was immigration. Although immigration may diminish racial distinctions in America in the long run, in the short run, as noted earlier, it can lower multiracial reporting because the foreign-born disproportionately marry coethnics (either before or after their migration) and thus usually are not "potential multiracials" (Waters 2000). From 2000 to 2008, the foreign-born increased from 11.0 percent to 12.5 percent of the population, which affected multiraciality rates for Asians and Latinos. As shown in table 3.1, 14.1 percent of Asian census listings in 2001 and 18.1 percent of "other" listings (almost all of which involved Latinos) were multiracial identifications, and 11.9 percent of Asian and 7.6 percent of other listings involved multiracial identifications in 2008. The decline in the percentage of Asian multiracial identications in 2008 is due in part to continued high immigration of Asians since 2000. Because the vast majority of foreign-born Asians are not multiracial (nor are they likely to identify in multiracial terms), the percentage of Asian multiracial identifications decreased between 2000 and 2008, even though the total number of Asians who identified multiracially increased slightly across these two periods.

Given these factors that affect multiracial reporting, what is most significant for our argument is that the absolute numbers of persons reporting a multiracial identity from 2000 to 2008 either increased or essentially remained unchanged within all groups over one million in size, except within the "other" group. This indicates rising multiracial identification in those racial categories not involving large foreign-born increases or ambiguities and confusion about the meaning of the census categories or their applicability to the responding group. And, perhaps most notable, among blacks (the group least likely to reflect changes in multiracial reporting tendencies) the percentage of multiracial identifications rose from 5.2 percent to 6.2 percent by 2008. Thus, we think the balance of the evidence indicates that multiraciality is increasing in the United States—a conclusion consistent with the findings from other research that black-white intermarriage increased between 2000 and 2008, while residential segregation slightly declined for blacks and all Latinos and slightly increased for all Asians (Farley 2009; Iceland 2009). In the cases of Latinos and Asians, clear-cut declines in residential segregation would have occurred except for the large and disproportionate initial settlement of foreign-born persons in both groups in areas of high coethnic concentration.

Population projections also suggest that the multiple-race segment of the U.S. population will increase by two to three percentage points each decade for the next century. If the assumptions underlying such projections are correct,

Table 3.1   *Numbers of Racial and Multiracial Identifications by Census Race Groups, 2000 and 2007–2008*

	Racial Identifications[1] (in Millions)		Multiracial Identifications[2] (in Millions)		Percent Change in Multiracial Identifications	Percent of Identifications that Are Multiracial	
	2000	2007–2008	2000	2007–2008		2000	2007–2008
White	217.1	231.4	5.78	5.80	0.3	2.7	2.5
Black	36.2	40.0	1.86	2.48	33.3	5.1	6.2
Asian	11.9	15.1	1.68	1.79	6.5	14.1	11.9
Other	18.8	18.2	3.40	1.39	−59.2	18.1	7.6
American Indian and Alaska Native	4.3	4.6	1.87	2.17	16.0	43.5	47.2
Native Hawaiian or other Pacific Islander	0.9	0.8	0.49	0.41	−16.3	54.4	51.3

Sources: Tabulations by authors based on data from the 2000 U.S. Census and the 2007–2008 American Community Surveys (Ruggles et al. 2009).
1. The numbers of racial identifications by racial group, when summed, exceed the size of the total U.S. population because multiracial persons are counted here in each of the groups with which they identify.
2. Multiracial persons are counted in each race category that a given person mentions.

by the year 2100, as much as 95 percent of the American Indian population, 70 percent of the Hispanic population, 43 percent of the Asian population, 37 percent of the black population, and 35 percent of the white population could identify as multiracial (Edmonston, Lee, and Passel 2002). And even if the overall multiracial population grows much more slowly in the foreseeable future, it may not increase at similar rates for all groups. Multiracial reporting is currently not equally distributed across all racial and ethnic groups. Such differences suggest that distinctive patterns across racial and ethnic groups among those who chose to mark two or more races provide clues about where the old color line is fading and where new ones may be forming, a topic we discuss more fully in later chapters.

Conclusion

The way the U.S. census has measured race has changed throughout its history, and two of the most notable factors that have influenced these changes are the black-white color line and immigration. Most significantly, census practices have reflected the centrality of racial status as an organizing principle of life in the United States, from the census's initial counting of a slave as only a fraction of a free person to its introduction of "Chinese" as a color category to the one-time listing of "Mexican" as a racial category to the classification of "Hispanic origin" as a set of national origins. These decisions were enormously significant, because counting one group as a fraction of another, or counting some groups as racial categories while counting others as a set of national origins, helped to institutionalize racial and ethnic boundaries in government policy and practice, as well as in the national consciousness.

The categorization of the U.S. population along racial lines by the census and by civil rights groups is more than simply an exercise in counting. The development of the categories themselves plays a key role in constructing our social reality through discourse about racial status, by instructing certain groups to identify themselves in particular ways in the census, and by coding ethnic groups into racial categories. Moreover, by linking political benefits to group identities, the census can become an active agent in identity formation. Although we recognize that what is measured by the census and civil rights categories is "a particular kind of politicized construction of reality" (Kertzer and Arel 2002, 35), we argue that these ethnoracial identities are meaningful to those who claim them.

Racial categorization is continuing to evolve, with the most recent change reflected in the 2000 census—the landmark decision to allow Americans to "mark one or more races" to identify themselves and members of their households. This option is significant because it gives official status and recognition to Americans who see their backgrounds as having involved racial mixing. The freedom to choose more than one racial category is momentous when one considers that the U.S. census previously attempted to measure and classify racial mixing between blacks and whites through mechanistic categories such as "mulatto," "octoroon," or "quadroon"—or, according to the one-drop rule of hypodescent, as simply "black." By allowing Americans to mark multiple races to identify themselves, the OMB recognizes the rise of intermarriage, acknowledges the growing multiracial population, and rejects the premise of the absolute mutual exclusivity of race that once characterized racial measurement in U.S. history. In short, the change may signal that racial boundaries are no longer as rigidly circumscribed and defined as in the past. At the same time, the fact that mixed-race categories like "mulatto" were at one time used and subsequently discarded in favor of a return to exclusivist bases of categorization suggests that having available the option of designating oneself as a mixed-race person may not always reflect a loosening of the boundaries dividing racial groups. Thus, we think it is important to probe more deeply into the cultural and structural significance of intermarriage, multiraciality, and multiracial identification before reaching conclusions about shifts in the U.S. color line and the ways today's immigrants both generate and accommodate themselves to such changes.

~ Chapter 4 ~

Immigration and the Geography
of the New Ethnoracial Diversity

*with James D. Bachmeier
and Zoya Gubernskaya*

More immigrants come to the United States than to any other country in the world (Brown and Bean 2005). According to the American Community Survey, by the year 2008, the foreign-born population in the United States exceeded thirty-eight million, and their native-born children were nearly as numerous, accounting for about another thirty-four million (Ruggles et al. 2009). Unlike the waves of immigrants who arrived in the early twentieth century, today's immigrants are mainly non-European. In 2008, only about 12 percent of legal immigrants originated in Europe or Canada, whereas about 80 percent came from Latin America, Asia, Africa, or the Caribbean (U.S. Office of Immigration Statistics 2009). As a result, as previously noted, nearly sixty million of today's newcomers are nonwhite; this group (including both immigrants and their children) now constitutes nearly a fifth of the total U.S. population (Bean et al. 2009). These new arrivals contribute substantially to the size of the country's overall Latino minority (15.2 percent of the national population in 2008, up from less than 5 percent in 1970), and of the country's Asian group (about 5 percent, up from less than 1 percent) (Ruggles et al. 2009). And these trends are likely to continue. According to conservative National Research Council projections, by the year 2050 America's Latino and Asian populations will make up at least 24 percent and 8 percent of the U.S. population, respectively (Lee and Zhou 2004; Smith and Edmonston 1997). Unquestionably, then, contemporary immigration is altering the racial and ethnic terrain of the United States.

This chapter has three overarching objectives. The first is to communicate forcefully that immigration has led to a great deal of ethnoracial change in the United States over the past forty years. The second is to demonstrate that considerable variation in the degree to which this change has occurred exists across localities—states and cities. The third is to reveal where the largest concentrations of intermarriage, multiracial identification, and diversity are located. The most diverse state turns out to be California, where we decided to conduct in-depth qualitative interviews with intermarried couples and multiracials. We probe in detail the material from these interviews in the four chapters following this one. In this chapter's sections, we outline changes in the size and composition of the U.S. population over the past forty years, showing how contemporary immigration has increased the size of nonwhite groups and led to the birth of "new diversity" states and metropolitan areas in many parts of the country. We map out the geography of intermarriage and multiracial identification using data from the 2007 and 2008 American Community Surveys to illustrate which states and metropolitan areas exhibit the highest rates of exogamy (Ruggles et al. 2009). Finally, we calculate and present a measure of diversity that indicates which states and cities in the country show the greatest ethnoracial heterogeneity.

Immigration and the Geography of the U.S. Population's Racial and Ethnic Composition

As already emphasized, the U.S. nonwhite population has increased extensively over the past forty years as a result of substantial immigration. The two largest immigrant groups, Hispanics (over half of whom report themselves as white) and Asians (all of whom are considered nonwhite according to Census Bureau categorization), constituted only a small fraction of the country's population in 1970, but since then they have more than tripled in size, accounting together in 2008 for one fifth of the country's total people. Most of this growth—virtually all of it in the case of Asians—is directly attributable to contemporary immigration (Bean et al. 2004). The Latino population has grown so rapidly that by 2008 there were more Latinos in the United States, over forty-six million, than blacks, who numbered about forty million, even after counting as black all persons who listed a multiracial identification of black and one or more other racial categories. Thus, Latinos today are the nation's largest minority group. In 2008, Asians, too, accounted for a sizable fraction of the population (Ruggles et al. 2009). Clearly, the United States has moved far beyond black and white and now boasts a population that is far more diverse in race, ethnicity, and national origin than it was even just a few decades ago.

America's white population, too, is by no means insignificant. In fact, about 75 percent of the U.S. population reported only a white identification in 2008 (Ruggles et al. 2009). If we exclude from this figure whites who also reported that they were Latino (about 8.8 percent of the population), non-Latino whites make up about two thirds of the population. This proportion may appear large, but it comes at the end of a steady decline over the past three decades. In 1970, 83 percent of Americans were non-Latino whites; by 1980 the figure had shrunk to 80 percent; by 1990, to 75 percent; and by 2008, to 66 percent (Ruggles et al.

2009). Thus, the non-Latino white population has declined by about seventeen percentage points since 1970. If whites had remained as relatively numerous in 2008 as they were in 1970, there would be more than fifty million more of them in the country today. This may help to explain some Americans' anxiety that whites may soon become a minority in the United States.

While the proportion of non-Latino whites in the country has steadily declined, the percentages of Asians and Latinos have grown considerably. Asians have increased their share of the population by about four percentage points and Latinos by about ten percentage points since 1970. Non-Latino blacks increased their shares by a modest two percentage points (Bean et al. 2004). Thus, the major gains in shares of the U.S. population since 1970 are accounted for by Asians and Latinos, the groups that have made up most of the shift in the composition of immigrants coming to the country since 1965, when the National Origins Quota Act was abolished and replaced by the Hart-Celler Act.

The rise of Asian and Latino groups has increased the racial and ethnic diversity of the whole country, yet these changes are particularly evident in some areas and nearly invisible in others. In other words, because the new immigration has been geographically concentrated and unevenly distributed, some states and metropolitan areas are disproportionately reflective of, and perhaps strongly affected by, Asian and Latino immigration, whereas others remain virtually untouched, so that the new racial and ethnic diversity brought about by contemporary immigration is most conspicuous in certain areas of the country. Even though immigration has become more spatially dispersed than previously (Massey 2008), it still remains geographically concentrated. The implications of the country's growing diversity may be most evident in areas of the greatest immigration, and many Americans may assume that the growing racial and ethnic diversity is more ubiquitous than is indeed the case, if they happen to live in an area where immigration is concentrated.

To begin to understand such possibilities, we first examine state-by-state distributions of the nonwhite population in 2008, which constitutes a crude indicator of diversity. (We also present and calculate a more refined measure that is more suitable for analytical purposes that require both the number of groups and their evenness of distribution be taken into account.) By "nonwhite" we mean all persons identifying as Latinos and those who indicate that they belong to at least one of the nonwhite racial groups used in the census. When we use the term "ethnoracial" groups we are referring to five categories: Latinos, whites, blacks, Asians, and others. By including those "nonwhite" Latinos who identify as whites in this definition, as well as white multiracials, we employ an upper-bound measure of nonwhite racial and ethnic status for purposes of mapping diversity. Using such a standard, when we examine the thirty states with the largest nonwhite populations (see table 4.1), we see that in percentage terms, the most nonwhite state is Hawaii, whose population is 75.1 percent nonwhite. The least nonwhite state (not shown in table 4.1) is Vermont, whose nonwhites account for a mere 4.9 percent of the state's population. The states with the second and third largest nonwhite concentrations are the District of Columbia

Table 4.1 Percentage of a State's Nonwhite Population, by Ethnoracial Group, and Percentage Foreign-Born Within Each Ethnoracial Group, (for States with at Least 20 Percent Nonwhite Populations), 2007–2008

State[a]	Black		Asian and Pacific Islander		Latino		NANLOR[b]		Total Nonwhite	
	Percentage	Percentage Foreign-Born	Percentage	Percentage Foreign-Born	Percentage	Percentage Foreign-Born	Percentage	Percentage Foreign-Born	Percentage	Percentage Foreign-Born
Hawaii	3.6	4.6	62.3	23.4	8.2	12.3	1.0	1.8	75.1	21.0
District of Columbia	54.6	5.4	3.7	51.3	8.5	59.3	0.7	22.2	67.6	14.9
New Mexico	2.5	5.7	1.6	54.6	44.7	16.2	9.3	0.3	58.1	14.3
California	6.6	5.4	13.5	61.2	36.4	40.4	1.3	10.1	57.8	40.6
Texas	11.7	4.6	3.7	65.1	36.1	32.2	0.9	7.5	52.5	27.9
Nevada	8.0	5.6	7.5	55.6	25.5	45.4	1.9	2.9	42.9	37.8
Maryland	29.7	9.7	5.5	67.7	6.4	53.9	0.7	15.7	42.3	24.0
Georgia	30.2	4.5	3.0	65.8	7.9	53.6	0.7	16.8	41.8	18.4
Arizona	3.9	7.2	2.9	57.1	30.0	35.3	4.8	0.9	41.7	30.3
Mississippi	37.8	0.2	1.0	52.6	1.9	49.8	0.7	3.6	41.3	3.7
New York	15.4	26.2	7.2	70.5	16.4	40.6	1.0	34.1	40.0	40.3
Florida	15.5	18.4	2.6	65.0	20.8	50.6	0.9	18.0	39.7	38.3
New Jersey	13.6	13.9	7.8	71.0	16.1	44.7	0.7	29.5	38.3	38.8

Louisiana	32.3	0.5	1.6	61.4	3.3	41.1	0.9	3.7	38.1	6.7
Illinois	15.0	2.7	4.6	65.2	15.1	42.2	0.6	16.1	35.3	28.0
South Carolina	29.0	0.8	1.4	58.8	3.9	50.9	0.8	10.2	35.0	8.9
Alaska	4.9	5.5	6.1	50.9	5.6	20.8	17.0	0.1	33.6	13.6
Virginia	20.3	5.3	5.4	65.9	6.6	49.3	0.8	9.9	33.0	24.0
North Carolina	21.9	2.2	2.1	62.4	7.2	54.0	1.6	3.6	32.8	17.5
Delaware	21.2	6.9	3.1	66.2	6.5	37.0	0.7	7.2	31.6	19.0
Alabama	26.7	0.6	1.2	61.0	2.7	48.5	1.0	1.4	31.5	7.0
Colorado	4.2	8.6	3.3	55.0	20.0	28.5	1.5	3.0	29.0	27.3
Oklahoma	8.4	2.3	2.1	59.3	7.5	38.0	10.4	0.4	28.4	15.3
Connecticut	9.7	18.7	3.7	66.8	11.9	27.1	0.9	27.0	26.2	29.7
Washington	4.3	13.0	8.3	56.4	9.6	38.9	2.5	3.1	24.6	36.7
Arkansas	16.1	0.8	1.3	55.6	5.3	48.1	1.5	2.1	24.2	14.1
Tennessee	17.0	1.8	1.5	61.1	3.6	49.1	0.8	3.6	22.9	13.3
Michigan	14.6	1.7	2.6	64.3	4.0	28.6	1.2	2.9	22.5	13.9
Rhode Island	5.6	27.1	3.1	56.4	11.5	45.1	1.2	21.6	21.4	40.7
Massachusetts	6.3	29.7	5.2	66.2	8.3	33.8	1.3	37.8	21.1	40.9

Source: Tabulations by authors based on data from the 2007–2008 American Community Survey (Ruggles et al. 2009).

a. "New-diversity" states in italics.

b. Native American and non-Latino "other" racial groups.

and New Mexico, at 67.6 percent and 58.1 percent, respectively. Neither of these, like Hawaii, has a very large population. California and Texas are the next two most nonwhite states, at 57.8 percent and 52.5 percent nonwhite, respectively, and the two most populous states in the country. New York and Florida, the third and fourth most populous states, rank eleventh and twelfth in percentage of nonwhite population. Hence, with the exception of a few small states, the nation's most heavily populated states also tend to be the country's most nonwhite states.

Significantly, this new "nonwhiteness" departs substantially from the traditional black-white geographic pattern of old. When we break down into the four major racial-ethnic subgroups (except white) the nonwhite population in the states in which that segment of the population exceeded 20 percent in 2008, we find four discernible patterns. First, although the old black-white binary pattern of diversity is still somewhat in evidence, it is found only in a few southern states: Alabama, Arkansas, Louisiana, Mississippi, South Carolina, and Tennessee. We refer to these as "black-white states." Even Georgia and Maryland, a southern state and a border state, both with relatively large black populations, have changed enough recently to have substantial percentages of Latinos. Second, a few places are emerging that tend to exhibit a new binary pattern of mostly whites and Latinos, a prime example being Arizona. We refer to these as "Latino-white states." These places where Latinos, not blacks, constitute the bulk of the minority population add a new and different dimension to the county's traditional, dual black-white racial division.

The third major pattern is that twenty-two of the high-minority states (nearly three-fifths of them, including the District of Columbia), now contain at least three major racial and ethnic groups, each representing 5 percent or more of the state's overall population. The twenty-two states are Alaska, Arkansas, California, Connecticut, Delaware, the District of Columbia, Florida, Georgia, Hawaii, Illinois, Maryland, Massachusetts, Nevada, New Jersey, New Mexico, New York, North Carolina, Oklahoma, Rhode Island, Texas, Virginia, and Washington (see figure 4.1). Following the terminology of Frank D. Bean and his colleagues (2004), we call these the country's "new diversity states." More startling, seven states (Alaska, California, Maryland, Nevada, New Jersey, New York, and Oklahoma) contain four groups, each with at least 5 percent of total state population, a pattern we designate as "hyperdiversity." These places reflect a changing racial and ethnic landscape stemming in most instances from Asian and Latino population growth resulting primarily from contemporary immigration. Fourth, the states with the most racially and ethnically diverse populations are also among the country's most populous and also most prosperous places. Thus, the new racial and ethnic diversity in the United States appears to characterize mainly states that are both large in size and also generally among the nation's richest.

We find similar patterns of binary concentration and new diversity when we examine metropolitan areas containing the largest nonwhite populations in the country (see table 4.2). Thirteen of the twenty metropolitan areas with

Figure 4.1   *New Diversity and Hyperdiversity States (Those That Are 20 Percent or More Nonwhite), 2007–2008*

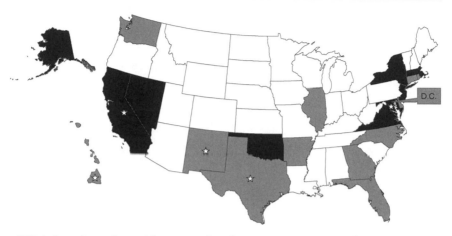

■ At least three ethnoracial groups each make up 5 percent or more of state's population
■ At least four ethnoracial groups each make up 5 percent or more of state's population
☆ "Majority-minority" states

Source: Tabulations by authors based on data from the 2007–2008 American Community Survey (Ruggles et al. 2009).

the relatively largest nonwhite populations, about two thirds, have at least three racial or ethnic groups constituting 5 percent or more of their populations. These urban locales are the loci of the country's new racial and ethnic diversity, and most are located in "new diversity states." They include Fresno, Honolulu, Houston, Jersey City, Los Angeles, Merced, Miami, New York, Riverside–San Bernardino, Salinas-Monterey, San Antonio, San Jose, and Stockton. The remaining seven of the top twenty nonwhite metro areas are "Latino-white": Brownsville, El Paso, Laredo, Las Cruces, McAllen, Visalia, and Yuma. Clearly, diversity is the emerging touchstone of the new racial-ethnic structure in the United States. California has the country's greatest number of high-diversity metropolitan areas, with seven of the top thirteen.

In addition to an apparent connection between diversity and overall population size, there also is an apparent link between diversity and immigration. When we examine the concentration of immigrants living in the states together with a simple nonwhite-percentage measure of diversity, we note that those states with the greatest diversity are also places with relatively large foreign-born populations (see also table 4.1). The top thirty states with the largest percentage of nonwhite residents tend also to contain higher percentages of foreign-born persons, except for the Latino-white states. Similarly, the low-diversity states have

Table 4.2   Percentage of a Metropolitan Area's Nonwhite Population, by Ethnoracial Group, and Percentage of Foreign-Born Within Each Ethnoracial Group for the Twenty Areas with the Highest Percentage of Nonwhites, 2007–2008

Metropolitan Area (MSAs & CMSAs)[a]	Black		Asian and Pacific Islander		Latino		NANLOR[b]		Total Nonwhite	
	Percentage	Percentage Foreign-Born	Percentage	Percentage Foreign-Born	Percentage	Percentage Foreign-Born	Percentage	Percentage Foreign-Born	Percentage	Percentage Foreign-Born
Laredo, Tex.	0.0	0.0	0.6	58.4	95.1	28.9	0.3	0.0	96.0	29.0
McAllen–Edinburg–Pharr–Mission, Tex.	0.4	4.2	1.0	82.7	89.6	30.6	0.3	11.7	91.3	30.9
Brownsville–Harlingen–San Benito, Tex.	0.3	7.3	0.8	76.9	86.1	27.8	0.4	9.7	87.7	28.1
El Paso, Tex.	2.8	5.7	1.1	60.8	82.1	30.4	0.6	0.7	86.6	29.8
Miami–Hialeah, Fla.	17.7	27.5	1.6	72.9	62.8	66.2	0.5	33.7	82.5	57.8
Honolulu, Hawaii	4.5	4.6	66.3	25.2	7.5	11.5	0.9	2.3	79.2	22.5
Los Angeles–Long Beach, Calif.	9.2	5.9	13.8	65.6	47.4	44.3	0.8	16.2	71.3	43.1
Las Cruces, N.M.	2.6	20.4	1.3	61.2	65.1	26.8	0.8	3.9	69.8	26.9
Jersey City, N.J.	12.7	18.2	11.2	77.0	40.8	55.3	1.2	30.0	66.0	51.4

Merced, Calif.	4.1	1.2	7.9	64.0	52.4	34.7	1.4	6.3	65.8	35.5
San Antonio, Tex.	6.8	4.2	2.3	55.2	54.3	15.9	0.9	5.9	64.4	15.9
Fresno, Calif.	5.2	1.7	8.4	51.6	49.1	31.4	1.7	8.3	64.3	31.0
Visalia–Tulare–Porterville, Calif.	1.8	13.6	3.8	51.6	56.6	35.3	1.4	3.9	63.6	34.9
San Jose, Calif.	2.8	9.5	32.2	65.1	26.4	39.7	1.0	19.9	62.3	51.1
Salinas–Sea Side–Monterey, Calif.	4.3	8.5	8.9	51.6	47.6	44.5	1.1	11.6	61.9	42.5
Stockton, Calif.	8.5	3.1	14.7	57.7	36.9	35.4	1.3	7.8	61.4	35.7
Yuma, Ariz.	2.2	2.7	1.4	52.1	56.1	36.6	1.4	0.0	61.0	35.0
New York–Northeastern, N.J.	22.4	31.1	11.2	72.1	26.1	42.3	1.2	49.4	60.9	43.8
Riverside–San Bernardino, Calif.	7.9	3.1	6.4	58.4	45.1	35.8	1.3	6.0	60.8	33.3
Houston–Brazoria, Tex.	17.5	5.9	6.4	68.3	34.8	44.3	0.7	13.7	59.4	35.2
Nonmetro areas	8.1	1.5	1.3	46.1	6.6	32.2	2.4	1.3	18.5	15.7

Source: Tabulations by authors based on data from the 2007–2008 American Community Survey (Ruggles et al. 2009).

a. Metropolitan statistical areas and consolidated metropolitan statistical areas; cities with four substantial minority groups in italics.

b. Native American and non-Latino "other" racial groups.

relatively few foreign-born persons. Thus, immigration is not only contributing to population growth but is also substantially responsible for the new racial and ethnic diversity in the country.

The Geography of Intermarriage, Multiracial Identification, and Diversity

Here we undertake an examination of intermarriage and multiracial identification and how they relate to contemporary immigration and the new racial and ethnic diversity, with the latter calculated in a more nuanced way than percentage nonwhite. We lay out the geography of intermarriage and multiracial identities using data from the 2007 and 2008 American Community Surveys. In the next section we discuss how racial and ethnic diversity seem to relate to both intermarriage and multiracial identities.

In our analysis of intermarriage we examined exogamy rates for couples, defined as the percentage of all current marriages where the partners are not members of the same ethnic or racial group. "Group" is defined as either all married couples in the total adult population or as all married couples in the adult population of a given major ethnoracial group. An ethnoracial group of couples is defined as all couples containing at least one person from the given group. In the case of multiracial persons, we treat them for purposes of defining intermarriage as belonging to the first group they listed in the data from the American Community Survey. We calculated exogamy rates per hundred marriages overall and for given racial-ethnic group for states (and the District of Columbia) and the fifty largest metropolitan areas in the country (tables 4.3 and 4.4). The overall exogamy rate is lower than it intuitively seems it should be, given the higher subgroup rates, but this occurs simply because in the subgroup rates each exogamous couple is counted twice, once in each subgroup represented by the couple's two ethnoracial identifications.

Not surprisingly, California shows one of the highest intermarriage rates of any state in the country, 18.1 percent of all marriages (figure 4.2). Among whites, over one fifth of all married couples have a spouse from a different ethnoracial group. A high prevalence of intermarriage in California is also demonstrated by the state's containing eight of the ten highest city intermarriage rates (table 4.3). In the sprawling Los Angeles–Long Beach area, over 25 percent of marriages among whites, more than 36 percent among Latinos, and 61 percent among Asians involve spouses from different ethnoracial groups. Even in Orange County, which has a reputation for conservativism, high rates of outmarriage obtain, especially among blacks, Latinos, and Asians, probably reflecting the selection into the county of highly educated intermarried minorities, but perhaps also reflecting the fact that the area's conservative reputation derives more from economic libertarianism than social conservatism.

Turning to the geography of multiracial reporting in the United States, we see, as in the cases of immigration and intermarriage, that multiraciality is not

Table 4.3   Intermarriage Rates and Diversity Index Scores, by State, 2007–2008

State	Intermarriage Rate[a]	Diversity Index	Intermarriage Rate[a] by Group				
			White	Black	Latino	Asian and Pacific Islander	Other
Hawaii	31.7	0.67	49.9	52.5	80.7	40.9	98.0
California	18.1	0.67	20.7	34.4	46.6	64.9	84.2
New Mexico	17.8	0.62	24.8	55.0	34.8	88.2	32.1
Nevada	16.1	0.60	16.8	34.4	62.1	78.7	77.9
Alaska	15.1	0.53	16.0	40.1	90.9	85.4	48.5
Arizona	12.5	0.57	13.4	48.5	49.0	84.7	34.9
Oklahoma	12.5	0.47	12.7	26.4	73.5	94.3	79.5
Colorado	11.7	0.45	12.2	45.9	55.9	86.1	85.8
Washington	10.8	0.41	10.6	57.6	75.2	79.4	81.6
District of Columbia	10.7	0.60	16.0	9.0	72.0	72.2	68.7
Texas	10.7	0.63	13.3	16.2	31.3	81.1	87.6
Oregon	9.0	0.34	8.9	52.2	77.6	89.6	84.5
Florida	8.8	0.57	9.5	17.8	47.7	88.7	88.1
Wyoming	8.1	0.24	8.0	54.4	80.3	91.9	74.7
Utah	7.8	0.31	7.8	67.9	73.2	79.1	68.7
New Jersey	7.7	0.57	7.8	18.5	53.0	72.7	76.5
Kansas	7.3	0.34	7.3	30.1	72.3	93.2	90.2
New York	7.1	0.59	6.8	23.5	50.4	68.4	76.1
Virginia	6.9	0.51	7.2	15.6	75.4	83.2	82.6

(Table continues on p. 66.)

Table 4.3   (Continued)

State	Intermarriage Rate[a]	Diversity Index	White	Black	Latino	Asian and Pacific Islander	Other
						Intermarriage Rate[a] by Group	
Maryland	6.6	0.58	7.3	10.9	75.8	80.6	81.3
Idaho	6.5	0.27	6.5	84.2	65.4	90.5	68.2
Connecticut	6.5	0.43	6.4	35.4	48.4	87.9	87.4
Illinois	6.4	0.54	6.7	13.8	52.1	79.1	85.9
Delaware	6.2	0.49	5.9	18.9	57.9	90.7	87.9
Montana	5.9	0.22	5.5	80.2	93.2	98.4	54.4
Rhode Island	5.2	0.37	4.9	43.1	61.5	82.4	95.9
Georgia	5.0	0.57	5.6	8.2	72.5	81.8	79.1
Massachusetts	4.9	0.36	4.7	38.3	60.7	77.9	76.7
Michigan	4.8	0.38	4.8	15.6	75.7	83.3	85.5
North Carolina	4.8	0.50	5.0	9.8	70.7	88.6	55.3
Louisiana	4.6	0.51	5.3	5.7	76.9	87.3	80.6
Nebraska	4.2	0.28	4.2	36.1	69.8	87.5	80.9
Arkansas	4.2	0.40	4.4	7.8	76.6	93.0	89.8
Indiana	4.1	0.30	4.1	22.6	68.9	88.2	87.8
Minnesota	4.1	0.27	4.0	52.5	77.4	86.6	76.3
South Dakota	4.0	0.25	3.9	100.0	82.3	83.3	51.5

Missouri	3.9	0.31	4.0	16.0	82.3	87.6	85.7
Wisconsin	3.9	0.27	3.8	26.6	68.8	76.3	78.6
Ohio	3.7	0.30	3.7	19.3	75.5	88.3	81.9
North Dakota	3.7	0.19	3.7	50.9	60.2	100.0	46.7
South Carolina	3.7	0.50	4.1	6.3	75.5	88.4	84.7
Tennessee	3.4	0.38	3.6	11.6	78.3	85.5	89.0
New Hampshire	3.4	0.13	3.4	82.8	77.7	71.8	89.2
Iowa	3.3	0.18	3.3	48.8	79.4	90.3	89.1
Alabama	3.2	0.46	3.5	6.3	74.3	89.6	75.8
Pennsylvania	3.2	0.32	3.2	18.4	59.0	80.6	79.5
Mississippi	2.8	0.52	3.3	4.1	80.7	86.9	69.7
Kentucky	2.8	0.22	2.7	24.2	79.2	90.5	91.3
Maine	2.6	0.10	2.5	99.2	84.6	95.0	88.8
Vermont	2.2	0.09	2.2	74.5	97.0	84.9	84.1
West Virginia	2.2	0.12	2.2	34.2	89.3	93.9	72.5
Average	.7.2	0.40	8.0	35.4	69.6	84.3	77.5

Source: Tabulations by authors based on data from the 2007–2008 American Community Survey (Ruggles et al. 2009).
a. Percentage of marriages that are ethnoracially exogamous.

Table 4.4   *Intermarriage Rates and Diversity Index Scores in the Fifty Largest U.S. Metropolitan Areas, 2007–2008*

Metropolitan Area	Intermarriage Rate[a]	Diversity Index	Intermarriage Rate[a] by Group				
			White	Black	Latino	Asian and Pacific Islander	Other
San Jose, Calif.	21.5	0.69	24.0	50.2	53.6	60.4	85.1
Oakland, Calif.	20.1	0.72	22.4	25.7	64.5	60.8	87.3
San Diego, Calif.	19.4	0.63	21.0	46.5	53.2	76.1	82.9
Los Angeles–Long Beach, Calif.	19.0	0.67	25.4	25.7	36.2	60.7	87.3
Riverside–San Bernardino, Calif.	18.5	0.63	23.0	31.1	41.4	74.5	72.0
Miami–Hialeah, Fla.	18.4	0.54	35.4	13.0	30.8	88.6	93.9
Orange County, Calif.	18.2	0.65	19.5	55.7	55.1	66.9	88.0
San Antonio, Tex.	18.0	0.57	27.9	33.2	30.0	78.2	91.4
Las Vegas, Nev.	17.8	0.64	19.2	33.7	58.6	77.1	78.0
San Francisco–Oakland–Vallejo, Calif.	17.6	0.66	19.1	41.7	69.5	49.5	76.6
Sacramento, Calif.	17.4	0.60	18.0	36.1	68.6	65.8	88.1
Austin, Tex.	15.3	0.59	17.1	27.4	51.6	85.5	97.3

Fort Lauderdale–Hollywood–Pompano Beach, Fla.	15.2	0.66	17.5	20.9	55.8	83.5	83.7
Seattle–Everett, Wash.	12.4	0.47	12.1	58.8	83.3	73.6	85.2
Denver–Boulder–Longmont, Colo.	12.3	0.52	12.9	37.4	53.4	79.5	86.2
Phoenix, Ariz.	12.0	0.55	12.5	44.4	49.9	80.0	61.2
New York–Northeastern, N.J.	11.8	0.72	12.7	21.3	41.2	62.9	79.7
Houston–Brazoria, Tex.	10.8	0.68	13.5	10.6	36.9	73.5	85.5
Portland–Vancouver, Ore.	10.5	0.38	10.4	50.8	78.4	88.8	91.7
Bergen–Passaic, N.J.	10.3	0.60	10.7	21.3	49.6	80.0	69.2
Fort Worth–Arlington, Tex.	10.1	0.59	10.9	18.8	48.0	84.6	85.5
Washington, D.C./Md./Va.	10.1	0.65	11.4	14.0	73.9	79.5	84.2
Dallas–Fort Worth, Tex.	10.1	0.65	11.3	13.3	45.8	80.1	83.9
Orlando, Fla.	9.9	0.60	11.0	23.1	35.8	88.0	80.8
Tampa–St. Petersburg–Clearwater, Fla.	9.4	0.47	9.8	19.9	55.7	87.2	87.5

(*Table continues on p. 70.*)

Table 4.4 (Continued)

Metropolitan Area	Intermarriage Rate[a]	Diversity Index	Intermarriage Rate[a] by Group					
			White	Black	Latino	Asian and Pacific Islander	Other
Norfolk–Virginia Beach–Newport News, Va.	9.2	0.55	9.8	15.2	76.1	88.5	90.2
Salt Lake City–Ogden, Utah	8.8	0.36	8.9	64.2	67.2	77.9	87.2
Chicago–Gary–Lake, Ill.	8.3	0.63	9.2	11.6	47.8	75.4	87.7
West Palm Beach–Boca Raton–Delray Beach, Fla.	8.0	0.54	8.6	16.2	53.0	92.2	93.2
Jacksonville, Fla.	7.7	0.50	8.2	13.2	64.6	88.6	94.2
Newark, N.J.	7.5	0.62	7.6	15.6	48.8	74.4	72.6
Nassau County, N.Y.	6.7	0.46	6.8	22.4	67.2	62.5	81.2
Kansas City, Mo./Kans.	6.7	0.41	6.9	20.2	78.1	83.5	90.1
Atlanta, Ga.	6.0	0.62	6.9	8.7	72.8	76.7	79.3
Milwaukee, Wis.	5.8	0.46	5.9	18.0	61.1	70.3	82.8
Raleigh–Durham, N.C.	5.8	0.55	6.2	9.6	71.3	89.5	72.9
Baltimore, Md.	5.7	0.53	6.4	10.6	75.1	77.2	74.3

Boston, Mass.	5.5	0.39	5.3	34.6	73.3	75.9	80.0
Columbus, Ohio	5.5	0.39	5.5	25.7	80.0	83.4	93.4
Minneapolis–St. Paul, Minn.	5.1	0.34	5.1	50.9	80.4	83.7	88.0
Charlotte–Gastonia–Rock Hill, S.C.	5.0	0.51	5.5	10.4	68.8	83.8	85.5
Philadelphia, Pa./N.J.	4.9	0.50	5.0	13.0	56.6	74.4	75.7
Detroit, Mich.	4.7	0.48	5.0	10.6	73.2	84.7	87.4
Indianapolis, Ind.	4.6	0.37	4.7	21.1	79.6	83.8	85.8
St. Louis, Mo.–Ill.	4.3	0.39	4.5	13.6	85.0	90.1	83.5
Nashville, Tenn.	4.2	0.41	4.3	16.1	77.9	78.4	89.8
Cleveland, Ohio	4.0	0.41	4.1	10.3	63.2	86.2	80.7
Greensboro–Winston Salem–High Point, N.C.	3.7	0.49	3.8	8.5	69.8	79.7	70.6
Cincinnati, Ohio/Ky./Ind.	3.1	0.33	3.1	17.1	74.7	92.2	74.1
Pittsburgh–Beaver Valley, Pa.	2.5	0.23	2.4	22.3	82.2	75.2	95.2
Average	7.1	0.43	7.6	19.5	54.1	66.9	70.0

Source: Tabulations by authors based on data from the 2007–2008 American Community Survey (Ruggles et al. 2009).
a. Percentage of marriages that are ethnoracially exogamous.

Figure 4.2   *Intermarriage Rate (Percentage of Marriages That Are Ethnoracially Exogamous), by State, 2007–2008*

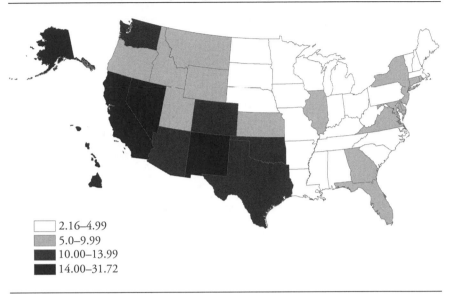

	2.16–4.99
	5.0–9.99
	10.00–13.99
	14.00–31.72

Source: Tabulations by authors based on data from the 2007–2008 American Community Survey (Ruggles et al. 2009).

uniform across areas. Overall, twenty-two of every thousand Americans identified with more than one race in the 2008 American Community Survey (ACS); of course, some states exhibit considerably higher rates of multiraciality than others. Rates of multiracial identification are high in Alaska (seventy-two per thousand), California (thirty-five per thousand) and Hawaii (218 per thousand), but low in Alabama, Georgia, Kentucky, Louisiana, Mississippi, New Hampshire, Pennsylvania, South Carolina, Tennessee, and West Virginia, where rates of multiraciality are only about nine to fourteen per thousand of state population totals (see table 4.5).

This illustrates a distinct pattern of multiracial distribution: the multiracial population is clustered in several states and metropolitan areas rather than evenly distributed throughout the country (figure 4.3). In fact, about two thirds of those who report multiracial identifications live in just ten states: California, Florida, Hawaii, Illinois, Michigan, New Jersey, New York, Ohio, Texas, and Washington. All of them have relatively large immigrant populations. Forty percent of those who report multiracial identifications reside in the West, a region of the country that has demonstrated substantially more tolerance for racial and ethnic diversity than other parts of the country (Baldassare 1981, 2000; Godfrey 1988). California leads the nation as the state with the largest number of multiracial persons and is the only state with a multiracial popula-

Table 4.5   *Multiracial Identification Rates, U.S. States, 2007–2008*

State	Multiracial Persons	Identification Rate[a]	Diversity Index
Hawaii	279,627	217.5	0.67
Alaska	49,294	72.0	0.53
Oklahoma	233,631	64.4	0.47
Washington	249,183	38.3	0.41
California	1,290,768	35.2	0.67
Oregon	125,627	33.3	0.34
Nevada	82,438	31.9	0.60
New Mexico	58,414	29.5	0.62
Wyoming	15,287	29.0	0.24
Colorado	139,619	28.5	0.45
Kansas	70,618	25.3	0.34
Idaho	37,216	24.6	0.27
Arizona	157,413	24.5	0.57
South Dakota	18,420	23.0	0.25
Montana	21,466	22.3	0.22
Maryland	116,045	20.6	0.58
Connecticut	72,171	20.6	0.43
Michigan	204,833	20.4	0.38
Virginia	156,251	20.2	0.51
Delaware	17,506	20.1	0.49
Rhode Island	20,965	19.9	0.37
New York	383,442	19.8	0.59
Utah	52,707	19.6	0.31
Massachusetts	125,909	19.4	0.36
District of Columbia	11,409	19.3	0.60
Texas	453,806	18.8	0.63
Missouri	109,108	18.5	0.31
Arkansas	52,417	18.4	0.40
Nebraska	32,669	18.4	0.28
Minnesota	94,411	18.1	0.27
Florida	329,893	18.0	0.57
Indiana	112,437	17.7	0.30
Ohio	202,608	17.7	0.30
New Jersey	153,066	17.6	0.57
Vermont	10,672	17.2	0.09
Maine	22,227	16.9	0.10

(*Table continues on p. 74.*)

Table 4.5   *(Continued)*

State	Multiracial Persons	Identification Rate[a]	Diversity Index
Illinois	211,721	16.4	0.54
North Carolina	147,953	16.2	0.50
Wisconsin	86,867	15.5	0.27
Iowa	45,572	15.2	0.18
North Dakota	9,221	14.4	0.19
Tennessee	86,949	14.1	0.38
South Carolina	61,461	13.8	0.50
Pennsylvania	171,595	13.8	0.32
Kentucky	57,141	13.4	0.22
Alabama	61,924	13.3	0.46
Georgia	127,524	13.3	0.57
New Hampshire	17,262	13.1	0.13
West Virginia	22,310	12.3	0.12
Louisiana	52,609	12.1	0.51
Mississippi	27,170	9.3	0.52

Source: Tabulations by authors based on data from the 2007–2008 American Community Survey (Ruggles et al. 2009).
a. Number per thousand of population.

tion that exceeds one million. Table 4.6 shows the metropolitan areas that exhibit the highest and lowest rates of multiraciality.

Ethnoracial Diversity Across Localities

We use a different measure of diversity for examining the linkage between geographic variation in diversity and multiraciality. This measure is more nuanced and is based on the Herfindahl Index, which takes into account the number of subgroups or subpopulations and the evenness of their representation in a group or population. Our measure is defined as 1 minus the Herfindahl Index of Concentration, or 1 minus the sum of the squared proportions in the subgroups or subpopulations. When this measure is used, California exhibits the highest diversity score in the country (table 4.3), reflecting not only its relatively large nonwhite population but also the fact that it contains several ethnoracial groups that are relatively evenly distributed. (All the groups are statistical minorities, meaning that none makes up more than half of the state's overall population.) In short, California possesses more racial-ethnic groups whose members are relatively more evenly distributed across groups than any other state.

Figure 4.3   *Multiracial Identification per One Thousand*
of Population, by State, 2007–2008

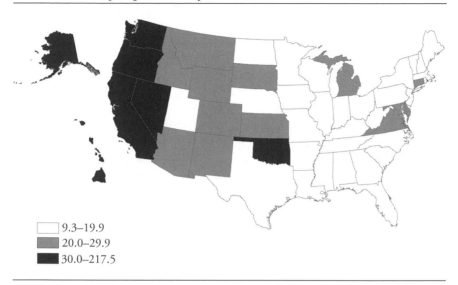

9.3–19.9
20.0–29.9
30.0–217.5

Source: Tabulations by authors based on data from the 2007–2008 American Community Survey (Ruggles et al. 2009).

It seems evident that states and cities with the highest intermarriage rates also possess relatively high Herfindahl Index–based diversity scores, which we call the diversity index. Often this is because these states contain substantial representations of at least three ethnoracial groups, as noted. It is also clear that many states in the western region of the country show higher levels of both diversity and intermarriage, something that reflects the generally lower levels of sociocultural (if not economic) conservatism there, with the notable exception of Utah, which is characterized by a high concentration of endogamous Mormons. States and cities with very low intermarriage rates tend to be either in the South, such as Mississippi, or overwhelmingly white, such as Vermont. Locations in the South with low intermarriage rates often are characterized by moderately high diversity scores because they contain two racial groups, the traditional black or white bipolarity, but are not generally reflective of the new multigroup diversity.

Examining multiraciality by place thus seems to reveal a positive association between immigration, racial and ethnic diversity, and multiraciality. Generally, we observe that states with higher levels of racial and ethnic diversity brought about by contemporary immigration, as reflected in the percentage of the population that is neither non-Hispanic white nor non-Hispanic black, boast larger multiracial populations than states that are less racially and

Table 4.6   *Multiracial Identification Rates in the Fifty Largest U.S. Metropolitan Areas, 2007–2008*

Metropolitan Area	Multiracial Persons	Identification Rate[a]	Diversity Index
Oakland, Calif.	104,329	41.8	0.72
Sacramento, Calif.	77,334	40.6	0.60
Seattle–Everett, Wash.	102,843	40.4	0.47
Riverside–San Bernardino, Calif.	161,326	39.4	0.63
San Diego, Calif.	114,562	38.3	0.63
Portland–Vancouver, Ore.	74,518	36.6	0.38
San Jose, Calif.	61,783	35.2	0.69
Las Vegas, Nev.	63,154	34.1	0.64
San Francisco–Oakland–Vallejo, Calif.	58,247	33.4	0.66
Los Angeles–Long Beach, Calif.	301,620	30.6	0.67
Fort Lauderdale–Hollywood–Pompano Beach, Fla.	46,188	26.3	0.66
Denver–Boulder–Longmont, Colo.	58,642	25.9	0.52
Orange County, Calif.	77,692	25.9	0.65
San Antonio, Tex.	45,929	25.1	0.57
Washington, D.C./Md./Va.	131,001	24.9	0.65
Orlando, Fla.	49,921	24.4	0.60
Kansas City, Mo.–Kans.	44,554	24.4	0.41
Austin, Tex.	36,824	24.3	0.59
Norfolk Beach–Newport News, Va.	38,357	23.6	0.55
Columbus, Ohio	35,932	22.7	0.39
Minneapolis–St. Paul, Minn.	68,931	22.3	0.34
New York–Northeastern, N.J.	214,406	22.2	0.72
Phoenix, Ariz.	85,536	21.8	0.55
Salt Lake City–Ogden, Utah	33,241	21.7	0.36

Table 4.6   *(Continued)*

Metropolitan Area	Multiracial Persons	Identification Rate[a]	Diversity Index
Boston, Mass.	73,210	21.0	0.39
Fort Worth–Arlington, Tex.	41,129	20.6	0.59
Dallas–Fort Worth, Tex.	80,593	19.8	0.65
Jacksonville, Fla.	25,289	19.7	0.50
Indianapolis, Ind.	33,608	18.8	0.37
Baltimore, Md.	48,583	18.5	0.53
Milwaukee, Wis.	27,551	17.8	0.46
Bergen–Passaic, N.J.	24,431	17.6	0.60
Detroit, Mich.	77,546	17.6	0.48
Raleigh–Durham, N.C.	26,120	17.2	0.55
Philadelphia, Pa./N.J.	87,856	16.9	0.50
Chicago–Gary–Lake, Ill.	144,045	16.8	0.63
Cincinnati, Ohio/Ky./Ind.	25,445	16.4	0.33
Tampa–St. Petersburg–Clearwater, Fla.	44,783	16.4	0.47
Newark, N.J.	32,676	16.0	0.62
Charlotte–Gastonia–Rock Hill, S.C.	29,685	15.9	0.51
St. Louis, Mo./Ill.	42,377	15.6	0.39
Houston–Brazoria, Tex.	78,059	15.5	0.68
Nassau Co, N.Y.	43,444	15.4	0.46
Cleveland, Ohio	33,648	15.3	0.41
Pittsburgh–Beaver Valley, Pa.	32,152	14.5	0.23
Atlanta, Ga.	67,583	13.6	0.62
Nashville, Tenn.	19,520	13.5	0.41
Miami–Hialeah, Fla.	30,688	13.1	0.54

(*Table continues on p. 78.*)

Table 4.6   *(Continued)*

Metropolitan Area	Multiracial Persons	Identification Rate[a]	Diversity Index
Greensboro–Winston Salem–High Point, N.C.	17,325	12.6	0.49
West Palm Beach–Boca Raton–Delray Beach, Fla.	15,637	12.4	0.54
Nonmetro areas	1,336,428	19.0	0.33

Source: Tabulations by authors based on data from the 2007–2008 American Community Survey (Ruggles et al. 2009).
a. Number per thousand of population.

ethnically diverse. This reveals why states such as West Virginia and Kentucky exhibit low rates of multiraciality: there simply are few racial and ethnic minorities in these states, little racial and ethnic diversity, fewer opportunities for racial mixing and intermarriage; therefore, the levels of multiraciality and multiracial identification are quite lower. An apparent link between the new racial and ethnic diversity and patterns of multiracial identification also appears to emerge at the metropolitan level; areas with greater levels of racial and ethnic diversity show higher rates of multiraciality.

This pattern of greater racial and ethnic diversity appearing to be related to higher levels of multiracial reporting does not hold in black-white diversity states. For example, Mississippi, Alabama, South Carolina, and Louisiana have relatively large black populations, yet the racial and ethnic diversity in these states takes the form of the traditional binary black-while model. Unlike the new diversity brought about by contemporary immigration, high levels of black-white diversity do not seem to be connected to high rates of multiracial reporting. So even though Mississippi, Alabama, and Louisiana have large white and black populations, the presence of these two groups is associated with low levels of multiracial reporting. Despite the fact that there has been a long history of racial mixing between whites and blacks in the South, the strong dividing line between these groups constrains multiracial identification, leading individuals to identify monoracially as either black *or* white rather than as black *and* white (Bean et al. 2004; Davis 1991/2001; Farley 2002; Harris and Sim 2002). In short, black-white diversity differs starkly from the racial and ethnic diversity brought about by contemporary immigration. Higher black-white diversity does not seem to be related to higher rates of multiracial reporting, whereas diversity resulting from contemporary immigration does result in higher rates of multiculturality and multiracial identification.

Conclusion

No longer black and white, the United States is now more racially and ethnically diverse than ever before, substantially as a result of contemporary immigration from Latin America and Asia. Today's Latino and Asian groups, which once constituted only minor fractions of the country's population, have tripled in size over the past few decades and now account for 15.2 percent and 5.0 percent, respectively, of the country's population. Contemporary immigration has moved the country far beyond black and white and has given rise to numerous "new diversity states," of which California, Florida, Illinois, Texas, and New York are only the largest. There are also now many "new diversity metropolitan areas," some of which, such as Houston, Los Angeles, and New York, have substantial representations of at least four major racial and ethnic groups, each accounting for relatively sizable percentages of the metropolitan area's total population. Clearly, diversity is the emerging touchstone of the new racial and ethnic structure in the United States.

Because the new diversity, like the new immigration, is geographically clustered, it is highly conspicuous in certain parts of the country, and less visible in others. Areas that are more racially and ethnically diverse also exhibit greater levels of intermixing, as evidenced by the higher rates of multiracial reporting. In short, states and metropolitan areas that are also home to the largest immigrant populations exhibit the greatest racial and ethnic diversity. Using the geography of intermarriage and multiracial identity as a guide, we find that higher levels of new nonwhite diversity tend to co-occur with higher levels of intermarriage and multiraciality. The reason for this may be that greater diversity fosters increased contact and tolerance. We explore these possibilities more explicitly in chapter 9, where we seek to assess systematically hypotheses about diversity's effects on boundary loosening.

Increased diversity may not operate similarly for all racial and ethnic groups. Greater levels of racial and ethnic diversity may loosen boundaries more under circumstances where whites' sense of superior group position is least threatened. Thus, boundaries may be most loosened for Asians, less so for Latinos, and maybe even not at all for blacks. Yet before we reach premature conclusions about the nature of change in attitudes and orientations toward intermarriage and how and why various factors might differentially condition diversity's influence on boundary dissolution, it is important to obtain a much more in-depth portrait of differences across major ethnoracial groups regarding experiences with and perceptions of intermarriage and multiracial identification. This is the subject matter of the next four chapters. These investigations reveal not only the nature of the boundary-changing dynamics associated with the new immigration, diversity, intermarriage, and multiracial identification but also how these vary across specific ethnoracial groups. By concentrating on how these phenomena play out in California, the most diverse state in the country, we are better able to understand the substance of the changes in attitudes and orientations that may be part and parcel of the structural and compositional changes noted in this chapter.

~ PART II ~

Individual Experiences of Diversity:
From Multiraciality
to Multiracial Identification

~ Chapter 5 ~

The Cultural Boundaries of Ethnoracial Status and Intermarriage

As early as 1941, Kingsley Davis and Robert K. Merton studied patterns of intermarriage as a way of measuring the social distance between groups and, in 1964, Milton M. Gordon extended this line of research by relating intermarriage to assimilation. Gordon theorized that because intermarriage follows other types of structural assimilation, exogamy marks one of the final stages of a minority group's assimilation into the majority-group host culture. Social scientists today follow Gordon's lead, viewing intermarriage as a sign of increased contact between groups, declining racial and ethnic prejudice, the breakdown of ethnoracial and cultural distinctions, and the fading of group boundaries (Fu 2001; Gilbertson, Fitzpatrick, and Yang 1996; Hwang, Saenz, and Aguirre 1997; Jacobs and Labov 2002; Kalmijn 1993, 1998; Lee and Bean 2004; Lee and Edmonston 2005; Lee and Fernandez 1998; Lieberson and Waters 1988; Moran 2001; Perlmann and Waters 2004; Qian and Lichter 2007; Romano 2003; Rosenfeld 2002; Tucker and Mitchell-Kernan 1990).

Sociologists have also documented how intermarriage—which often involves historically disadvantaged minorities marrying into the native-born majority group—creates opportunities for mobility in the United States. One way that intermarriage fosters mobility is by creating opportunities for the formation of "social bridges" between families and acquaintances of different ethnoracial backgrounds (Laumann et al. 1994; Goldstein 1999). Intermarriage not only enlarges and diversifies one's social networks but also increases one's cultural capital because of those extended networks, thereby enhancing opportunities for mobility (Patterson 1997). Pointing to American Jews and Japanese Americans as exemplars, Orlando Patterson (1997) asserts that their extraordinary successes can be explained in part by their high rates of intermarriage and concludes, "The lesson of these successful ethnic groups is unambiguously clear: If you want in, you marry in. And if you come from a group with impoverished networks, you have even more reason to do so" (197). Social scientists have used intermarriage as a barometer for declining group prejudice and assimilation, but few have empirically examined whether the incorporative power of intermarriage works in the same manner and to the same degree for different ethnoracial groups (Moran 2001).

We examined this question by comparing patterns of intermarriage among Asians, Latinos, and blacks, assessing what intermarriage means to the people involved and how they think others see their relationships. We also examined what intermarried couples believe intermarriage means for incorporation. We prefer the term "incorporation" rather than "assimilation" because the latter connotes absorption into the host society, suggesting the loss of distinctive ethnic qualities on the part of immigrant groups. "Incorporation" refers to the more general process of convergence, or perhaps divergence, between immigrants and the native-born, which can include a focus on the similarities and differences between foreign- and native-born populations (Alba and Nee 2003; Bean and Stevens 2003; Zhou and Lee 2007).

Much social science research has focused on the structural opportunities and constraints that affect trends in intermarriage. We seek to add a new dimension to the literature by examining the cultural boundaries that guide decisions about the choice of marital partners. By means of the concept of "social-construction differentials"—differences in the ways the members of a given racial or ethnic group view the members of their own group vis-à-vis the members of another—we investigate the cultural boundaries that individuals construct and navigate when choosing marital partners (Link and Oldendick 1996). We conducted in-depth interviews with thirty-six interracial couples who had at least one biological child together. We examined how these couples constructed and defined ethnoracial status, how their understanding of such definitions and categories affected the cultural boundaries they drew when deciding on a suitable marriage partner, and whether intermarriage facilitated incorporation in the cases of various ethnoracial groups (see table A.1 in the appendix for a breakdown of interracial couples we interviewed).

Sociologists agree that intermarriage is an indicator of incorporation, but they have not fully examined whether the incorporative power of intermarriage functions similarly across all groups. In this chapter we take up this issue and address two specific research questions. What are the cultural boundaries of racial status that intermarried couples construct to guide their choice of marital partners? And how does their experience of exogamy and their view of cultural boundaries and intermarriage affect how they see their own incorporation experiences? Answering these questions provides insight into the incorporative power of intermarriage and the ways intermarriage functions for different ethnoracial groups.

Intermarriage and Incorporation

In 1921, Robert E. Park and Ernest W. Burgess (1921, 735) defined assimilation as "a process of interpenetration and fusion in which persons and groups acquire the memories, sentiments, and attitudes of other persons and groups and, by sharing their experience and history, are incorporated with them a common cultural life." Milton M. Gordon (1964) added nuance to the definition by postulating that intermarriage marks one of the final steps of structural assimilation of a minority group into the majority host culture. Gordon's thesis has been widely influential among social scientists who recognize that intermarriage signifies not only the extent to which a minority group has achieved social, economic, and political parity with the majority group but also the degree to which members of different groups accept one another in the most intimate of relationships (Hwang, Saenz, and Aguirre 1997; Kalmijn 1993, 1998; Lee and Bean 2004; Lee and Edmonston 2005; Lee and Fernandez 1998; Lieberson and Waters 1988; Porterfield 1978; Qian and Lichter 2007; Rosenfeld 2002).

The change in intermarriage rates among European ethnics provides support for this thesis. At the beginning of the twentieth century, intermarriage between European ethnics was rare and relations between different groups was almost caste-like, especially relations between older European ethnics, such as descendents of the English, French, Scandinavians, and Germans, and newer arrivals from eastern and southern Europe, such as Italians, Russians, and Poles (Bugleski 1961; Pagnini and Morgan 1990). Today, European ethnics intermarry at such high rates that only one fifth of European-origin Americans have spouses with identical ethnic backgrounds, reflecting the virtual disappearance of group boundaries among them as well as their complete incorporation (Alba 1990; Lieberson and Waters 1988; Waters 1990). In fact, so prevalent is intermarriage and so complete is European Americans' incorporation that the racial, ethnic, and cultural boundaries among European ethnics have receded to the point that they are now symbolic, costless, and voluntary, rather than ascribed, instrumental, and consequential (Gans 1979; Waters 1990).

Recent research on intermarriage indicates that today's Asians and Latinos show rates of intermarriage that parallel those of their European predecessors. Joel Perlmann and Mary C. Waters (2004) find that the patterns of intermarriage among second-generation Mexicans today are similar to those among second-generation Italians in the early to mid-twentieth century. Not only are Asians and Latinos intermarrying non-Hispanic whites in high numbers, but their rate of intermarriage also increases with each succeeding generation and with increases in income and education (Gilbertson, Fitzpatrick, and Yang 1996; Jacobs and Labov 2002; Kalmijn 1993; Lee and Edmonston 2005; Lee and Fernandez 1998; Liang and Ito 1999; Qian 1997; Qian and Lichter 2001, 2007; Rosenfeld 2002; Sanjek 1994). Given these trends, we may be witnessing what Roger Sanjek (1994) refers to as a "race-to-ethnicity" conversion for Asians and Latinos whereby these immigrant groups heretofore perceived as nonwhites are increasingly perceived as ethnic groups, not separate racial groups.

Trends in Intermarriage

Marriage across racial groups, while on the rise, is still relatively uncommon, and remains at levels far below those that would be expected from chance alone, signaling that racial status continues to matter in the marriage market (Alba and Golden 1986; Kalmijn 1993; Moran 2001; Qian and Lichter 2001, 2007; Sandefur and McKinnell 1986). It should come as little surprise that inter-racial marriage is still relatively uncommon, given that as of 1967, marriage across racial lines was still banned in sixteen states. Not until the 1967 ruling *Loving v. Virginia* did the Supreme Court overturn the country's final antimiscegenation laws, thus ending all race-based legal restrictions on marriage.

The appellants in *Loving,* Richard and Mildred Loving, were arrested in their Virginia home in 1958 for being married because he was white and she was black. To avoid incarceration, the Lovings moved back in with their respective parents and then moved together to Washington, D.C., where they lived for several years. While there, they called upon Robert Kennedy, then the attorney general of the United States, who referred them to the American Civil Liberties Union (ACLU). With the help of the ACLU, Richard and Mildred Loving overturned the country's final antimiscegenation laws (Funderburg 1994).

The decriminalization of intermarriage, occurring in the context of the civil rights movement, had a dramatic impact on the rise of intermarriage. Within a decade, the number of interracial marriages doubled, from 150,000 in 1960 to 300,000 in 1970, when interracial marriage accounted for 0.7 percent of all marriages (Lee and Edmonston 2005; Root 2001). One decade later, the number of intermarriages had tripled, to 900,000. Yet despite the rapid rise in these figures, interracial marriages constituted a mere 1.3 percent of all married couples in 1980 (Root 2001). Though still a relatively small fraction of all marriages, interracial marriage has increased dramatically since 1960. Between 1960 and 2000, the number of intermarriages increased by a factor of about 20, from 150,000 to 3.1 million, and accounted for 6.2 percent of all American marriages (Bean and Stevens 2003; Jacoby 2001; Lee and Bean 2004; Lee and Edmonston 2005). By 2008 the percentage of intermarriages had increased to 7.6 percent, meaning that one in every thirteen marriages in the United States involved partners from different racial backgrounds—a significant increase that cannot be attributed to population growth alone.

Although marriage between individuals of different ethnoracial backgrounds has increased overall, there are significant group differences among America's native-born population. In 1990, only 4.8 percent of marriages involving whites and 8.2 percent of those involving blacks were racially exogamous unions, whereas the corresponding figures for marriages involving Asians and Latinos were 69.3 percent and 46 percent, respectively (see table 5.1). By 2000,

Table 5.1   *Percentage of Couples That Are Exogamous with at Least One U.S.-Born Spouse, by Race-Ethnicity, 1990 to 2008*[a]

| | 1990 | 2000 | | 2007–2008 | |
	All Married Couples	All Married Couples	Single-Race Married Couples	All Married Couples	Single-Race Married Couples
Total	4.6	6.1	5.6	6.9	6.5
White	4.8	6.3	5.8	7.1	6.7
Black	8.2	13.3	11.8	17.4	15.9
Asian and Pacific Islander	69.3	73.5	72.5	72.5	71.8
Latino	46.0	47.6	46.4	52.5	51.2
AINLOR[b]	75.0	72.1	71.1	71.7	71.0

Source: Tabulations by authors based on data from the 1990 and 2000 U.S. Censuses and the 2007–2008 American Community Survey (Ruggles et al. 2009).

a. Numbers are derived from census questions on race and ethnicity. All people who identified themselves ethnically as "Hispanic" are classified as Latino. All others are classified by race. Thus, Latinos are included only in the Latino group and may be of any race. In the 2000 census and 2007–2008 ACS, non-Latinos reporting multiple races were classified as belonging to the largest of the racial groups with which they identified. Percentages are computed by dividing the number of exogamous marriages involving a given race by the total number of marriages involving any person of that race. Thus, for example, a marriage involving one white spouse and one black spouse would be included in both the numerator for each of the white and black intermarriage percentages, and in the denominator for each.

b. American Indian, Alaska Native, and non-Latino "other" racial groups.

intermarriage rates had increased for all groups, to 6.5 percent of marriages involving whites, 13.3 percent of those involving blacks, 73.5 percent of Asians, and 47.6 percent of Latinos. By 2008 the intermarriage rates for native-born Americans increased even further for white, black, Asian, and Latino couples, to 7.1 percent, 17.4 percent, 72.5 percent, and 52.5 percent, respectively. Thus, the relative numbers of intermarriages as defined by major ethnoracial census categories have increased over the past two decades. And in the cases of Asians and Latinos, this has occurred despite the fact that the relative sizes of these groups have also increased considerably, trends that exert a depressing effect on exogamy when all else is equal because larger groups provide more potential coethnic marriage partners.

That both blacks and whites evince increases in their rates of intermarriage appears to signal that the black-white color line that has so tenaciously gripped our country may finally be losing its hold. However, when we compare the black intermarriage rate to the intermarriage rates of other nonwhite native-born groups, such as Asians and Latinos, we reach a different conclusion. In 2008, 72.5 percent of native-born Asian marriages and 52.5 percent of native-born Latino marriages were exogamous, meaning that nearly three-fourths of marriages of U.S.-born Asians and over half of marriages of U.S.-born Latinos involved a partner of a different ethnoracial background. Meanwhile, for black marriages the corresponding figure was only one in six. Moreover, among young native-born Asian and Latino individuals (twenty-five to thirty-four years of age), the intermarriage figures are also high (Qian 1997). By comparison, less than 10 percent of young blacks marry someone of a different racial background (Perlmann 2000). That America's newer nonwhite groups exhibit considerably higher rates of intermarriage suggests that the boundaries for Asians and Latinos are more porous than they are for blacks. Racial status may be declining in significance more rapidly for these groups than for African Americans.

Not only is intermarriage more common among Asians and Latinos than among blacks, but the rate at which they marry whites is also much higher. Of intermarried Asians, 87 percent marry whites, and among intermarried Latinos, the figure is 90 percent. Although 69 percent of intermarried blacks marry whites, this figure is lower than that of Asians and Latinos (Lee and Bean 2004). The comparatively higher rates of intermarriage among native-born Asians and Latinos also indicate not only that as these groups acculturate they become more receptive to intermarriage but also that whites increasingly perceive them as suitable marriage partners (Moran 2001).

Social scientists have largely focused on structural explanations emphasizing differences in such factors as educational attainment, levels of residential segregation, income inequality, and group size to account for the disparity in the rates of intermarriage among various ethnoracial groups (Blau 1977; Blau, Blum, and Schwartz 1982; Hwang, Saenz, and Aguirre 1994). For instance, researchers have noted that intermarriage is more common among the highly educated because college campuses and professional workplaces are often sites of intergroup contact (Kalmijn 1993; Liang and Ito 1999; Lieberson and Waters 1988; Qian 1997). Intermarriage may be more prevalent among the highly educated because increased education promotes greater tolerance for difference, thereby making intermarriage more acceptable (Jacobs and Labov 2002). More highly educated ethnoracial minorities are also more likely to live in less segregated neighborhoods, further increasing the probability of contact across group lines (Charles 2003; Massey and Denton 1993; Zhou and Logan 1991). Finally, group size matters; the smaller the group size, the greater the likelihood of intermarriage, since small groups offer fewer opportunities to find a suitable marriage partner within the group (Blau 1977; Hwang, Saenz, and Aguirre 1994; Jacobs and Labov 2002; Kalmijn 1991; Lee and Fernandez 1998; Sandefur and McKinnell 1986).

As relevant as these structural factors may be in explaining some of the variation in intermarriage rates, they do not fully account for intergroup differences.

For example, Latinos have surpassed blacks as the largest minority group, and they also have lower levels of educational attainment than blacks. The differences in group size and education would predict that a higher fraction of blacks than Latinos would marry whites. However, the opposite is true; Latinos in the United States exhibit very high rates of intermarriage despite their relatively large group size and low levels of educational attainment. This trend is even more apparent among native-born Latino females, indicating that the barriers for intermarriage are very low for this group (Qian and Lichter 2001).

Social scientists have focused on the structural factors that contribute to divergent intermarriage patterns and have paid far less attention to cultural ones. Yet this pattern and others suggest the need to examine factors beyond the structural ones to account for group variations in intermarriage. Structural factors may affect the opportunities for members of different groups to come into contact, but cultural constraints and culturally acceptable parameters affect the willingness of members of different groups to date and marry across ethnoracial lines (Moran 2001). For instance, polls show that as many as 20 percent of white Americans continue to disapprove of intermarriage and believe that interracial marriage should be illegal, despite its legalization more than four decades ago (Kennedy 2003b). Cultural constraints may also affect members of ethnoracial minority groups. In the early twentieth century, loyal members of European ethnic groups, such as Jews, Italians, Poles, and Irish, perceived coethnics who intermarried as "traitors to their way of life," especially when their ethnic group faced discrimination (Perlmann 2000, 517). Scholars have noted a similar finding among some contemporary blacks who view coethnics who intermarry (especially with whites) as racial defectors who lack pride in their race (Kennedy 2003b; Patterson 1997; Porterfield 1978; Romano 2003).

Renee C. Romano (2003) explains that blacks' disapproval of interracial relationships soared after the civil rights movement, in tandem with the resurgence of black nationalism in the mid-1960s. As blacks began to slowly penetrate white-dominant institutions, they came to view marriage across the color line as a deliberate attempt to assimilate into the white culture and society—an act tantamount to racial disloyalty and inauthenticity. On the line was the duty of individual blacks to the larger black community, especially the duty among black males to date and marry within their own racial community rather than across the color line (Romano 2003). This explains in part why black females were vehemently opposed to interracial marriage between black males and white females (Porterfield 1978).

The fact that some blacks view intermarriage (especially with a white partner) as a sign of racial disloyalty or inauthenticity is a cultural constraint that may also contribute to the low rate of intermarriage among blacks. Investigating whether this and other types of cultural constraints exist among members of different ethnoracial groups may also help to explain the different patterns of intermarriage in different ethnoracial groups. The data we collected through in-depth interviews of interracial couples provide some insight into the way that these men and women construct and view cultural and racial boundaries, which in turn guide their choices of marital partners.

The Cultural Boundaries of Racial Status and Intermarriage

That Asians and Latinos have higher rates of intermarriage than blacks suggests that the social construction of racial status may play a pivotal role in influencing partner preferences in the marriage market. More specifically, individuals may view some racial boundaries as more salient than others, thereby shaping the cultural parameters around which they make decisions about whom to marry. To explore this possibility, we asked the interracial couples how they perceived and defined themselves and each other in racial terms and also how their families and friends reacted to their unions. We found significant differences between the Asian-white and Latino-white couples on the one hand and the black-white couples on the other in the way that they construct racial status and racial differences. These differences affect whom they and their families believe to be a suitable marriage partner.

The most striking finding is that for most of the Asian-white and Latino-white couples, "race" is a nonissue in their relationship. Some of these couples said that they never really thought nor talked about race, nor did issues of racial differences come up with their family members and friends when they had decided to marry. This was particularly true of the Latino-white couples, in part, because many Latinos identify as white. Some explicitly stated that they do not feel that they are in an "interracial" relationship and even wondered whether they qualified to participate in a study of intermarriage. When the subject came up during the interview, a white female married to a second-generation Mexican male wondered aloud, "Well, I was curious because you were saying the term 'interracial,' and I always think of inter-racial as identifying by race. And looking at the two of us and how we identify ourselves—," and then her second-generation Mexican husband interjected, "We're both part of the white race." She then continued, "Well, Caucasian. So I see us more in ethnic terms, as bicultural."

Another Latino-white couple expressed a similar point of view. When asked whether they felt they are a part of an interracial couple, a white female who is married to a foreign-born Mexican male noted, "No, not at all," and her husband quickly reiterated, "Not at all." The wife then continued, "The most my parents thought is that he speaks Spanish. But they didn't see it as a difference; they saw it as a bonus. Like, 'Oh, how great, he speaks Spanish, too.' You know, they didn't see it as a difference. There was nothing that was really a difference." The Latino-white couples did not recount experiencing any opposition stemming from their unions because both they and their families regarded their differences as "cultural" or "linguistic," rather than as "racial."

None of the Latino partners in our study marked their race as "black" when they identified themselves. They identified as being of Hispanic origin and then marked their race as "white" or "other." In part this results from the fact that since we drew our sample from California, the Latinos we interviewed are of Mexican origin, and Mexicans are less likely to identify as black than some other Latino ethnic groups who have more African ancestors in their background (for a more detailed discussion of this point, see chapter 6). Hispanics who identify themselves and are identified by others as black may have different experiences altogether. This may be particularly relevant in other parts of the country, such as New York, where there are Latinos who are Puerto Rican, Dominican, and Haitian.

Like the Latino-white couples, the Asian-white couples also feel that there is little social distance and difference between whites and Asians. For instance, when we asked a second-generation Chinese man how he feels about being married to a white woman, he replied, "It's just like regular, like there's no sense that somebody's looking at us. It's like we're one race, basically." Similarly, when we asked a white woman married to a 1.5 generation Japanese man (born abroad but raised in the United States) whether her parents expressed any concerns about the racial or ethnic status of her husband, she said, "It never even came up." She added that their different ethnic backgrounds did not cause any concerns because her parents wanted her to marry someone who was "similar" to her: "It was never talked about, but I think my parents wanted me to date or be with someone similar to, or as close to, myself. You know, if I were to get involved with an African American or something it would be, well, especially an African American, it would have been hard."

When we probed further as to why her parents would have opposed the idea of her marrying an African American man but raised no objections to her choice of a Japanese partner, she explained that in her view, Asians are much closer to whites than African Americans are to whites. Commenting on the cultural similarities between whites and Asians, she found little difference between these two groups. In stark contrast, she felt that the African American culture is "the opposite," and sets African Americans apart from both whites and Asians:

> Well, our whole culture is much more prejudiced against African Americans than Asians. Asians are perceived as hardworking, ambitious, scholastically inclined, strong family, and the African American culture is the opposite. Plus Asians look more Caucasian than black people. I don't really distinguish much between Asians and Caucasians. It seems to me, anyway, that it's very blended. Plus the African Americans came to our country as slaves. Now the Asians came to our country practically as slaves, but I think there was still a distinction.

This white woman saw Asians as more phenotypically and culturally similar to whites than blacks are to whites, and saw virtually no difference between Asians and whites. Most Asian-white couples did note differences between themselves and their partners, yet they defined their differences as cultural rather than racial. For instance, when we asked a second-generation Filipina how her parents felt about her marrying a white man, she replied that although her father warned that she was marrying someone from a different "culture," her parents did not voice any objections to their marriage. She then quickly added, "But my parents are blunt about *interracial* marriage. They look accepting, but no." Perplexed by her statement, we asked how her parents define "interracial marriage." She explained that in her parents' view (and her own), interracial marriage means marriage to a black partner. Her white husband concurred with her assessment, and then elaborated: "I know my mom and my dad and their family, they definitely wouldn't want me to bring home certain races, but with her, they're fine." When asked what races, he replied with a laugh, "Well, like, you know, African American, a black girl. That's the one that sticks out in my mind. I mean, maybe if she looked like Whitney Houston or something, it would be okay," he said with a laugh. In order for his parents to approve of a black partner, she would have to be exceptional.

Three notable findings emerged from the interviews with the Asian-white and Latino-white couples concerning the way in which these couples construct racial status and racial differences when it comes to intermarriage. First, they viewed Asian-white and Latino-white intermarriage as intercultural rather than interracial. That these couples define their differences in cultural rather than racial terms suggests that they view the categories of "Asian" and "Latino" as both mutable and assimilable rather than static and fixed. This is critical because cultural boundaries in the United States have been far more permeable than racial ones.

Second, and in a related vein, these couples believe that Asians and Latinos are more culturally similar and closer to whites than they are to blacks. That Asian-white and Latino-white couples perceive little or no difference between themselves supports the thesis that the boundaries between Asians and whites and Latinos and whites may be fading more rapidly than the boundary between these groups and blacks. Consequently, Asian-white and Latino-white intermarriage occurs within what members of these groups deem as culturally acceptable parameters.

Third, Asian-white and Latino-white couples perceive very little difference between Asians and Latinos on the one hand and whites on the other, but they regard African Americans as both culturally and racially distinct. In their view, the "social-construction differential"—the difference in the way a group views their race vis-à-vis another race—is narrower between Asians and whites and Latinos and whites than between blacks and all other groups (Link and Oldendick 1996). The large social-construction differential between blacks and other groups (including other nonwhite groups) indicates that the black category appears to carry more social significance and greater social stigma than the Asian and Latino categories (Loury 2002; Yancey 2003, 2007). Hence, unlike Asian-white and Latino-white unions, marriage with blacks appears to fall beyond the culturally acceptable boundaries of racial status and intermarriage, even among interracial couples and their families, who would presumably hold the most progressive views about crossing color lines.

Black Exceptionalism in the Marriage Market

Intermarried couples explained that their parents were generally open about their dating people of different racial, ethnic, or cultural backgrounds, but they were also quick to point out that their parents would have raised serious objections if they had chosen a black partner. Marrying someone black was where most individuals and families drew the color line, and was where the theme of black exceptionalism in the marriage market consistently emerged. A twenty-four-year-old woman born to a white mother and a Mexican father explained:

> I was never brought up to hate or dislike black people, but if I dated a black man, my white side of the family and Mexican side of the family would disown me. And they've made it very clear. My dad told me if I ever brought a black guy home, he would kill him, and my grandma told me if I ever brought a black man home that she would kill me. As long as he wasn't black. Never said anything about any Asians or Indian or Pakistani, nothing. As long as he wasn't black.

When we asked a twenty-six-year-old woman born to a Vietnamese mother and a white father whether her parents had a racial or ethnic preference for her choice of dating partners, she said:

> Yeah, they didn't like black. My dad had a big problem about me dating blacks in high school and right after high school. And my mom, I tried to see how she would accept me dating black people, and she said that if I ever got married to a black guy, I wouldn't be accepted in her house anymore. And then I said, "What about our grandchild?" and she said, "No," so I'm not really attracted to black guys anymore.

We then asked whether her parents would have any problems with her dating white, Latino, or Asian men, and she responded without hesitation, "No problems." In another instance, when we asked a white woman married to a first-generation Mexican man how she would react if her adult daughter chose to marry a black man, she laughed nervously and exclaimed, "What a question! Well, to be perfectly honest, it wouldn't go over real well."

What is especially noteworthy about the three previous respondents is that the first two are multiracial and the second is a white woman who is married to a Mexican man. In the case of the multiracial women, their parents refuse to allow their children to cross the black color line, even though they themselves crossed a color line with their unions. In the third instance, the native-born white woman is married to a foreign-born Mexican man, yet she is uncomfortable with even the thought of a possible marriage between her adult daughter and a black partner. These candid reactions reflect a pattern that consistently emerged from the interviews: parents directly and indirectly socialize their children to exclude blacks from their pool of suitable marriage partners, which affects their children's dating preferences and eventual partner selection.

Furthermore, Asian-white and Latino-white couples stated that their family members did not raise objections to their unions, but all the inter-married black couples spoke of the negative reactions they received from both blacks and nonblacks. A thirty-eight-year-old African American male married to a white woman said that the first time his wife showed a picture of him to her mother, "she had, like, a fucking stroke. Can you believe this? She almost keeled over and died." When her parents first learned that she was pregnant, "her father said, 'Well, maybe you should have an abortion,' and that kind of shit. He's fucking sick. He didn't want any black grand-children or something."

Although this reaction was particularly extreme, it was not very different from some of the other negative reactions of nonblack family members whose children had chosen to marry a black partner. Some nonblack parents had gone as far as to sever all ties for years with their children, often until their first grandchild was born (Porterfield 1978; Rosenblatt, Karis, and Powell 1995). Such deep fissures have a lasting effect on black partners and their spouses, long after their parents reconcile with their adult children.

It is not only the nonblack partner's family that raised objections to inter-marriage with a black partner; the family and friends of black partners voiced similar objections. African Americans mentioned that coethnics had accused them of being "race traitors," of "weakening the race," and of "adding cream to their coffee" when they chose to date and marry across racial lines. Black men who get involved with nonblack women have been particular targets of poignant and confrontational questions, especially from black women, such as "Why are you dating her?" or "Why are you disrespecting your people?" At times, coethnic strangers feel they have license to make pejorative comments about interracial black couples. An African American man who married a white woman explained, "In the black community, white is not good, you know.

That is like the devil. I may walk into a restaurant with my wife and two kids, and it's like, 'You frickin' sellout!' And it's all I can do not to reach back and grab somebody's dreadlocks."

Through stares and offensive comments, coethnics can drive up the cost of interracial intimacy and scare off individuals who might otherwise explore the possibility of dating and marrying across the black-white color line (Kennedy 2003b). These findings confirm the view that some blacks perceive intermarriage with a white partner as a sign of racial disloyalty or inauthenticity (Kennedy 2003a, 2003b; Patterson 1997; Romano 2003; Smith and Moore 2000). These types of negative reactions on the part of both blacks and whites reinforce the social-construction differential between blacks and whites and function as cultural constraints that place black-white intermarriage outside the realm of what is deemed culturally and normatively acceptable.

By contrast, none of the Asian-white and Latino-white couples mentioned that they had been targets of negative comments from friends, family, or coethnics. Unlike the blacks who married white partners, the vast majority of the Asians and the Latinos with white spouses do not feel that coethnics view them or their unions as symbols of racial disloyalty. Only one Asian woman admitted to experiencing discomfort while she was with her white partner, and that was when they dined at a Korean restaurant in Koreatown in Los Angeles, where she felt the glaring and disapproving eyes of her coethnics. But it was only within the confines of an ethnic restaurant, located in an ethnic neighborhood, that she had ever felt disapproval from coethnics, many of whom were immigrants. In general, most Asians and Latinos do not feel that their coethnics make them feel that their choice of a white partner makes them less racially or ethnically authentic, and none of them felt this way either.

The vastly different reactions to Asians' and Latinos' intermarriage with whites on the one hand and blacks on the other stem in part from the fact that most Asians and Latinos are new immigrants or the children of immigrants, whose understanding of racial and ethnic relations are shaped by a different set of circumstances than those of African Americans. Most significantly, the Asian and Latino experiences are not rooted in a historical legacy of slavery, Jim Crow segregation, and the resultant consequences of legal and persistent discrimination that gave rise to and cemented the tenacious black-white divide. Because of the historical differences in relations between whites and Asians and Latinos on the one hand and between whites and African Americans on the other, Asians and Latinos do not view intermarriage with a white partner as an act of racial disloyalty or inauthenticity, as some African Americans view black-white intermarriage.

Outsiders' approval and disapproval of partners have very real consequences on dating and intermarriage practices. When parents, friends, and coethnics overtly or covertly disapprove of intermarriage with members of certain racial or ethnic groups and not others, they effectively draw a line around the people they consider to be culturally suitable partners. Black-white intermarried couples receive the most opposition, not only from family members but also from coethnic friends and strangers, indicating that the stigma and sanctions against black-white intermarriage are stronger than they are for Asian-white and Latino-white intermarriage.

The existence of cultural boundaries that influence one's choice of a marital partner indicates that marriage and other romantic unions do not occur simply because of romantic individualism (Moran 2001). Even love—which many believe is strictly an individual choice—occurs within parameters that are shaped and determined by structural and cultural opportunities and constraints. Structural barriers such as residential and occupational segregation fortify and further highlight cultural differences, which in turn strengthen cultural boundaries. The cultural boundaries in the field of romance that arise out of historical and structural circumstances partially explain the pattern of black exceptionalism in the marriage market, even decades after the countrywide legalization of intermarriage. Hence, black exceptionalism in the marriage market not only reflects ethnoracial differences but also reinforces them, strengthening the divide between blacks and nonblacks in the United States.

Intermarriage and Mobility

Sociologists have used rates of intermarriage as a barometer of incorporation, but so far they have neglected to ask whether intermarried couples view their unions as a vehicle for mobility. The in-depth interviews of the interracial couples revealed two themes. First, none of the intermarried Asian and Latino partners expressly associate marriage with a white partner as a route to upward mobility. Rather, they view their marriages as a natural and inevitable step in their process of "becoming American." Second, most of the Asian, Latino, and white respondents (and particularly their parents) associate marriage with a black partner as a direct pathway to downward mobility.

Although many of the Asian and Latino partners stated that their parents, the majority of whom are foreign-born, may have preferred that they had chosen a coethnic spouse because of cultural compatibility, they also explained that their parents were not surprised that they had chosen to marry an "American," with "American" meaning white. Because many of the Asians and the Latinos in our sample are second generation (U.S.-born with at least one foreign-born parent), they are more acculturated than their foreign-born parents. The parents—knowing that their children had grown up in the United States and lived in middle-class neighborhoods—were neither surprised nor dismayed to learn that their children had chosen white spouses. In the parents' view, choosing to marry a white partner was simply a natural and inevitable step in their process of becoming American.

But they failed to recognize that the very process of "becoming American" is in itself a form of upward mobility because it connotes a movement from immigrant to native and from foreign to familiar, so in this sense intermarriage with a white partner can accelerate incorporation, whether that goal is intended or not. This echoes Richard Alba and Victor Nee's (2003, 38) view that immigrants and ethnoracial minorities "may not intentionally seek to assimilate" but may do so nevertheless, as an unintended consequence of making pragmatic decisions to successfully adapt to the host society. Applying their framework to intermarriage patterns among Asians and Latinos, we posit that although these groups may not choose to marry a white partner because they view it as a vehicle for incorporation and mobility, their choice nevertheless accelerates incorporation into native-born, white culture.

More generally, the theme of mobility was one that surfaced prominently and repeatedly during the interviews with the interracial couples, especially among the Asian and Latino respondents. For example, they explained that their foreign-born parents constantly reiterated that they had immigrated to the United States to provide "more opportunities" and "a better life," not just for themselves but especially for their children. Growing up in immigrant households, the Asian and Latino respondents often heard their foreign-born parents speak of the importance of moving up and getting ahead. From this perspective, parents raised no objections to their children's marriages with white partners, but they staunchly believed that marriage with a black partner was a sure and direct path to downward mobility. One second-generation Chinese woman who did marry an African American explained that her immigrant parents opposed her marriage because they believed that such a marriage would close off opportunities for her to move up in society:

> Of course within our U.S. society there's a pecking order where whites are at the top of the socioeconomic ladder, and then probably Asians, and Latinos, and then blacks, and then I don't know where Native Americans fall—in there somewhere. So I think their concern was—what did they say?—"We've worked so hard to give you all these opportunities, to open doors to you, and now you are marrying someone African American and those doors are going to close." Her African American husband added, "Yeah, you're limiting yourself." And she continued, "Because [of] the prejudice that exists in our society, and the racism that exists in our society."

For this second-generation Chinese woman, her parents' message was clear: marrying an African American partner will not only stunt her prospect of upward mobility but will also actually lead to downward mobility. And not only the foreign-born assume that intermarriage with a black partner will lead to downward mobility; the native-born whites we interviewed also share this view. For instance, the father of a white woman who had decided to marry a black man asked whether she was prepared to be treated like a black person. The white father's question implied: Are you prepared to experience the social stigma associated with blackness, as well as the supposed downward mobility in status that ensues from marriage to a black partner? Other parents expressed this concern by asking pointed questions such as "How do you think society will treat you?" or "What are people going to think of you?" The assumption was that they would be regarded and treated as black, which in their view constituted incorporation into a stigmatized and racialized minority group.

Intermarried blacks were also the only couples who were questioned by family members as to how their unions would affect their children; often, "concern for the children" became the way that parents voiced their disapproval of these unions. Kimberly DaCosta (2007) argues that children are used as a lightning rod around which concerns about racial status and family gravitate because raising concerns about innocent children is an acceptable justification of people's opinions about contentious issues such as interracial and gay marriage. People who oppose these unions can project their negative feelings of anxiety, fear, and disapproval as positive, protective feelings about children.

Marriage with a black partner is the only type of interracial relationship where parents raised concerns for the children or fears about the possibility of downward mobility or incorporation into a racialized minority status. Neither the Asian-white nor Latino-white couples reported this type of cautionary reaction from their friends or relatives; nobody asked the white spouse of an Asian or Latino partner whether he or she is ready to be treated like an Asian or a Latino. Nobody asked the white spouse of an Asian or Latino partner how they thought society would treat their children. The concern about downward mobility into a racialized status applies only to marriage with a black partner, an indication that family members perceive marriage to a black—but not to an Asian or a Latino—as a route to downward mobility, once again firmly demarcating a cultural boundary between blacks and nonblacks in the marriage market. This also suggests that the incorporative power of intermarriage operates differently for black-white couples than it does for Asian-white and Latino-white couples, with Asian-white and Latino-white couples following one pathway, and black-white couples following another. Interracial black unions are the only type of unions that generate anxiety about incorporation into a downward, racialized status and a closure of the possibility of incorporation into a white or nonblack status.

Conclusion

Because intermarriage is an indicator of incorporation, we study patterns of intermarriage among Asians, Latinos, and blacks, which become analytical lenses through which we gauge the pathways and processes of incorporation.

We raise the question of whether today's nonwhite newcomers, the vast majority of whom are Asian or Latino, are following the traditional pathway of their European predecessors or are incorporating as racialized minorities whose experiences have more in common with those of African Americans. The statistical trends in intermarriage and data from our in-depth interviews of thirty-six interracial couples provided little evidence to support the thesis that today's nonwhite immigrants are incorporating as racialized minorities. They provided more evidence supportive of the hypothesis that the experience and social status of Asians and Latinos are closer to those of whites than to those of blacks at this point in time. Three critical findings support this thesis.

First, Asian-white and Latino-white intermarried couples feel that there is little or no racial difference between them, but rather view their group differences as cultural or linguistic. These couples claim that their racial differences have been a "nonissue" in their relationships, while stipulating that racial status would have been an issue had they chosen to marry a black partner. In other words, in their view marriage with a black partner is what they define as "interracial" marriage. They also add that although their families accepted their Asian-white and Latino-white unions, they would have strongly opposed a marriage with a black partner, illustrating that today's new nonwhite immigrant groups view African Americans as a racialized out-group and pointing to a distinct pattern of black exceptionalism in the marriage market.

Second, the black intermarried couples experienced the strongest opposition to their unions from both blacks and whites. The negative reactions, stigma, and sanctions against intermarried black couples exemplify the ways in which racial status and racial divides are constructed differently for blacks than for Asians and Latinos. These divides in turn shape the cultural boundaries around which members of different groups define whom they consider suitable and unsuitable marital partners. Structural factors affect the opportunities for members of different groups to come into contact with one another, and culturally accepted parameters affect the willingness of members of different groups to marry across racial and ethnic lines.

These findings help explain the different patterns of intermarriage among nonwhite groups and underscore the point that even though antimiscegenation laws have been legally eradicated for more than four decades, informal practices continue to operate to keep the rate of black intermarriage relatively low. In the absence of antimiscegenation laws, cultural boundaries and cultural constraints against black intermarriage become effective tools to recreate and reinforce the low rate of black intermarriage. The findings also emphasize the point that even love and romantic unions are not simply the products of romantic individualism, but rather are influenced by structural constraints and cultural boundaries.

Finally, from our examination of the relationship between intermarriage and mobility, we found that although the Asian and Latino intermarried couples may not consciously view intermarriage with a white partner as a route to upward mobility, they associate it with becoming American. However, we posit that becoming American in itself is a form of mobility because it signals a movement from foreign to native, so in this sense, inter-marriage with a white partner can accelerate incorporation, whether intended or not. Asians' and Latinos' choice of white marital partners leads to further incorporation into white American culture. In sharp contrast to this, the Asian and Latino respondents and their parents regard intermarriage with a black partner as a direct path to membership in a racialized minority culture and status because they perceive blacks as the out-group in the United States. In essence, because black intermarriage symbolizes a direct path to downward mobility, most whites, Asians, and Latinos draw the color line at marriage with blacks.

~ Chapter 6 ~

What About the Children? Interracial Families and Ethnoracial Identification

The family, both nuclear and extended, is an important site of ethnoracial identity formation, since cultural traditions and identities are first learned in the home (Alba 1990). When both parents share the same ethnoracial background, there is little discrepancy about how the parents will choose to identify their children, but when parents come from different backgrounds, the choice is far less obvious. Will they prioritize one ethnoracial identity over another, or will they choose to combine both parental backgrounds to identify their children? What are some of the factors that guide the choices parents make?

Historically, the legacy of the "one-drop rule" of hypodescent determined the ethnoracial identification of children born to black-white unions, but the children born to Asian-white and Latino-white unions have not been subject to the same constraining principle. One reason for this is that the ethnoracial identification of multiracial Asian and Latino children did not become salient until fairly recently as a result of the rapid growth of the Asian and Latino populations after the 1965 Immigration Act (Xie and Goyette 1997). Another reason is that Asians and Latinos are neither white nor black and therefore lack a historical precedent that governs the identification of children born of Asian-white and Latino-white unions. It is not clear whether their identities will be closely circumscribed, like those of multiracial black children, or whether their identities will be more flexible, fluid, and perhaps even symbolic, like those of European white ethnics. The ways interracial couples identify their children and the ways these children are perceived by others have important implications for the incorporation trajectory of new nonwhite immigrant groups. Whether the children of Asian and Latino intermarriages view themselves and are perceived by others as white will determine to a large extent whether the "racial distinctions" between Asians and whites and Latinos and whites disappear (Alba and Nee 2003).

In this chapter we combine background data from the 2000 census with information gained from the in-depth interviews we conducted with thirty-six interracial couples who have at least one biological child together and with forty-six multiracial adults, in order to provide insight into this question. The data from the 2000 census provides a snapshot of how interracial couples identify their children and reveals differences among intermarried Asians, Latinos, and blacks. The in-depth-interview data allows us to better understand the subjective process that guides the ways parents choose to identify their children and the meanings that they ascribe to their choices. Our interviews were geared to eliciting information with three research questions in mind: First, how do interracial couples identify their children, and what are the factors that guide their decisionmaking process? Second, how do the gendered patterns of intermarriage affect the ethnoracial identification of children born to interracial unions? Third, what is the role of the ethnic community and ethnic institutions in shaping the ethnoracial identities of multiracial Americans?

Previous Research on the Ethnoracial Identification of Multiracial Youth

Much of the earlier research that focuses on how interracial couples identify their children was conducted before 2000, prior to the 2000 census with its new option that allowed Americans to mark "one or more races" to identify themselves and members of their households ethnically and racially. In this earlier body of research, social scientists noted several factors that influence the way interracial couples identify their children, including the gender of the minority parent, the presence of coethnics in the metropolitan area, the diversity of the community, and the generational status of the child. For instance, Asian-white or Hispanic children who live in metropolitan areas with a large presence of coethnics are more likely to be identified as Asian or Hispanic (Eschbach and Gomez 1998; Saenz et al. 1995; Xie and Goyette 1997). Rogelio Saenz, Sean-Shong Hwang, Benigno E. Aguirre, and Robert N. Anderson (1995) speculate that this may be because a large coethnic population cultivates coethnic networks and institutions, which provide avenues for multiracial children to maintain their minority ethnic identity and culture.

A large concentration of coethnics also facilitates the acquisition and maintenance of an ethnic language, enhancing the likelihood that multiracial children will identify with the minority parent's ethnic origin (Eschbach and Gomez 1998; Harris and Sim 2002; Jiménez 2004; Korgen 1998; Saenz et al. 1995; Stephan and Stephan 1989; Xie and Goyette 1997). Studies of the Asian and Latino second generation confirm the importance of speaking a language other than English in shaping an individual's ethnic identity; children of immigrants who are fluent in their parents' mother tongue are more likely to adopt an ethnic rather than an American identity (Portes and Rumbaut 2001; Zhou and Bankston 1998). By contrast, Asian-white and Latino-white couples who

live in metropolitan areas with relatively few coethnics are more likely to identify their children as white, presumably because they lack the ethnic resources
necessary to transfer and maintain Asian and Latino ethnic identities for their
children (Eschbach and Gomez 1998; Saenz et al. 1995).

Ethnoracial diversity also plays a role: the more diverse the community, the
more likely it is to accommodate multiple identities, including multiracial identities, a point underscored by Cookie White Stephan and Walter G. Stephan's
research (1989). They find that Japanese multiracial youths are more likely to
identify multiracially in Hawaii than are Hispanic multiracial youths in New
Mexico because Hawaii's ethnoracial diversity fosters a milieu for a range of
identity labels for the children of mixed heritages. In New Mexico, by contrast,
where intermarriage is less common, multiracial Hispanics lack a commonly
used vocabulary to designate their mixed heritages, thereby making it more difficult for multiracial Hispanics to identify and be identified as such (Stephan
and Stephan 1989).

Finally, the gender of the minority parent plays a role. Asian-white children
who have Asian fathers are more likely to be identified as Asian than those who
have Asian mothers. Saenz and his colleagues (1995) and Yu Xie and Kimberly
Goyette (1997) hypothesize that this may be because children tend to adopt
their father's surname, so if the father is Asian, the children tend to bear an
Asian ethnic surname. Because surnames are visible and audible ethnic identifiers, bearing an ethnic surname often leads others to make assumptions
about an individual's racial and ethnic identity (Waters 1990).

We add to this body of research by providing new analyses from the 2000
census and by incorporating a qualitative dimension drawn from our interviews. We focus on the process by which interracial couples identify their children, the way that multiracial adults self-identify, and the meaning that they
attach to these identities.

America's Multiracial Youth: A Portrait

In 2000, when the U.S. census allowed Americans to mark "one or more races"
to identify themselves and members of their households, 40 percent of interracial couples with children under the age of eighteen chose this option and
checked more than one racial category: 49 percent of black-white couples,
52 percent of Asian-white couples, and 25 percent of Latino-white couples
identified their children multiracially (Tafoya, Johnson, and Hill 2005).
Among the couples who did not avail themselves of the "one or more races"
option but chose only one racial category to identify their children, stark differences arose. Most black-white couples chose black, whereas most Asian-white
and Latino-white couples chose white rather than Asian or Latino, respectively
(Tafoya, Johnson, and Hill 2005). These findings are in line with those reported
by David R. Harris and Jeremiah J. Sim (2002), who found that when multiracial adolescents were asked about the single best race to describe themselves,
75 percent of black-white multiracials chose black, whereas 52 percent of

Asian-white multiracials chose Asian (see also Farley 2004; Saenz et al. 1995; Xie and Goyette 1997).

America's multiracial population is an overwhelmingly young one; 42 percent are under the age of eighteen. Yet even among those under eighteen we find that multiracial reporting declines with age. Fifty-five percent of one-year-old children born of black-white unions are identified as multiracial, compared to 35 percent of seventeen-year-old children born of black-white unions. Among one-year-old children of Asian-white unions, 57 percent are identified as multiracial, compared to 45 percent of seventeen-year-olds, and a similar pattern emerges for the children of Latino-white unions (Tafoya, Johnson, and Hill 2005). Hence, even among multiracial youths, older children are less likely to be identified as such.

In California, the state with the largest multiracial population, 1.6 million people, or one in every twenty-one Californians, identified multiracially, accounting for 4.7 percent of the state's population. Among Californians under the age of eighteen, the ratio rises to one in every fourteen, or 7.3 percent of young Californians. In fact, the number of multiracial births already exceeds the number of black and Asian births in the state (Tafoya, Johnson, and Hill 2005). So notable is the growth of California's young multiracial population that the demographers Sharon M. Lee and Barry Edmonston (2005, 33) have remarked, "It would not be surprising if the average person were to conclude that intermarriage and multiracial and multiethnic children are the norm."

The greater proportion of young multiracial births in California and across the country more generally is attributable in part to the increase in the number of interracial marriages, especially among the young Asian and Latino populations, and in part to the greater likelihood of the parents of multiracial children to identify their children as multiracial, compared to parents of earlier cohorts. Parents are choosing their children's ethnoracial identities on official documents, such as the census form, and also are shaping the way their children identify themselves, making it critical to understand the process by which parents make these choices. Drawing on our interview data, we look in depth at three different groups of parents and their families: Asian-white and Latino-white; Asian-Latino; and black-white and black-nonblack.

Asian-White and Latino-White Couples and Their Children

All the interracial couples we interviewed acknowledged their children's multiracial and multiethnic heritages. Although many reported trying hard to instill and reinforce their multiracial identities, they have not always succeeded. In fact, most Asian-white and Latino-white couples reported that the incorporative power of intermarriage is so strong that even though they may identify their children as multiracial or multiethnic and go to great lengths to instill this identity in them, they believe (and in some cases fear) that their children will soon identify as simply "American" or "white." Black-white couples also acknowledge their children's multiracial heritage, yet none identify their children as simply American or white; rather, most perceive their children as black, which is how outsiders view them. In short, although all interracial couples acknowledge their children's multiracial heritage, they assert that both they and their children do not necessarily identify multiracially in their everyday lives. Rather, the children of Asian-white and Latino-white couples are more likely to end up claiming a white or American identity, whereas the children of black-white couples are more likely to claim a black one.

Because the Asian-white and Latino-white children in our sample were born in the United States, are strongly influenced by American culture, and speak only English, the Asian and Latino interracial couples maintain that their children "act white." These parents explain that regardless of how hard they try to instill a strong sense of their Asian or Latino ethnic ancestries, they have resigned themselves to the fact that their children will identify with the majority host culture—and will see themselves as white or as American, often using these terms interchangeably. For example, a white woman married to a second-generation Indonesian man explained that her children will probably identify as white because "they know more about the American lifestyle than they do of their dad's culture because they are not living in Indonesia, if that makes sense. They know more customs here." Similarly, a second-generation Asian Indian woman married to a white man agreed that their children would probably identify as white because "they were born here, and it's not like they're going to India." Her husband then added, "I get the feeling that they'll probably identify themselves as white mostly because they probably won't speak Hindi. Plus, all of their friends are white, and, you know, that will probably be the way they identify themselves."

The Asian-white couples acknowledged that because their children are English monolingual and have little direct, sustained contact with the Asian parent's ethnic culture, they felt that their children would simply identify as white as they grow older. These patterns of identification are consistent with previous research that has demonstrated that English monolingualism and little exposure to the minority parent's culture increases the likelihood that Asian-white and Latino-white children will adopt a white identity rather than an Asian or Latino one (Eschbach and Gomez 1998; Harris and Sim 2002; Korgen 1998; Saenz et al. 1995; Stephan and Stephan 1989; Xie and Goyette 1997).

The pattern of ethnoracial identification among the children of Latino-white couples is similar to that of children of Asian-white couples. For instance, a white woman married to a first-generation Mexican man explained, "I would always identify [my children] as white. I always considered them to be white. And to me, what does white mean? Caucasian is probably more specific." Others said that outsiders identify their children and the family as a whole as white, which shapes the way they see their children and themselves as a family unit. When a Latino-white couple was asked how outsiders react to them when they are together with their son, the second-generation Mexican husband said, "Just a regular American family." When we asked how people identify their son, he responded simply, "White, Caucasian," signaling that he was using the terms "American," "white," and "Caucasian" interchangeably. Others specified that although their children have both white and Mexican "cultures," they viewed their children (and their children were viewed by others) as simply white or American.

Sociologists have long noted that ethnoracial identity formation is a dialectical process—one that involves both internal and external opinions and processes (Nagel 1994; Rodríguez and Cordero-Guzman 1992; Waters 1990, 1999a). Thus, outsiders' ascriptions powerfully affect people's choices of ethnoracial identity, and the Asian-white and Latino-white couples we interviewed recognized that outsiders identifying their children as white strongly influenced the way their children chose to identify. These couples had more or less resigned themselves to the seemingly inevitable fact that their children will probably identify as simply white or American, regardless of how hard they try to maintain the distinctive elements of their Asian or Latino cultural backgrounds. These findings point to the robust strength of the incorporative power of intermarriage for Asians and Latinos when they choose white partners, for it leads others to see their offspring as white.

Some of the Asian-white and Latino-white couples actually consider their children's Asian and Latino ethnoracial identities largely symbolic and situational. In these cases, the parents may regard their children as white or American in everyday life but will choose to identify them as Asian or Latino when they believe that a minority status will bring benefits. A Mexican-white couple underscored this point when they debated how they should identify their daughter, Ana, on the 2000 census form. The exchange between the white wife and the Mexican husband was recorded on tape.

> WIFE: I don't know for Ana. Would you say that Ana is Hispanic? I would say no, not Spanish.
> HUSBAND: I would say no, she's not Spanish, but it depends. If this was a college—
> WIFE: I would say she has a Spanish, Hispanic parent, but I don't think she is.
> HUSBAND: But would that make her Hispanic or not?
> WIFE: No.
> HUSBAND: But how are you defining Hispanic? Based on birth, yeah, because that's how I'm defining it. But if this was a college application, we'd say yeah.
> WIFE: Oh yeah, we'd say yeah.
> INTERVIEWER: Why would you say yes if it was a college application?
> HUSBAND: Because she'd get into a better school because of it.

INTERVIEWER: Why?

HUSBAND: Because she's a minority. It would do more for her getting into a better college. I mean, opportunities.

Clearly, they understand that by identifying their daughter as Hispanic in certain contexts, they are maximizing the opportunities that are available to her, even if they do not identify her as Hispanic on other documents or in everyday life. They recognize and take full advantage of their daughter's multiracial background, which provides the option of privileging one identity over the other depending on the context and the benefits associated with that choice. The parents' decision to change their daughter's identity from white to Hispanic is a strategic adaptive response to a specific situation (Saenz and Aguirre 1991).

Asian-Latino Couples and Their Children

We found it striking that the experiences of the Asian-Latino couples we interviewed paralleled those of the Asian-white and Latino-white couples. Their interview responses suggested that the children of Asian-white, Latino-white, and Asian-Latino unions are incorporating more strongly as white than as Asian or Latino. Asian-Latino intermarried couples feel that their children will grow up to identify as American or white, rather than as Asian, Latino, or multiracial. For instance, when we asked a 1.5 generation Japanese woman married to a second-generation Mexican man how she thinks her children will identify themselves as they grow older, she explained, "I think American, because they are born here and go to school here." She used "American" interchangeably with "white." Similarly, a second-generation Chinese woman married to a second-generation Mexican man stated that even though the neighborhood in which they live has a sizable Latino population, and therefore her son may "have more of a Hispanic influence," ultimately she thought he would "just be more white."

Like the Asian-white and Latino-white couples, the Asian-Latino couples feel the sheer force of incorporation when it comes to their children's identification. A second-generation Mexican man married to a second-generation Korean woman explained that he believes his children will soon forget that they are both Hispanic and Asian and will adopt an American or white identity.

> Before you know it, my kids wouldn't even remember that they're half anything. I think they would be American. They would just not even think that they are half this or half that. And I've seen it happen. Even if you're one hundred percent Hispanic, they kind of forget that they're Hispanic. They're just accepted as being one of the majority teenager group. They're more just white. Now, I'm not saying that would happen to my kids because we would try. But I think that chances are that they become white are really strong.

His second-generation Korean wife agreed that regardless of how strongly they may try to instill and reinforce a multi-ethnic or multicultural identity, their children would "be accepted as just one of the group, and they wouldn't make it an issue."

That Asian-white, Latino-white, and Asian-Latino couples believe that their children would soon identify as white or American indicates the sheer force of the incorporative power of intermarriage for the children of these interracial unions. These couples have resigned themselves to the seemingly inevitable fact that their children will identify as white, both culturally and racially, regardless of how hard they may try to prevent this.

Black Interracial Couples and Their Children

Unlike the Asian-white, Latino-white, and Asian-Latino couples, none of the black-white couples that we interviewed identified their children as simply white or American, nor did they claim that their children identified this way, a finding supported by Barbara Tizard and Ann Phoenix (1993) with their in-depth interviews with black-white couples. While black-white couples recognize and celebrate the ethnoracial mixture of their children's backgrounds, they tend to identify their children as black rather than as white, nonblack, or American. One African American man explained that he identified his children as black, "because I see myself as mostly black, and I tend to see them that way."

This black man's response echoed those of all the black parents who have children of mixed racial backgrounds. A multiracial male whose mother is white and whose father is black acknowledged that he identifies as "black American—homegrown, one hundred percent." His wife is white, and they have two sons together. When asked how he chose to identify them, he explained, "I would say that they're half and half on the purest level, but still, for some reason, I just look at them as black." Thus, even though he could claim a multiracial identification for himself and his children, he identified both himself and his children as black. When asked whether he ever identifies his children as white or something other than black, he stated candidly, "You know, I've never had an occasion to do that. Maybe it's just the eyes that I'm looking through. I just haven't at all, and that's probably not a good thing." When probed further, he and the other black-white couples emphasized the point that nobody would take them seriously if they tried to identify their children as white. This underscores the power of external ascription to determine the latitude that black interracial couples feel they have in choosing how to identify their children.

The black-white couples further explained that the subtle and not-so-subtle reactions of others to their unions and their multiracial families are palpable clues hinting at other people's ambivalent feelings. For example, interracial black couples often receive perplexed reactions from service workers in restaurants and stores, who consistently assume that they are not together and often ask to help one person before asking the other. Black multiracial respondents described the puzzlement of strangers and also of their friends when they are seen with their nonblack parent, as a twenty-six-year-old black multiracial male explains:

> I remember being with my dad, even if we were standing in a line together, people would help him and then ask if I was next. They couldn't connect that we were together. It got to the point where I would almost not want to go with my dad. I mean, I got to deal with this—people looking at us funny? What's this white guy doing with this black kid? I think a lot of the time people have no idea that my dad is my dad, and that did kind of bother me when I was younger. People would say, "Oh, who's that?" And I would say, "Oh, that's my dad!"

When we asked whether he received similar reactions when he went out with his black mother, he looked puzzled, as if the answer was so obvious that he did not understand why we had bothered to ask. Then he answered simply, "No, not at all."

From a parent's perspective, a black parent of a multiracial child normally does not have to contend with the perceptual split along racial lines between him- or herself and the child, regardless of how fair-skinned the child may be, but the same does not hold for a white parent of a multiracial black child (Wilson 1981). This is because historically, the children born to black-white unions stayed with the black parent (usually the black mother), so even today, when interracial marriage is on the rise for all groups (including blacks), many Americans still find the pairing of white parents and multiracial black children unusual and vexing.

And not only black and white pairings but also black and nonblack pairings generally cause confusion. A black-Chinese male stated, "When I'm with my [Chinese] grandpa, especially now that he's older, people will ask if I'm doing some kind of community service. People always ask me, 'Wow, are you doing some kind of community service?' And I'm like, 'No, that's my grandpa.'" He then added that when he is with his black grandfather or his father, "people don't say anything."

Given the confused reactions they receive when they venture out with nonblack family members, the children of black interracial unions choose to identify as black rather than as multiracial or nonblack. The bewildered reactions, stares, and questions that black interracial couples and black multiracial families receive illustrates that outsiders see certain racial combinations together as foreign, unfamiliar, and seemingly illogical, especially in the most intimate of relationships. This is what we refer to as "a racial disconnect." From an outsider's perspective, there is a racial disconnect between black and nonblack, which underscores the idea that multiracial black families endanger the color line (Dalmage 2000).

Black interracial couples, however, choose to identify their children as non-white for reasons other than external ascription. Choosing to identify their children as white holds a different meaning for black-white couples than for Asian-white and Latino-white couples. Given the legacy behind the one-drop rule and the meaning and consequences behind the historical practice of "passing as white," choosing to identify one's children as white may signify not only a rejection of the black community but also a desire to be accepted by a group that has legally excluded and oppressed blacks in the past (Davis 1991/2001 Kennedy 2003b).

Furthermore, none of the black-white couples choose to identify their children as simply American because as native-born Americans they feel that the American label is already an implicit part of their and their children's identities. The children of Asian-white and Latino-white unions in the sample are also native-born, but because many of the Asian and Latino parents are either immigrants or the children of immigrants, the American label is not an implicit part of their identities, as it is for native-born whites and blacks (Zhou and Lee 2007). Another critical distinction between the Asian-white and Latino-white couples on the one hand and the black-white couples on the other is that the latter do not equate "American" with "white." For black-white couples, "American" also equals "black." For all these reasons, intermarried black couples are less likely to identify their children as white or American.

The interviews illustrate that when marrying across the color line, interracial black couples are the least likely, least able, or least willing to transfer a nonblack identity and status to their children. Unlike Asian-white, Latino-white, and even Asian-Latino couples, who believe that their children will most likely adopt a white or American identity, none of the black-white or black-Asian couples identified their children as simply white, American, or nonblack. Although they may acknowledge their multiracial backgrounds, interracial black couples are acutely aware that their children are often identified as black by others. The findings indicate that the cultural persistence of the one-drop rule of hypodescent still strongly operates to reinforce the practice of identifying Americans with any trace of black ancestry as racially black (Davis 1991/2001; Hollinger 2003; Lee and Bean 2004, 2007; Roth 2005).

Gendered Patterns of Intermarriage and the Significance of Surnames

The gendered patterns of intermarriage also affect the racial identification of the children of interracial unions, most notably through the patrilineal passing on of surnames to the children. Because surnames are strong visible and audible ethnic identifiers, bearing an ethnic surname often invites others to make assumptions about one's ethnoracial identity (Waters 1990). Having an ethnic surname such as Rodriguez, Gonzalez, or Hernandez suggests that the person may be of Hispanic origin, whereas a surname such as Yamaguchi,

Kim, or Chang suggests an Asian origin. Ethnic surnames constrain identity choices in a way that Anglo surnames such as Smith or Jones do not. This explains why the father's racial identification is a stronger predictor of the children's racial identification than the mother's identification and also why the children of interracial unions in which the father is nonwhite are more likely to be identified as nonwhite (Waters 2000; Xie and Goyette 1997).

A woman born to a Mexican mother and a white father illustrated this point as she explained that her Anglo surname had caused her to constantly have to prove that she is not "just white": "I felt like, growing up, I kind of had to prove my being Mexican to a lot of my peers and stuff. You know, people see you and they just hear your name, and when you have an English last name, they assume that you're just white, and they categorize you as white."

Other Latino-white and Asian-white multiracials also note that having a nonethnic last name has pushed them to adopt white rather than Latino or Asian ethnic identities. For instance, an Asian-white woman born to a Japanese mother and a Norwegian father stated that she identified more strongly with her father's ethnoracial background because she inherited his distinctive Norwegian surname. In a similar vein, a Latino-white male who bears a German surname strongly identified as white, but upon reflection acknowledged that he might have identified more strongly as Latino if he had a distinctively ethnic last name, such as Rodriguez or Gonzalez.

The significance of surnames as ethnoracial identifiers is particularly relevant in light of the gendered patterns of intermarriage among different groups. Gender differences in intermarriage are modest among whites, Latinos, and American Indians, but they are substantial among Asians and blacks. Notably, the gender differences operate in opposite directions (Qian and Lichter 2007). Among Asians, females are more likely to out-marry than males, whereas among blacks, males are more likely to out-marry than females (Fryer 2007; Hwang, Saenz, and Aguirre 1994; Jacobs and Labov 2002; Kalmijn 1993; Lee and Edmonston 2005; Lee and Fernandez 1998; Liang and Ito 1999; Moran 2001; Qian and Lichter 2007; Schoen and Thomas 1989). Asian American women (except for Asian Indians) are more likely than Asian men to out-marry, regardless of ethnicity and nativity (Lee and Fernandez 1998). In 2000, over twice as many Asian women (22 percent) than Asian men (10 percent) were in interracial marriages (Lee and Edmonston 2005). These proportions are reversed among blacks: black males are more than twice as likely to out-marry than black females; in 2000, 10 percent of black men, but just 4 percent of black women, had a nonblack spouse, and the gap has widened in recent years (Fryer 2007; Lee and Edmonston 2005).

The gender differences are even more evident among younger married Americans, those twenty-five to thirty-four years old. In 2000, only 5 percent of young African American women and 14 percent of young African American men were in racially mixed marriages. Again, for young Asian Americans the gender difference is in the opposite direction: 39 percent of young Asian women married interracially but just 26 percent of young Asian men (Jacobs and Labov 2002; Qian and Lichter 2007). The gender difference for Latinos, while not significant, leans in the same direction as that of Asians: Latino females are more likely to intermarry than Latino males (Qian and Lichter 2001). However, Asians, Latinos, and blacks have similar patterns when they do out-marry: the majority of all three groups choose white spouses (Lee and Bean 2004).

The gendered patterns of intermarriage are germane because they have implications for the ethnoracial identification of the children of Asian-white and Latino-white unions, who tend to bear Anglo surnames rather than Asian or Latino ones. Having an Anglo surname pushes multiracial Asians and Latinos to identify more strongly as white, partly because others identify them as such on the basis of this Anglo racial and ethnic identifier. By contrast, black multiracial children are more likely to adopt the father's racial identity rather than the mother's, and since more fathers than mothers in black-white interracial couples are black, this results in a black racial identification on the part of the children. For all these reasons, the gendered patterns of intermarriage reinforce the outcome that Asian and Latino multiracial respondents identify as white and black multiracial respondents identify as black.

Surnames, however, do not always work in the same manner for multiracial black children. For example, one second-generation Chinese woman married to an African American attempted to transfer her Chinese ethnic identity to her son by giving him her ethnic surname as well as a Chinese ethnic first name:

> I figured having a Chinese last name or Chinese first name would make him a little more identifiable as Asian or Chinese. Because when I was in college and involved in the Asian American Alliance at school, we went through the enrollment lists and looked for last names and first names that might give us a clue. And then we would invite them to events. And I thought that I would want him to be invited on the basis of his last name. So if we gave him my husband's last name, you know, you wouldn't know that he was Asian.

When we asked her African American husband how he felt his son would be perceived by others, he had a different take on the subject altogether:

> I think he'll be perceived as black when he's seen. That's my expectation. If he goes into one of those Chinese immersion programs, or whatever, like all of those Chinese after-school programs in Chinatown, or even takes a martial-arts class, how will he be perceived by the other children there? He'll be seen as black.

This African American father has grasped that surnames do not function the same for multiracial blacks as they do for multiracial Asians and Latinos.

An Asian or Latino surname does not pull a black multiracial away from adopting a black identity, nor does it guarantee a particular ethnic identification for black multiracials (Roth 2005). To further emphasize this point, a twenty-nine-year-old black-Latino male, whose father is Mexican and whose first, middle, and last names are ethnically Latino, explained that regardless of his Latino names, he does not identify as Latino, nor do others identify or accept him as Latino:

> I am José Santos Gonzalez—took me a long time to get that one. José was one thing, but, like, Santos, too? I don't look like a José. José is a Mexican name. I don't see Santos when I look in the mirror. To me, I look in the mirror, I look like a black kid. So this was my thinking, I don't look Mexican, Mexicans don't accept me. They know I'm half Mexican, but they don't accept me.

Hence, regardless of whether multiracial blacks bear Latino or Asian ethnic identifiers, other mechanisms such as outsiders' ascription and ethnic exclusion too often powerfully constrain multiracial blacks from freely adopting a nonblack racial identity and, just as important, from having that nonblack identity accepted by others.

The Ethnic Community and Ethnic Institutions

Previous research has shown that living in a neighborhood with a large coethnic population leads multiracials to more closely identify with the identity of the minority parent. For instance, Asian-white children who live in metropolitan areas with a large concentration of Asians are more likely to be identified as Asian than as white, and the same holds true for Hispanic youths (Eschbach and Gomez 1998; Saenz et al. 1995; Xie and Goyette 1997). This may be because a large coethnic population fosters the creation of ethnic institutions, which in turn allow multiracial children to more easily maintain their minority ethnic identity and culture (Saenz et al. 1995).

However, the data from our in-depth interviews with multiracial Asians reveals that ethnic institutions can also have the opposite effect for multiracial Asians; ethnic clubs, ethnic churches, and ethnic businesses can pull multiracial Asians away from adopting Asian ethnic identities and push them into adopting multiracial, white, or American identities. The multiracial Asians we interviewed openly discussed how they have been excluded by members of Asian ethnic organizations, such as university clubs, ethnic churches, and ethnic stores, simply because they are not "full Asian." Comments such as "The Asian kids didn't see me as Asian" were not uncommon among the Asian multiracial individuals we interviewed. Such comments reflect the sentiment that monoracial Asians often embrace a narrow definition of Asian identity, resulting in the exclusion of multi-racial Asians. The ethnic exclusion in turn leads many Asian multiracials to choose a non-Asian identity because they do not feel accepted by other Asians.

For example, when we asked an Asian-white female born to a Japanese mother and a white father how she chose to identify, she revealed that she identified as white more often than as Asian because of the negative encounters that she experienced with Asians: "I think, honestly, I identify a little bit more with white just because the only times I've ever felt badly about my mix is from full Asians. They are the only ones that have ever made me feel uncomfortable." When we asked her if she could recall a specific example, one in particular came to mind: "My mom and I would go shopping, and I think we went to Chinatown or whatever. We went to a store and the saleslady—she was a hundred percent Chinese—and she just kept looking at my mom and looking at me, and she finally just said, 'We can't help you here.' "

Similarly, a multiracial male born to a Japanese mother and a white father told us that he felt more alienated by Asians, particularly by other Japanese, than by whites and recalled specific instances in which he felt excluded by members of his karate club in college: "Again, this whole thing of feeling alienated. They were actually meaner to me than they were to the white kids. That's when I got really ticked off at the Japanese. Instead of seeing me as part Japanese, they didn't accept me, and hated me even more [than whites]." So memorable and hurtful were these instances that they strongly shaped the way these multiracial Asians now choose to identify.

When we asked the Asian multiracial respondents their opinion as to why Asians excluded them from coethnic institutions and social circles, they said that they felt the behavior stemmed from a belief in the superiority of ethnic purity. One Asian multiracial woman attributed the exclusion of multi-racials by some Asians as "elitism": "I think there's some sort of elitism that some Asians may have, that if you're mixed with some other race or something, then you're not fully Asian." A black-Korean multiracial female echoed this: "The Korean people are more like, they don't mix race that much so they're more opposed to it, I guess, not as accepting of it." The exclusion that multiracial Asians experience from their monoracial Asian counterparts pushes them to embrace other ethnic identities, including white, American, or multiracial.

The History of Multiraciality of Asians, Mexicans, and African Americans

The tendency of some Asians to exclude multiracials can be traced back to the history of mixed-race children born to Asian women and military men from the United States and other countries. In Korea, thousands of Korean-

American children were fathered by American troops who began arriving in the country in 1950. Most of the Korean women who bore these children were destitute during wartime conditions, and the Korean-American children were born under conditions of extreme poverty. Some of the American military servicemen married the Korean women with whom they had relationships during the war, but many did not, and the women were left to raise their children on their own. Stigmatized because they were poor, born out of wedlock, and of mixed race, Korean-American children faced the sting of prejudice and exclusion from Korean society, including from the women's own families, many of whom had refused to accept the multiracial children (Davis 1991/2001).

Compounding their disadvantage was their ambiguous citizenship and social status. Because citizenship in Korea is based on the father's status, the Korean-American children fathered by American GI's were defined as American rather than as Korean. But unless the American father could be found and a valid marriage between the Korean mother and American father was legitimated, these children were not granted American citizenship because they had been born out of wedlock and outside of the United States. Consequently, most Korean-American children were denied citizenship from both the United States and Korea (Davis 1991/2001). Furthermore, because one's social status in Korea is based on being registered under one's father's name, children born out of wedlock did not carry their father's name and were treated as nonpersons lacking any type of legitimate lineage. The children born to Vietnamese women and American servicemen during the Vietnam War suffered a similar fate. Given the moniker the "dust of life," Vietnamese-American children were treated as outcasts and denied citizenship and social status in Vietnam. Because of the history of mixed-race children fathered in Asian countries by members of the U.S. military, some Asians (particularly older Asian immigrants in the United States) continue to regard multiracial Asians with prejudice and contempt and exclude them from their ethnic circles.

The history of racial mixing in Mexico has a far more positive connotation than in Asia, resulting in the concept of "mestizaje" or "mestizo," meaning "mixed" and implying racial and cultural synthesis. After the sixteenth-century Spanish Conquest of Mexico, the country evolved into a nation with intertwined European and Indian roots (Nash 1995; Rodriguez 2007). Interracial unions involving Indians, Europeans, Africans, and Asians were common following the Spanish Conquest, and intermarriage was accepted in the latter half of the seventeenth century in Mexico. Hence, unlike the United States, which had long obstructed interracial marriage and frowned on racial mixing (especially between blacks and whites), Mexico recognized and celebrated its mestizo history, or history of racial mixing.

Having grown up with the concept of mestizaje, many Mexicans who come to the United States feel that they do not fit into the racial categories presented to them by the census. This may explain why more than 40 percent chose to identify as "Some other race" in the 2000 census. Rather than identifying as either black or white, many Mexicans (and Latinos more generally) embrace a kaleidoscope of ethnoracial identities that transcend the sharp boundaries of America's racial categories. This explains why Mexican multiracials feel they can easily blend into both Mexican and white cultural circles, and also why the Latino multiracials we interviewed do not feel excluded from Mexican or Latino ethnic communities in the same way that Asian multiracials do.

Like Mexicans, African Americans have had a long history of racial mixing in their backgrounds; consequently they accept black multiracials into their social and institutional circles more readily than Asians. This became evident when we spoke with a multiracial woman whose mother is Korean and whose father is African American. She explained that she had always felt that it was more "natural" for her to socialize with blacks rather than with Koreans. She never feels "out of place" with blacks, but she has felt this way with Koreans: "Well, if I was around Asian people—well, Korean people— I felt more out of place. When I'm with a lot of black people, I don't feel out of place." Asked to elaborate on why she felt "out of place" with Koreans but not with blacks, she explained that it was partly because of the language barrier with Koreans, but, more important, because Koreans seem less accepting of racial mixing than blacks:

> It was just more natural for me to hang around black people. There's no language barrier. Like, as far as I know, there are young Korean people my age who speak English, but if you go into their culture, they're very, like, we're all Korean. The Korean store, they're all Koreans, and if you look different, they're, like, wait a minute. But black people, they're more used to being around more different types of people. Black people always tended to be more, like, oh, you have black, so you're black . . . .
>
> The Korean people are more, like, they don't mix race that much so they're more opposed to it, I guess, not as accepting of it. And the older-generation Koreans probably look down on me a little bit. I don't think they're into the whole race-mixing thing. A lot of them look at me, like, confused. I go to a Korean store with my mom and they're, like, trying not to look but they want to look, like, is that her daughter?

The inclusion this woman felt with blacks and the exclusion she felt from Koreans led her to identify more strongly as black rather than as Korean.

This experience was similar to that of a female graduate student of African American and Chinese descent who explained that whereas black organizations have been very inviting and inclusive of her, Asian ethnic clubs have been "very exclusive":

> They don't even invite me to stuff. I mean, most of the black students do, but the Asians, and I've talked to them about this a lot, they're so exclu-

sive that unless you're, like, all Asianed out, they don't invite you. I don't ever get invited to any of their events. But the black student organization, they're totally like, yeah.

Blacks appear to be much more accepting than other groups of black multiracials; consequently, multiracial blacks find it easier to blend into black social circles and friendship networks, as a black-white multiracial woman confirmed:

> African American people, I often find, accept me more readily into a friendship group. Whether this is intentional or not intentional as far as other groups are concerned, I'm not quite sure, but I often find myself having friend groups that are African American. I don't set out to do this, it just happens pretty much. African American people I've hung out with or been friends with, they always seem to accept, okay, she's black and white, so let's go with this. As far as other groups are concerned, I don't think I've been alienated by them, but I don't think there's been that relationship where we identify.

Yet immediately after explaining how African Americans have more readily accepted her within their social circles, she adds, "Although I was accepted more by an African American group, occasionally I get the fact that I'm not African American enough. 'You're not black enough. You don't do this, and, you know, why don't you talk more like this?'" Although multiracial blacks may feel more included in black than in nonblack social circles, at times they also face questions from other blacks about their racial authenticity.

Ethnic Language and Ethnic Identity

Being able to speak the language of one's minority ethnic group is another factor that affects identify formation among multiracial Americans, particularly Asian and Latino multiracials. Social scientists have noted that the ability to speak an ethnic language is a primary component of one's internal ethnic identity construction, and speaking the minority parent's language increases the likelihood that multiracial children will identify with the minority parent's ethnic identity (Eschbach and Gomez 1998; Harris and Sim 2002; Jiménez 2004; Korgen 1998; Saenz et al. 1995; Stephan and Stephan 1989; Xie and Goyette 1997). Conversely, Asians or Latinos who do not speak an ethnic language are less likely to self-identify as Asian and Latino because they are less likely to feel ethnically authentic. This sentiment was expressed by a Japanese-white female who elaborated why she feels more white than Japanese: "I feel more white because I grew up more in a white situation. I think I adopted more of a white culture than I did a Japanese culture. I don't speak Japanese, and I don't follow Japanese religion or anything like that."

The black-Korean woman who stated that she felt it was more natural for her to be with blacks than with Koreans also said that the language barrier with her Korean relatives limited her ability to communicate and socialize with them. Consequently, she felt more distant from them and closer to her black relatives, even though she saw her black family infrequently:

> I just feel more comfortable identifying with my black part. I didn't grow up around my black part of the family because they lived in Illinois. My Korean part of the family all live out here [in Los Angeles], but they don't speak very good English, and I don't speak Korean. So even at family gatherings we didn't talk much. We were the only ones that didn't speak Korean so we didn't really talk to anybody during family functions so we kind of just sat there, sat there and ate. My mom speaks better English than the other members of our family. But when I go back to see my family in Illinois, which was only, like, two or three times, it's, like, instant. I talk to all of them, and it's more comfortable, even though I've only met them, like, three times.

In some cases the multiracial Asians and Latinos complained that their Asian and Latino counterparts deliberately used ethnic language as a tool to exclude them. For instance, a woman of Filipino and white ancestry discussed how she decided not to join the Filipino club on her college campus after the members gave her the cold shoulder because she could not speak or understand Tagalog. Similarly, an Asian Indian–white female explained that her white mother often felt deliberately excluded by Asian Indians (particularly women) in social contexts when they began to speak in Hindi, even though they were fully aware that her mother did not speak the language. The woman noted, "You know, it's hard for my mom sometimes because Indian women have often closed the circle on her by speaking in Hindi, fully aware that she doesn't speak it. She felt kind of rejected by members of that culture, by my dad's family, and I think she's always felt left out when we go to Indian functions."

By contrast, a twenty-seven-year-old Latino multiracial male was able to join and participate in the Latin American club during college, even though the club was considered "cliquey," because he, like the other members of the club, spoke Spanish when they convened. Hence, ethnic clubs and ethnic language can operate as institutional mechanisms of exclusion for multiracial Asians and Latinos who do not speak the ethnic language, thereby making it less likely that they will adopt an Asian or Latino ethnic identity. But they can also operate as mechanisms of inclusion for multiracials who do speak the ethnic language.

It is critical to note that many second-generation Asians and Latinos who do not speak their parents' native language do not have the choice to "opt out" of their Asian or Latino racial or ethnic identities and adopt an alternate one.

For example, American-born Mexicans and Chinese who do not speak a language other than English do not feel they have the option to identify as white. They may not speak Spanish or Chinese, practice ethnic cultural traditions, or have Mexican or Chinese friends, and they may even feel more culturally similar to whites than to other racial or ethnic groups, but they do not feel that they can freely choose a white racial identity or an American national identity because others do not view them as such (Lee and Zhou 2004; Zhou and Lee 2007). By contrast, Asian-white and Latino-white multiracials feel that they have the choice to opt out of an Asian or Latino identity and assume a white or American identity precisely because they are multiracial. Interestingly, even the Asian-white and Latino-white intermarried couples discussed how their children "act white" or will most likely grow up to identify as white or American because they speak only English. In this instance, the interracial couples use the racially coded phrase "acting white" to refer to linguistic and cultural behavior rather than racial status (Carter 2005).

In short, English monolingualism works to pull multiracial Asians and Latinos away from adopting monoracial Asian and Latino identities. At the same time, it actively works to push them to embrace multiracial, white, American, or non-Asian or non-Latino identities. Ethnic language can become a clear marker demarcating a sharp boundary between in-group and out-group memberships. An interesting point of comparison is that African Americans do not have a foreign language from which they can derive a non-black identity, so language does not serve a parallel function in the identity construction of multiracial blacks as it does for Latinos and Asians. Whereas Asian-whites and Latino-whites who do not speak another language feel more white, black-white multiracials do not have the similar option of feeling more white or less black because there is no alternate foreign language on which they could base an alternate identity.

Conclusion

America's multiracial population is young—42 percent are under the age of eighteen—so the parents are the ones choosing their children's ethno-racial identification on official documents, such as the census form. The way interracial couples choose to identify their children attests to the incorporative power of intermarriage. Many Asian-white and Latino-white couples who recognize and identify their children as multiracial or multi-ethnic feel nonetheless that the sheer force of incorporation into the non-Hispanic white culture is so powerful that their children will soon adopt a white or American identity, regardless of how hard they try to instill in them a multiracial or multi-ethnic culture and identity. The gendered pattern of intermarriage and the exclusion that some multiracials (especially Asian multiracials) experience from coethnic institutions further pushes them to adopt a white or American identity.

Black intermarried couples feel differently. Although they, too, recognize the multiracial backgrounds of their children, they are more likely to identify their children as black, in part because they claim that others identify them as such. Whereas the Asian-white, Latino-white, and Asian-Latino couples believe that their children will soon identify as white or American, none of the black intermarried couples identified their children as white, nonblack, or simply American, suggesting that the incorporative power of intermarriage operates differently for blacks than it does for Asians or Latinos. Interracial black couples are the least likely, the least able, and possibly the least willing to transfer a white or nonblack ethnoracial identity to their children. The findings suggest that intermarried black couples appear to be traversing a unique pathway, one that leads to incorporating into a racialized, minority status. We found not only that the culturally acceptable parameters of intermarriage exclude blacks but also that intermarried black couples are least able or least willing to transfer a nonblack status onto their children.

~ Chapter 7 ~

Who Is Multiracial? The Cultural Reproduction of the One-Drop Rule

As noted earlier, the 2000 census allowed Americans to mark "one or more" races to indicate their racial identification. This landmark change in the way the census has measured race was significant not only because it represented official recognition of racial mixing in the United States but also because it validated the view that racial categories are no longer strictly bounded and mutually exclusive (DaCosta 2000; Farley 2002; Hirschman, Alba, and Farley 2000; Hollinger 2003; Morning 2000; Waters 2000; Williams 2006). This was a momentous step, for the United States has historically denied the reality of racial mixture and instead adhered to the view expressed by Madison Grant (1916, 16), a well-known eugenicist and "scientific racist," who proclaimed in the early twentieth century, "The cross between a white man and an Indian is an Indian; the cross between a white man and a Negro is a Negro; the cross between a white man and a Hindu is a Hindu; and the cross between any of the three European races and a Jew is a Jew."

In 2000, 7.3 million Americans—one in every forty, or 2.6 percent of the population—identified multiracially (Ruggles et al. 2009). In 2007 the figures were 6.5 million, or 2.2 percent (U.S. Census Bureau 2007). As we noted in chapter 3, multiracial reporting varies widely by group, with blacks exhibiting the lowest rate among all nonwhite groups. In fact, their rate of multiracial reporting is much lower than those among Asians and Latinos, even after controlling for differences in age, education, nativity, gender, and region of the United States (Tafoya, Johnson, and Hill 2005). It is particularly puzzling, given that the Census Bureau estimates that at least three quarters (and very likely 90 percent) of the black population in the United States is ancestrally multiracial, that just 5.8 percent chose to identify as multiracial in 2008 (Ruggles et al. 2009). Clearly, most African Americans do not identify themselves strictly on the basis of their genealogy. Instead, most rely on the social construction of racial status and, in particular, the legacy of the one-drop rule of hypodescent, whereby anyone with as little as one thirty-second black ancestry or any traceable amount of black blood is categorized as racially black (Davis 2004; Haney-Lopez 1996; Nobles 2000). The relatively higher rates of multiracial reporting among Asians and Latinos suggests that the absence of the one-drop rule of hypodescent for these groups leaves them with more options to choose from among various ethnoracial identities (Farley 2004; Harris and Sim 2002; Stephan and Stephan 1989; Xie and Goyette 1997).

In this chapter we use the data we collected from the forty-six in-depth interviews we conducted with multiracial adults to examine some of the mechanisms and processes that lead to different rates of multiracial reporting by different ethnoracial groups. Two broad research questions guide the analyses that follow. First, how do we explain the different rates of multiracial reporting among Asians, Latinos, and blacks? Second, in the absence of the legal implementation of the one-drop rule of hypodescent, what cultural and institutional mechanisms may now be in place to effectively keep the rate of black multiracial reporting relatively low and, conversely, the rate of black monoracial reporting unexpectedly high?

The Cultural Reproduction of the One-Drop Rule

We found that in the absence of the legal invocation of the one-drop rule of hypodescent, ethnoracial identification is still highly contextualized and governed by cultural parameters (Moran 2001). Culturally and institutionally embedded practices such as external attributions of identity and interactions within institutional contexts, such as schools and the criminal-justice system, continue to operate effectively to constrain the multiracial identities of blacks in the United States and keep the likelihood of their multiracial identification relatively low, especially compared to that of Asians and Latinos. In fact, cultural and institutional factors operate in the opposite direction for multiracial Asians and Latinos. Ethnic organizations and networks often exclude multiracials from their circles, consequently pulling Asians and Latinos with multiracial backgrounds away from choosing monoracial Asian and Latino identities and pushing them instead in the direction of adopting multiracial, white, or American identities.

External Ascription

From our interviews we found that multiracial Asians and Latinos have much more flexibility in their choice of racial and ethnic identities than multiracial blacks, in large part because of the sheer force of outsiders' ascription, which constrains the racial options of multiracial blacks. Although black Americans may acknowledge their mixed ancestry, they are the least likely to identify multi-racially because others identify them as black, which in turn affects the way they choose to identify. For instance, when we asked a twenty-seven-year-old black multiracial woman about her ethnoracial background, she said:

> One of my mom's grandmothers and one of my dad's grandmothers are Native American. And on my mom's side, she has a grandmother who is German Irish, married to a French black guy. I just don't go around saying, "Oh yeah, I'm black, white, Native American." If it comes down to it where someone says specifically, "What do you have in your genetic background?" then I do tell them, "I have Native American and Caucasian," but I have always identified as African American."

When we asked a thirty-three-year-old woman born to a white mother and a black father why she chose to identify as black, she said:

> I feel if somebody is going to look at me, they're not going to think I'm white so I put black. I don't think I'd identify as white very often, but I guess if it's very specific, then I'm going to indicate that I'm both black and white. I mean, I know that I'm mixed, but if it were to come up and it were to be a choice, one or the other, I would say I'm black.

Other multiracial adults who had one black and one white parent had similar sentiments. Although they do not deny the racial mixture in their backgrounds, they chose to identify as black because, as a twenty-six-year-old male noted, "I think the main reason I identify as black is if someone looks at me, I don't really necessarily look white." So powerful is the force of outsiders' ascription that he chose to identify his son, whom he conceived with a white woman, as black rather than as multiracial or white. This man admitted that he chose a black identity for himself and his children because he did not believe that others would accept his claim of a white racial identity.

Sociologists recognize that ethnoracial identity formation is a dialectical process—one involving both internal and external opinions and processes (Nagel 1994; Rodríguez and Cordero-Guzman 1992; Waters 1990, 1999a). The way an individual chooses to identify is strongly affected by the way others choose to identify him or her. While this is true for all individuals, the consequences of external racial ascription for nonwhite groups are more costly than for whites (Jiménez 2009; Kibria 2002; Lee and Zhou 2004; Waters 1999a; Zhou and Lee 2007). This is especially the case for blacks in the United States—both African Americans and black immigrants—as Philip Kasinitz (1992), Nancy Foner (2005), and Mary C. Waters (1999a) have shown in their research on West Indian immigrants and their children. Immigrants from the Caribbean make ethnic distinctions among themselves and also draw a line between them and African Americans, but they soon come to realize that the power of race—of blackness, in particular—often overrides differences in nativity, ethnicity, class, and skin tone in the United States. By the second generation, more than half identify as black American (Waters 1999a).

Like black-white multiracials, black multiracials with Asian and Latino backgrounds similarly feel that people often see and identify them as black. One black-Korean multiracial man we interviewed explained that others, including Asians, do not see him as Asian or as multiracial, but as black. This became painfully clear in the context of relationships he has had with Asian women whose parents would not accept him because they perceived him as black rather than as multiracial or Asian.

> Since high school I've had four girlfriends—three were pretty serious relationships—all of them with Asian women. One girl was mixed, and the only one whose family accepted me was the girl who was mixed. And none of the parents had even met me but maybe once. But the reason all three of the other ones had said no is because I'm half African American. And so they just said, "We don't want you dating somebody who's half black." And the argument the girls would make is "He's half Korean, too. It's not like he doesn't understand Asian culture," and they'd be like, "No, he's half African American, too, and that's just too much."

When we asked whether he felt that it would have made a difference if he were half white rather than half African American, he immediately responded, "Oh yeah, definitely! If I was half white, half Korean, that would have been a totally different story. It was the fact that I was half black, half Korean that they couldn't deal." What was most frustrating for him was that although he has always acknowledged his Korean heritage, others, including Asians, refuse to recognize his Korean ancestry, but instead identify him as black. This black-Korean male candidly revealed how black can be an all-encompassing category in the way that others choose to perceive, identify, and treat him, stating: "I'm half Asian, half Korean, but Asian people don't even recognize that. They don't care. They don't see that. All they see is a black man. That's it." Multiracial Asians, especially if they are part black, have very limited entry into Asian American communities because Asians have historically refused to recognize mixed-race children as Asian (Hall 1992; Nakashima 1992). Blacks have been much more accepting of multiracial children than either Asians or whites (Spencer 1997).

External ascription can also take other forms, including the reactions that others have when they see certain interracial unions and multiracial families. This is particularly true for interracial black couples and black multiracials, who explained that they often receive perplexed reactions to their mixed unions. Black-white couples in particular said that service workers in restaurants and stores consistently assume that they are not a couple and often ask to help one and then the other. Black multiracial respondents also described the puzzlement that friends and strangers feel when they see them with their white parent. The bewildered reactions, stares, and questions that black inter-racial couples and multiracial individuals receive illustrates that for others, see-ing certain racial combinations together is foreign, unfamiliar, and seemingly illogical. From an outsiders' perspective, there is a clear disconnect between black and white, especially in the most intimate unions.

The Inclusivity and Exclusivity of Racial Categorization

Multiracial Asian-whites and Latino-whites feel that they have much more lee-way and freedom than multiracial blacks to choose among different racial options, including multiracial and white identities. Some choose to identify as half Asian or half Latino and half white; more important, outsiders do not chal-lenge these identities, nor do they immediately assign a monoracial Asian or Latino identity to them. Rather, their multiracial identities are more readily accepted than the multiracial identities for blacks. Moreover, outsiders often identify Latino-white and Asian-white multiracials—but not black-white multiracials—as white, which affects the way they choose to self-identify. For instance, many of the multiracial Latino-whites feel that they look "white" without a hint of Latino ethnicity. Their perception that they look white is rein-forced by others who are shocked to learn that they have a Latino parent. One twenty-three-year-old Mexican-white multiracial woman explained:

> I feel like I'm white with a hint of Mexican. That's not usually what I identify with, and that's not how people identify me either. I feel mostly Caucasian, but I do have a Mexican background and family and her-itage, but I identify with being white more just because that's the way I look. I mean, people are always surprised to find that my mom is Mexican. They say, "Oh my god, I never would have known. You look like a total white girl."

Similarly, another young woman with a white father and a Mexican mother explained that others, including other Mexicans, often assume that she is non-Mexican because of her Anglo appearance.

> I don't look Mexican, but I feel it within me. I cook Mexican food, and I listen to my Spanish stations. But a lot of people identify me as white because my appearance. I always shock them when I say, "Oh yeah, I'm Mexican." I go to a restaurant or food place that's Mexican and always order in Spanish, and they go, "Oh, habla español?" and I go, "Sí!" and then we start speaking.

The Latino multiracials we interviewed explained that others are consis-tently surprised to learn that they have a Latino parent. The surprised reaction stems in part from the fact that many non-Latinos (and even some Latinos) have a very narrow and specific vision of what a Latino, especially a Mexican, should look like. When we asked a Mexican-white couple what they thought the stereotypical image of a Mexican is, the Mexican husband replied, "Darker skin to begin with." His wife then chimed in, "I know for a fact when I tell people that my husband is Mexican, I know in their mind that they have an image of dark skin, sombrero, the totally classic—what's his name?—the coffee guy? Juan Valdez." Her husband corrected her, "He's Colombian." She then continued, "Well, whatever, but that's the stereotype." Latinos recognize that they span the color and feature spectrum—with many having fair skin and light eyes—but non-Latinos often have a very narrow vision of what a Latino should look like (Jiménez 2004). One Mexican woman married to a white man elaborated:

> In Mexico there's no one look. It's not all dark skin or dark eyes or look-ing Indian. One of my sisters has green eyes, and my other sisters have fair skin. I think that here people think all Mexicans have dark skin and brown eyes. In Mexico you see a lot of kids that look like Anthony [her son] or are lighter. There's this concept, this stereotype, that you look Mexican.

Non-Latinos are often surprised to meet Latinos and Latino multiracials who do not have dark skin, dark hair, or dark features. Similarly, non-Asians (and even some Asians) are surprised to meet multiracial Asians who do not have black hair, an olive complexion, and dark eyes. A man born to a Japanese father and a white mother explained that because of his blond hair and blue eyes, people assume that he is white and treat him accordingly: "Most of the time people assume that I'm white. I mean, it's just the fact that I look white. People just think or they have a stereotype of somebody that's white, so they will kind of treat me the same way."

In short, these multiracials challenge most Americans' expectations of what Latinos and Asians should look like. It is striking that whereas most Americans have a very narrow and specific vision of what Latinos and Asians should look like, we have a much broader vision of what blacks look like and define the category "black" very loosely. There is no stereotypical black look; we recog-nize and label as "black" people whose appearance spans the color and feature spectrum. For example, we readily identify Halle Berry as black, but we do not immediately identify Christina Aguilera or Cameron Diaz as Latina, even though both Aguilera and Diaz have distinctively Latino surnames. Similarly, we do not immediately identify Keanu Reeves, whose father was Chinese, as Asian, even though the name Keanu is Hawaiian. Cameron Diaz and Keanu Reeves both portray white characters in films, but Halle Berry so far has not, and it remains to be seen whether she will ever play a white character and be accepted by audiences as such.

Sports announcers consistently identify the American tennis player James Blake as African American, even though his mother is white. When Blake recently played in the U.S. Open, the commentators ignored his multiracial background altogether, even while they acknowledged that his mother, who is white, was seated in the audience with Blake's friends, the majority of whom were also white. Even given the clear and visible indicators of his white ethnoracial background, the sports commentators continued to refer to Blake as African American and dub him as "the next Arthur Ashe." In fact, a recent *New York Times* article compared Blake to Ashe with a headline that read, "Does James Blake Have What It Takes to Assume Arthur Ashe Jr.'s Stature?" (William C. Rhoden, *New York Times,* September 6, 2005).

The differences in ethnoracial identification and ascription point to what we refer to as the "inclusivity and exclusivity of racial and ethnic categorization." Whereas outsiders' ascription of black identity is broad and inclusive, their ascription of Latino and Asian identity is narrow and exclusive. In other words, most Americans are acutely aware of identifying black ancestry in a way that they are not similarly accustomed to identifying Asian or Latino ancestries. Hence, it is not simply that Asian and Latino multiracials "look more white," but rather that we are not as attuned to identifying and committed to constraining Asian and Latino ancestries in the same manner that we identify and constrain black ancestries. We immediately recognize any trace of black ancestry on sight and then ascribe a black racial identity to multiracial blacks, often ignoring their white, Latino, or Asian ancestries. By contrast, most Americans are not as attuned to recognizing traces of Asian and Latino ancestries with the same facility, and when they do, they are not as determined to constrain these identities. As a consequence, Asian-white and Latino-white multiracials feel that they have more freedom to choose among a variety of ethnoracial options.

The difference stems in part from the relative newness of the Asian and Latino multiracial populations, but it also stems from the invidiousness of the one-drop rule, whereby blackness, historically, has been treated as an all-encompassing, monolithic category combining people of diverse features and skin tones. The inclusivity of racial categorization among blacks is a product of three and a half centuries of miscegenation, including coerced unions between black female slaves and white male slave owners, combined with the legally enforced one-drop rule. These two factors produced a wide spectrum of color and physical features among people labeled black, or African American (Davis 2004). Furthermore, even though many blacks understand full well that their heritage includes white ancestry, the historical and coercive nature of these unions has meant that this knowledge has been divorced from any meaningful connection to whites (Waters 2000).

The one-drop rule in the United States and the resultant stigma attached to blackness have made multiracial blacks feel more limited in their choice of ethnoracial identification than multiracial Asians and Latinos. For instance, African Americans have not been able to claim that they are one-eighth African American without giving up the other seven eighths of their ancestry (Hollinger 2003). More precisely, multiracial blacks may acknowledge and claim their multiracial backgrounds, but others fail to recognize and accept their mixed ancestries. By contrast, nonblack Americans can claim to be one-eighth or one-quarter Asian or Latino and seven-eighths or three-quarters white and, more important, have those identities readily accepted by others. The combination of these factors gives multiracial Asians and Latinos more freedom to choose among various racial and ethnic options, including white and multiracial identities.

Immigrant status is another relevant factor. Most of the Asian and Latino multiracials in the sample come from families where the Asian or Latino parent is foreign-born (an immigrant). These multiracials view their claim to a white, American, or multiracial identity not as a rejection of their Asian or Latino ancestries, but rather as a step in their path toward becoming American. Many of the respondents and especially the Asian and Latino parents of the respondents used the terms "white" and "American" interchangeably, signaling that they equate white with American. By claiming a white racial identity, they feel that they are also claiming an American one.

By contrast, African Americans in the sample are native-born with a native-born legacy that dates back for generations, and so for them, adopting a white racial identity means something entirely different than becoming American. They are without a doubt American. But given the history behind the one-drop rule and the meaning and consequences behind the practice of "passing as white," for black multiracials to adopt a white identity may signify not only a rejection of the black community but also the desire to be accepted by a group that has legally excluded and oppressed them in the past (Davis 1991/2001; Kennedy 2003a). Hence, choosing to "exit" a black identity involves greater costs, consequences, and significance than choosing to "exit" an Asian or Latino identity.

Institutional Contexts

External ascription and outsiders' reactions are not the only forces that powerfully affect one's choice of identities. In addition, social institutions, such as schools and the legal system, shape, constrain, and reinforce particular ethnoracial identifications. These institutional contexts play a pivotal role in culturally reproducing the one-drop rule of hypodescent.

Schools   Teachers and guidance counselors take an active role in ascribing and forcing a monoracial black identity on multiracial blacks. One fifty-one-year-old black multiracial woman said that when she was in school, teachers explained to her, "Anytime you have, from what they told me, a certain percentage of black in you, you are considered black." When we asked her whether things are different today, she said that her children have also been labeled as black by their teachers: "My kids, when they were in Catholic school, they would have to answer one or the other: black or white. The teachers would say, 'Well, we'll just put you down as black.' " When asked how she felt about teachers identifying her as well as her children as black, she said, "Didn't bother me. I mean, you can say what you want. A lot of people, like I said, say if you have any black in you at all, you are black. Whether you want to say it or not, you are." So ingrained and accepted is the one-drop rule that this multiracial woman did not even question or challenge the teachers' decisions to label her or her children as black. We thought it was possible that younger black-white multiracials today may have had different experiences, yet we find that they, too, have experienced forced black monoracial identification in both subtle and not-so-subtle ways. One eighteen-year-old multiracial black female college student told us, "During high school, when I was made to do standardized testing and I had to pick one [race], teachers would fight with me about only picking one. Oftentimes I learned that my tests, when I marked two [races], they would send it in and erase one." When asked which race they erased, she replied, "White."

A white woman married to an African American man told us, "When I enrolled my daughter in school, I put her down as biracial black-white. When she went to junior high, when they brought her in to counsel her, they had marked off the 'white' and just marked the 'black.' She was offended by it, and she told them to change it, and so they did." When we asked whether there was an option for "biracial" or "multiracial," her African American husband responded, "No, not in Virginia. It wasn't an option. It was either black or white." When asked why they thought school administrators would deliberately change the enrollment form and, more specifically, why they would choose black, the African American husband and the white wife had the following exchange:

WIFE: You know the one-drop rule, right? Okay, well, in America, it still works.

HUSBAND: We're the only culture that it applies to. That's pretty bad, isn't it? Isn't that like institutionalized racism? Yes.

INTERVIEWER: Do you think most black people are aware of the one-drop rule?

HUSBAND: A lot.

WIFE: Oh yes, because it applies to them [blacks]. I think white people use it all the time.

Another black-white multiracial woman explained that her teacher indirectly identified her as black by asking her, in front of the class, whether she likes watermelon, playing off the stereotype that all blacks like watermelon. "He was talking about stereotypes, and that whole day, he was like, 'Don't you like watermelon?' That type of thing. It was kind of odd. I was like, 'Yeah, but that really doesn't mean anything.'"

Teachers, guidance counselors, and school administrators who encourage students to identify as black, erase "white" on school forms, and subtly and not so subtly identify multiracial students as black are active institutional agents who constrain the identity choices of multiracial blacks. They often encourage or even force multiracial blacks to adopt a monoracial black identity, despite the fact that the one-drop rule of hypodescent is no longer legally codified. Yet its legacy has lasting effects in important institutional contexts such as schools, effects that influence not only the way nonblacks choose to identify multiracial blacks but also the way multiracial blacks perceive and identify themselves. None of the Asian or Latino multiracials mentioned that their identities were challenged or questioned in this way in school, even when their parents marked them as white on school forms. In short, black multiracials find their identities contested and constrained in a way that Asian and Latino multiracials do not.

Legal System   Another institution that constrains the multiracial options for blacks, especially black males, is the legal system—in particular, the criminal-justice system. All the multiracial black males whom we interviewed discussed the run-ins that they had with police officers and security guards. Accounts of being pulled over, frisked, and harassed by police officers were not uncommon among black multiracial males, regardless of their ethnoracial mixture. A black multiracial male told us what happened to him and his friends as they were about to leave the parking lot of a mall in an affluent neighborhood:

> One time I went with some friends to the mall, this is when I was in high school. I wanted to buy my mom a Christmas present; I wanted to buy her a diamond pendant. You know, I had a job and I had been saving up my money. So we walked around the mall and went to different jewelry stores, and when we were leaving—it was myself, my girlfriend, and another one of my friends, he's African American—we were leaving the parking lot of the mall and pulling out. Just then, security and cops came out. 'Get out of the car! Put your hands on the steering wheel!' And it ended up some jewelry stores had called security, and some people fitting our description were casing out jewelry stores.

When we asked him why he thought the security guards decided to target him and his friends, he calmly explained, "Because I guess you don't see young blacks in jewelry stores, unless they're rappers or something, or unless they have something in mind. I was going to different jewelry stores to find something for my mom, and I actually bought her a diamond pendant that day."

A black-Korean multiracial male also told of the numerous occasions when he had been pulled over by police, especially when driving in predominantly white neighborhoods in Los Angeles. One particular incident stood out in his memory. He was with two of his friends and they decided to pay a visit to the sister of one of the friends, who happened to live in a predominantly white neighborhood in Orange County:

We went to visit his sister. It was the three of us. Got out of the car, went up to her apartment, knocked on the door, kind of, like, tapped on the window, and she wasn't there. So we were standing there, we walked downstairs and walked down to my car, and we were like, okay, we'll wait until she gets back.

And on the way back to my car, this lady pulls up—it was a white lady—and she was like, "I just called the police and gave them all your description. They will be here in five minutes." We were like, "What?" And one of my friends started cussing her out and before we even got to the car it was, like, [mimics a siren sound] cops and guns out, and they were like, "Put your hands on your head!"

And I had a pull-out stereo—you know those stereos, before they were a detachable face, you had to pull the stereo out, and I had a pull-out—and they sat us down. They checked every car in the parking lot. One of my friends was just, I mean, upset, and I was telling him, "You're not going to win any arguments." All three of us, he was the one who is full African American, the other one was half Mexican, half African American, and I'm half Korean, half African American.

And he was all irate, and I was like, "Man, you need to relax because we didn't do anything, so let them do what they have to do, but if you start shit, you know, what I'm saying, it may end up bad." So I finally calmed him down, and the cops searched every car in the parking lot and they said that they got a call that some guys fitting our description were breaking into cars and stealing car radios. That was like a half hour, forty-five minutes.

What is particularly poignant about the role of law enforcement in influencing multiracial black male identification is that it is precisely when young adolescent males begin to seriously question their ethnoracial identities that police officers begin to treat them as they treat black males—that is, with suspicion and threat. For instance, when we asked a twenty-nine-year-old multiracial man with a Mexican mother and a black father when he began to identify as black, he responded, "In elementary school, I always said I was Mexican and black, but in high school, I was black. That was it. I wanted to be the black kid." After more in-depth questioning, he described how he began to identify as black in his early teens, partly because he noticed a change in the way police officers reacted to him:

You probably never had to experience or worry about the police. You see the police, and that's just a cop. I see the police, and that's not a cop, that's the fucking enemy. I always wondered, okay, damn—how come when I'm six, eight, nine, ten, I wave at the fucking policeman and he waves back. It's all good. But why when I'm fourteen, fifteen, sixteen, and now, you look at me like I'm gonna do something. I ain't did nothing. I ain't got no record. Then you find out: No man, we don't like who you are, or who you might be, or who we think you are. So all of a sudden, it's me against you.

Another black-white multiracial male told us how, after leaving a convenience store with a friend in Simi Valley, he was pulled over by the police: "There were squads of police cars; it was crazy! Words were exchanged, and I got really, really heated. We were facedown, you know, boots smashing in our head. You know, they are talking all this crap. You know, 'You niggers.' It was really, really nasty." He and his friends were held for an hour and a half. When asked what he thought the reason was for his being pulled over, he stated, "Well, people, like I said, think I'm black, and to them, obviously, I blend into the same category."

All the black multiracial men recounted incidents like these. Such encounters with police officers lead black multiracial males to feel more black rather than multiracial or nonblack because their experiences with law-enforcement agents mirror those of black males, regardless of class background (Anderson 1990; Bonilla-Silva 2003; Feagin 1991). Like school officials, law-enforcement agents reinforce the one-drop rule of hypodescent by treating black multiracial males as black; this type of harassment by police officers is so common that multiracial black males have grown accustomed to it. As one young man said resignedly, "It gets to the point now when you get pulled over by cops, you know the procedure, you know everything that has to do with it, and it's just no big deal."

As multiracial children grow older, they increasingly interact with others outside the home, leading to more opportunities for outsiders to affect their ethnoracial identification. Interactions with authority figures in institutional contexts—whether in schools or law enforcement—strongly shape an individual's choice of identities, which helps to explain why older black multiracials are less likely to identify and be identified as multiracial and more likely to identify as black than their younger counterparts. This finding is consistent with David R. Harris and Jeremiah J. Sim's (2002) research showing that black-white biracial youths over the age of fifteen were more likely to choose black as the single race that best describes them than younger biracial youths. Regardless of the desire of multiracial blacks, especially males, to identify as multiracial, institutional constraints make it difficult for them to do so (DaCosta 2007).

The Question of Authenticity

Multiracial blacks are more readily identified and accepted as black by both blacks and nonblacks, but they are not always embraced by and welcomed into the black community as one of their own. This reluctance touches on the history of the necessity of proving one's authenticity as black (Kennedy 2003b). The question of authenticity recently came to the fore during discussions about President Barack Obama's ethnoracial identity. The son of a black African father and a white American mother, Obama identifies as black, but some blacks have charged that he is "not black enough" or "black, but not like us." It was Alan Keyes, the Republican candidate who ran and lost against

Obama in the Illinois Senate race in 2004, who first publicly raised the issue of Obama's background in the context of that race. Keyes accused Obama of not being black because, unlike Keyes, Obama is not a descendant of slaves, an opinion endorsed by some members of the media, including Stanley Crouch (2006), who in an op-ed piece in the New York *Daily News* suggested that Obama was not black because he had not "lived the life of a black American," by which he meant that Obama's family history did not include the shared African American experience of slavery, segregation, and discrimination. Some African Americans do not regard Obama, the son of a black Kenyan father and a white American mother, as authentically black American.

Obama's response to his critics is that his credentials of blackness are never in question when he attempts to hail a cab in Chicago or New York. His response underscores that external ascription can powerfully constrain one's identity choice. Second, he communicates that blackness is not exclusively defined by the shared, historical group experience of slavery and its consequences but also by the shared experience of living every day as a black man and dealing with interpersonal racism that ensues from that racial status.

What is peculiar about Obama's critics is that they question his black racial identity, even though Obama himself has unwaveringly chosen to identify as black, rather than as multiracial, nonblack, or white. His choice to identify as black is even more remarkable in light of the fact that he spent a part of his childhood in Hawaii, where racial mixture is more common and more readily accepted than in any other state in the country. Although Obama has always acknowledged his ethnic and racial mixture, his decision to identify as black is a traditional one that stems from the legacy of the one-drop rule of hypodescent as well as his day-to-day experiences of living as a black male in the United States.

Perhaps what is most noteworthy about Obama's decision to identify as black rather than as multiracial or nonblack is that he challenges the oft-held stereotype of blackness that links race with class, specifically that which associates blackness with the urban underclass. As a highly educated, professional, upper-middle-class black male who was not born and raised in inner-city poverty, Obama—like many middle-class African Americans—does not fit the common stereotype of a black American. Thus Obama departs from the stereotypical definition of a black American not only because of his non-native-born status and his multiracial, multicultural heritage, but also because of his status as a highly educated and successful professional black male. Questioning the black racial identity of Obama is to reinforce the stereotypical notion of blackness, which associates black with a distinct set of class experiences (Carter 2005). It is ironic that some of Obama's coethnics are choosing to impose this stereotype on him.

Our multiracial black respondents reported similar experiences of being accused of "not being black enough," "acting white," or "thinking you're better than us" because of their multiracial backgrounds. The charge of not being black enough or acting white in fact stems more from differences in class, as manifested in distinctive speech and behavioral patterns, rather than from their nonblack multiracial backgrounds per se. For instance, a black-white multiracial woman described the hostility of some of her high school classmates:

> In school, even though they were kids, they still had that hostility. They were are all Ebonics, and they didn't like the way I spoke because it was too white-girl for them. I'm very well pronounced. I'm very well educated. I use full words, I don't say "dis" and "dat." And I don't drive a low rider, and I don't listen to rap music really loud, and I don't take part in tennis shoes and all that jewelry, and I don't get into all that facade of wearing Tommy Hilfiger.
>
> The way that I dressed, the way my hair looked, the way I speak, the way I carried myself, the way my family is—all that would come out in me. I wasn't black enough to be in their friend realm. And my mom wasn't the typical black mom wearing house slippers at the grocery store and the hair in curlers. It was never like that. We were just different in general. We were uppity for black people.

Blacks did not feel that this woman was "black enough" to be included in their social circle, yet she distinguished herself from other blacks on the basis of her white, middle-class behavior, speech, and dress preferences. She drew a clear divide between herself and other blacks, whom she viewed as categorically different, and in the process she treats black as a monolithic category and subscribes to a stereotypical notion of blackness regarding other kids in school. By stating that she is uninterested in loud rap music, ostentatious jewelry, and designer sportswear, she reifies what it means to be black, which in her view is someone who is inarticulate and poorly educated and also someone who likes rap music, jewelry, and designer sportswear. In the process of distancing herself from other blacks, she reinforces a stereotypical definition of blackness that conflates race with class (Carter 2005; Waters 1999a). It is important to note, however, that even though multiracial blacks may have experienced resentment and taunts from blacks that they are "not black enough," this does not lead them to reject their black racial identity altogether. Although they may experience questions about their black authenticity from time to time, they acknowledge that they are more readily accepted in African American social circles than nonblack ones.

Conclusion

Not only are Asians and Latinos more likely to report multiracial identification than blacks, but Asian-white and Latino-white multiracials are also more likely to identify and be identified by others as white than as Asian or Latino. By contrast, blacks are less likely to identify multiracially and more likely to identify and be identified as black. In fact, none of the black-white multiracials identified monoracially as white, nor did the black-Latino and black-Asian multiracials identify as monoracially Latino or Asian. This suggests that although the one-drop rule is no longer legally enforced, it continues to be reproduced by culturally embedded practices at the institutional level and through everyday interactions. Thus, informal cultural mechanisms have taken the place of the historical "rule" and have similar consequences: they effectively keep the rate of black multiracial reporting relatively low.

These cultural premises and practices work in one direction for multiracial blacks and in the opposite direction for multiracial Asians and Latinos. Ethnic institutions, ethnic communities, and ethnic language discourage multiracial Asians and Latinos from adopting monoracial Asian and Latino identities and encourage them to choose multiracial and white identifications. The Asian and Latino multiracials we interviewed, hailing from immigrant backgrounds, are more likely to regard the claim of a multiracial or white identity as part of the process of becoming American. African Americans, on the other hand, as native-born Americans with a long and turbulent legacy in the United States, hold a different view: they do not equate a "white" racial identity with an "American" one. These divergent processes illustrate how the incorporative power of ethnoracial mixing and the ability to claim a multiracial identity differ by group. Blacks feel that they have fewer ethnoracial options than Asians and Latinos have—options from which they may freely choose and which will be accepted by others. Black immigrants to the United States are subject to the force of racialization, making it unlikely that their or, especially, their children's experiences would differ from those of African Americans.

Multiracial blacks may be more readily identified and accepted as black than as either white or nonblack, yet they are not always embraced by the black community as one of their own. Even though they may experience questions about their black authenticity from time to time, they also acknowledge that they are more readily accepted in black social and institutional circles than nonblack ones. Sometimes accused of "not being black enough," the onus is on multiracial blacks, as it is on middle-class blacks, to prove their racial authenticity. Yet questions about multiracial blacks' blackness are not so strong as to keep them outside the black racial category. Indeed, most multiracial blacks feel closer to blacks than to nonblacks.

~ Chapter 8 ~

From Racial to Ethnic Status:
Claiming Ethnicity Through Culture

In an oft-cited passage about group boundaries, the social anthropologist
Fredrik Barth (1969, 15) noted:

> The critical focus of investigation from this point of view becomes the eth-
> nic boundary that defines the group, not the cultural stuff that it encloses.
> The boundaries to which we must give our attention are of course social
> boundaries, though they may have territorial counterparts. If a group main-
> tains its identity when members interact with others, this entails criteria for
> determining members and ways of signaling membership and exclusion.

Barth recognized that ethnic boundaries are not static, fixed, and permanent,
but rather continually transform through expression, validation, inclusion,
and exclusion.

Racial and Ethnic Boundary Change

Today, social scientists agree that "race," like ethnicity, is a social rather than
biological category and have documented the processes by which racial boundaries have changed in different contexts and over time. In fact, changes in racial
classification have been an inextricable part of the immigrant incorporation
experience in the United States, and the European-immigrant incorporation
experience exemplifies the way the boundaries of racial status can expand to
absorb new groups. Groups such as Irish, Italians, and Poles, who once were
perceived as "unassimilable," became "white" because the boundaries of whiteness changed to incorporate them.

European immigrants adopted certain behaviors to speed their own incorporation, such as actively distancing themselves from African Americans to

attain whiteness. Another factor that helped their transition to whiteness was the cessation of large-scale European immigration in the 1920s. The closing of America's doors to massive waves of new European ethnics not only diminished fears about an overflow of allegedly racial inferiors but also facilitated the economic incorporation and mobility of European newcomers, especially during the flush years following World War II (Foner 2000, 2005), when the economy was booming. With economic mobility came the decoupling of national-origin differences from the idea of "racial" differences, contributing to the development of the idea that for many European immigrants, racial status was achieved rather than ascribed (Alba 1990; Gans 1979; Haney-Lopez 1996; Perlmann and Waldinger 1997; Waters 1990). In other words, as economic and cultural differences diminished and eventually faded between white and nonwhite immigrant groups, the Irish, Italians, and eastern European Jews became racially reclassified as white.

Herbert J. Gans aptly describes this process as "social whitening" or "social blanching" and makes clear that what changed was not the phenotype (skin color and physical and facial features) of previously nonwhite European groups, but the social construction (or, rather, reconstruction) of their skin color from nonwhite to white. As nonwhite immigrant groups achieve social and economic mobility and become more like native-born white Americans, they become reclassified, redefined, and accepted as white.

"Social whitening" may have been a part of the immigrant incorporation experience, but many social scientists caution that the very fact that Irish, Italians, and Jews were not subject to the same type of systematic legal discrimination as African Americans were illustrates that they had a different status from blacks to begin with, a standing that facilitated their eventual racial treatment as whites (Alba 1985, 1999; Fields 2001; Foner 2000, 2005; Guglielmo 2003; Lieberson 1980). Although members of some European immigrant groups may not have been considered white when they first arrived on these shores, they were viewed as nonwhite rather than as black by the country's Anglo-Saxons. This critical distinction should be underscored since in that time period's rigidly compartmentalized black-white world governed by the one-drop rule (which implied two poles—pure whiteness versus everything else), not being white did not necessarily equal being black, even if it was similar to being black. But because European ethnic immigrants were not in fact black, their status eventually changed, thus hastening the evolution and acceptance of the idea that at least some racial categories—maybe all except black—could eventually change.

Researchers have shown that European ethnics are not the only groups to have changed their status from nonwhite to white. Asian ethnic immigrant groups, such as the Chinese in Mississippi and the Japanese, also changed their racial status from almost black to almost white (Loewen 1971; Spickard 1989). James Loewen (1971) documented how Chinese immigrants in the Mississippi Delta made conscious efforts to change their lowly status by achieving economic mobility, emulating the cultural practices and institutions of whites, intentionally distancing themselves from blacks, and rejecting fellow ethnics who married blacks as well as their Chinese-black multiracial children. As a consequence of their deliberate efforts, the racial status of the Chinese in the region changed from almost black to almost white.

Today, so extreme is the shift of Asians in America's ethnoracial hierarchy that they now bear the titles of "model minorities" and "honorary whites," against whom other nonwhite groups are often judged and compared—a far cry from the derisive designation "yellow horde" once used to describe Asian immigrants at the turn of the twentieth century (Gans 2005; Lee and Zhou 2004; Zhou 2004). Again, what changed was not Asian immigrants' skin color or other physical characteristics but the way they are now perceived by native-born whites after having achieved both economic and social mobility. So dramatic is the turnaround that some social scientists are beginning to ask whether Asians are the next in line to become white.

As the historian Gary Gerstle (1999) has articulated, whiteness as a category "has survived by stretching its boundaries to include Americans—the Irish, eastern and southern Europeans—who had been deemed nonwhite. . . . Contemporary evidence suggests that the boundaries are again being stretched as Latinos and Asians pursue whiteness much as the Irish, Italians, and Poles did before them" (289). By placing Latinos and Asians in the same category as Irish, Italians, and Poles, Gerstle forecasts that Asians and Latinos are following the same incorporation trajectory as earlier immigrant ethnics and may, like their European predecessors, eventually become white.

Thus, changes in group boundaries clearly are a fundamental aspect of the immigrant incorporation experience. Based on the European-immigrant incorporation model, the decoupling of national-origin differences from racial differences resulted from economic and social mobility in the form of deliberate distancing from African Americans. Both of these processes have been an inherent part of the immigrant incorporation experience in the United States, leading previously nonwhite immigrant groups to cross over the color line to become white.

Today, so complete is the assimilation of European ethnics that few would disagree with the claim that European ethnics, such as Irish, Italians, and Poles, are white. In fact, the boundaries separating them are no longer defined as racial differences, but instead as ethnic differences that are merely symbolic (Gans 1979; Waters 1990). Ethnicity has faded into the twilight for white Americans, as Richard D. Alba (1985) vividly illustrates, meaning that ethnic identity no longer structures Americans' everyday lives: ethnicity does not determine where whites live, where they work, or whom they marry. Instead, ethnicity for white Americans is symbolic—lived, expressed, and celebrated through symbols such as food, festivals, holidays, and leisure-time activities. In short, rather than being ethnic, white Americans can simply feel ethnic whenever they choose, by frequenting a French restaurant, spending a day in Little Italy, or attending the St. Patrick's Day parade. Because the ethnic identities for white

Americans are not visibly evident, they feel faintly constrained in the way they choose to identify, thereby making their identities more malleable, situational, and voluntary than nonwhite identities (Alba and Nee 2003; Lee and Zhou 2004; Waters 1990; Yancey, Ericksen, and Juliani 1976; Zhou and Lee 2007).

Social scientists have documented the symbolic nature of white ethnicity, but they have paid far less attention to the nature of nonwhite ethnicity. When we began this project, we were interested in not only studying the patterns of multiracial identification based on the 2000 census, but also understanding the meaning and content that multiracial identification holds for multiracial Americans. We wondered whether "more than one race" was simply an answer to a census questionnaire or an idea that is instrumental in the everyday lives of multiracial Americans. In other words, is multiracial identity instrumental, symbolic (Gans 1979; Waters 1990), constrained by outsiders' ascription (Nagel 1994; Waters 1999b), situational (Okamura 1981; Yancey, Ericksen, and Juliani 1976), or some combination of these? In the process of examining the meaning and the consequence of multiracial identification, we were able to gauge which group boundaries are most resilient, which are most malleable, and what the findings suggest about the incorporation of new nonwhite immigrants and their placement along America's color line.

Symbolic Identities for Multiracial Americans

In chapter 7 we noted that Asian-white and Latino-white multiracials have more leeway in choosing among a variety of ethnoracial options—including multiracial and white identities—than black multiracials. In this chapter we investigate the meaning that ethnoracial and multiracial identification holds for multiracial Americans. From our interviews we found that many of the Asian-white and Latino-white multiracials' Asian and Latino ethnic identities are symbolic rather than instrumental. None of our respondents denied the ethnoracial mixture of their backgrounds, but most felt that their racial status holds little relevance or consequence in their everyday lives. For instance, when we asked a Mexican woman married to a white man how they identify their daughter, the woman explained:

> I want her to know where she comes from. I think it's important not to forget her mom and her mom's side of the family. I wouldn't want her to deny that she's half Mexican. I think she should be proud of it, just the same way that I wouldn't want her to deny that she's half white either. I want her to be proud of that, but I've never really thought race is a big issue.

The statement that she "never really thought race is a big issue" implies that this woman does not believe that her daughter's multiracial, multiethnic, or Mexican ethnic background will constrain her life chances. This is because she perceives Mexican ethnic identity as similarly symbolic and voluntary in nature as white racial identity—that is, lacking cost or consequence.

Other Asian-white and Latino-white multiracials echoed the belief that race will not affect their life chances. One Japanese-white male said:

> I don't think race matters that much. I don't think your race matters that much if you're really good at what you do. Well, at least in the U.S. you can be very successful. So I don't think how I look on the outside affects it. It should depend more on, like, the things that I'm able to do. I don't really feel it's going to affect me. I don't see limits.

Most Asian-white and Latino-white interracial couples and multiracial adults appear not to believe that "race" matters for their or their children's life chances: they do not conceal their ethnoracial backgrounds because there is no reason to do so. On the contrary, they readily acknowledge and are proud of their multiple heritages.

Even though their Asian and Latino identities may not be a salient feature in their everyday lives, the Asian and Latino multiracials often choose to mark their ethnoracial ancestries on official documents. For instance, when we spoke to a man born to a white mother and an Asian Indian father, he explained that while he identifies as white in his everyday life, he always marks both white and Asian Indian on the census and on other forms, saying, "I always felt like a regular kid, other than being just tanner than other people. But other than that I probably identified with being one hundred percent white. I don't identify that strongly with being Indian, but every time I put anything down on the census or anything, I'm Indian. That's it."

It is remarkable that he states that he has always identified as "one hundred percent white" throughout his life but consciously chooses to identify as Indian on the census and on other official documents. Similarly, many Asian-white multiracials do not think much about racial or ethnic status at all, nor do they strongly identify with their minority ethnic identity in their everyday lives, even though they acknowledge their Asian ethnic backgrounds on census forms and during interviews. This became even clearer later during the interview, when we asked this multiracial Asian Indian–white man about his plans to identify his son. The following exchange ensued between him and his wife, who is white and was eight months pregnant at the time:

> WIFE: Personally, I would still consider our child Indian, even though the Indian side is watered down considerably. I don't want to ignore that. I think it's still important.
>
> HUSBAND: I wish I had a stronger identification with being Indian. I really like learning about it, and I wish I knew more. For me, it's important, and I really need to know about it, so I think it's important for our child to have that same thing.

Neither partner had a sense of what it means to "be Indian," but both felt that it was important to learn more about being Indian so that they could pass on the heritage to their child. This couple treated Asian Indian ethnicity as a foreign culture that can be learned and acquired rather than an ascribed identity that is lived, experienced, and passed down in everyday life.

A similar point of view was expressed by a Japanese-white woman who said, "I don't carry a lot of the culture with me. I don't really think that my ethnic background is too important to who I am or what I do. But I'm finding more desire to have more culture." To these Asian-white multiracials, their Asian ethnicity was an additive component of their identity rather than something that structured or constrained their everyday lives. They emphasized that one can learn to be Asian Indian or Japanese and acquire elements of an Asian ethnic identity without having to forfeit one's white racial identity, reflecting the voluntary character of their Asian ethnic identities. In fact, some Asian-white multiracials even admitted to forgetting about their Asian ethnic ancestry altogether at times. A Vietnamese-white woman told us:

> Say we're in a room full of all white people, and I'm, like, the only Asian, I almost always forget that I'm Asian, or half Asian. Almost always. I consider myself white. I act very white as far as I'm concerned because that's all I know. So I don't have very much Vietnamese culture in me.
>
> I don't like Asian food, I have no Asian culture, I have no Asian traditions, and I know absolutely no Vietnamese. The only thing Asian about me is the fact that my mother is Vietnamese. I do everything white. I have all white traditions, I speak English. Everything about me is white, except for my car; it's a Honda! [She laughs.]

Latino-white multiracials responded similarly about their Latino ethnic backgrounds. One Mexican-white male even referred to himself as "whitewashed": "I think I'm more of like a crossover-type Hispanic. I don't speak Spanish, you know, a little bit, but I'm not fluent. So I've become more, you know, whitewashed. But I still try to stay true to my upbringing and Hispanic background." When we asked him to elaborate on what he means by "whitewashed" and a "crossover-type Hispanic," he said:

> I think there are two different types of Mexicans. There are immigrant Mexicans who come to the States and they speak Spanish, and their children speak Spanish and English probably, but associate themselves with those type of Hispanics. And then there's the other Hispanics who are more second- and third-generation Hispanics that are more "crossover Hispanics" that cross over to the white race, that don't really speak Spanish, but still maintain cultures of their Hispanic heritage. I feel like I'm more of a crossover-type Hispanic.

This Mexican-white man notes, acutely, that one can claim a Mexican ethnicity and also claim a white racial identity, just as one can claim an Irish or Italian ethnicity and also claim a white racial identity.

An additional factor in "crossing over" is that most of the Asian-white and Latino-white multiracials we interviewed have little direct exposure or connection to coethnic communities, so they feel more culturally similar to native-born whites than to other Asian or Latino ethnics. Their cultural affinity with white American culture and their corresponding detachment from Asian or Latino ethnic culture lead them to feel more culturally white and to adopt a white racial identity. The weakening attachment to ethnic identities is a normal part of the incorporation process; it is strengthened in the case of these multiracials who are also white, and they begin to identify more strongly as white than as Asian or Latino. Ethnic attachment also weakens for most U.S.-born monoracial Asians and Latinos, but because they do not have another racial or ethnic status to base their identities on, they do not perceive and identify themselves as racially white (Lee and Zhou 2004; Zhou and Lee 2007). Monoracial Asians and Latinos find their Asian and Latino ethnoracial identities far more binding and consequential than multiracial Asians and Latinos, in that their identities close off the option of claiming a white or unhyphenated American identity (Jiménez 2009; Kibria 2002). Perhaps more important, even if second-generation monoracial Asians and Latinos were to choose to identify as white, others would fail to recognize them as such and would not accept their claim of a white racial identity.

Claiming Ethnicity Through Culture— Tamales, Piñatas, Sushi, and Chopsticks

Although few of the Asian-white and Latino-white multiracials believe that their ethnoracial backgrounds structure their everyday lives, many genuinely appreciate their ethnic backgrounds and cultural traditions. Most of the multiracial respondents said they wanted to learn more about their ethnic culture because learning about and practicing these cultural traditions made them feel unique and special and, more important, set them apart from other white Americans, who, they believed, lack culture. Tapping into their ethnic cultures offers an antidote to having "no culture" and provides a reprieve from the "boring lifestyle" associated with being just white (Waters 1990). The desire to connect more strongly with their ethnic backgrounds seems to grow in intensity with age. One Japanese-white woman said:

> I'm finding more desire to have more culture. Just because I think the way that I live today, there is no culture, and I think it's kind of a boring lifestyle. When I meet someone from a different country, I see all these really interesting things that they do. It's because of how they were brought up, and I think the way I was generally brought up or wanted to be brought up was just kind of basic, you know, nothing really special to it. And I want to see, and maybe try more cultural things from the Asian descent to make it more interesting, to give my boyfriend and myself some more character.

This woman made several striking points about her multiracial background. First, as someone who has identified and has been identified as white throughout her life, she felt that her lifestyle was ordinary and boring. Second, in order to make her lifestyle more interesting and appealing, she would like to add some distinctive cultural elements to it, yet these elements would come from her "Asian descent," rather than her specific Japanese ethnicity. In other words, she lacks specific knowledge about her Japanese ethnic ancestry and conflates Japanese ethnicity with Asian racial identity. Third, she felt that she could adopt and try "cultural things" to add a new and interesting dimension to her lifestyle, illustrating the belief that Asian ethnicity is something recreational and fun that can be easily acquired, learned, and adopted.

Although most of the Asian-white multiracials we interviewed said that they knew little about Asian ethnic cultural practices, some said that they felt particularly unique because they had been able to practice and enjoy distinctive cultural elements, such as food, music, and entertainment. A Korean-white woman told us, "I'm white, but I also enjoy the fact that I'm Korean, because whereas a lot of Caucasian people, they don't have any culture, I can enjoy the dances, the food, the music, the entire culture that my mother's side has to offer me—that uniqueness." A Mexican-white male said he felt that "it's more of a privilege to have an ethnic type background than just white. I feel like there's more to me because I'm Hispanic, because of the culture and stuff, instead of just being white."

Both the interracial couples and multiracial adults emphasized the feeling of uniqueness they got from their culture; being "part Asian" or "part Hispanic" made them feel different and special, and set them apart from other white Americans, whom they viewed as ordinary. A white woman married to a Mexican man explained that she would like their son to identify with the Hispanic culture:

> I think I'd like him to identify more as Hispanic and fit the culture in and stuff. Just the different nuances and lifestyle and things like Spanish music, and the language, the different foods, to know what certain things are in the culture, like piñatas and things like that. And I would totally love for him to speak Spanish. I just think it would be so cool.

In her view, Hispanic culture and identity are defined by music, language, food, and piñatas. This woman did not view her son's Hispanic identity as constraining in any way; she saw Hispanic culture and identity as both additive and positive.

Most of our Asian-white and Latino-white multiracial respondents could tell us very little about any ethnic traditions that they practiced on a regular basis. When we probed the multiracial adults as well as the interracial couples about their ethnic culture—how they defined and practiced it and what cultural traditions they followed—most named elements such as ethnic foods, holidays, and music, which they enjoyed and celebrated on special occasions rather than in everyday life. The Latino multiracials pointed mainly to tamales at Christmas, piñatas at birthday parties, and Spanish or Mexican music, and the Asian multiracials mentioned going to Asian restaurants, using chopsticks, and celebrating the Chinese New Year.

A Mexican-white woman said, "I guess growing up we'd have piñatas, and we'd make tamales at Christmas, just kind of those little things that identify us as being from Mexico. I think those little traditions I would like to pass on just because they're fun, and it's just good." By describing the ethnic traditions as "little," "fun," and "good," she highlighted the recreational, peripheral, and positive role that they have in her life. Asian-white multiracials told of cultural practices that were limited to special holidays, such as celebrating the Chinese New Year, receiving money on holidays in red envelopes, eating Asian ethnic food, and taking off one's shoes in one's home. A Korean-white woman described her family's cultural traditions:

> As a child for my first birthday there was a feast. There was just about as much food as there would be at a Korean wedding—the works! Me in like a gown and everything. And then there is the Korean Children's Day in May every year. Other than the American Thanksgiving, there's a Korean Thanksgiving as well, and they have a whole bunch of food for that. It's all about food. And then the Chinese New Year and stuff, so bowing for money and more food. And taking off shoes.

When we asked whether these practices were important to her, she answered, "It added a little spice to life, but it wasn't, like, I have to do it." When we asked whether she wanted her children to grow up with these traditions, she said, "I want them to have knowledge, just like, you know, what their grandmother was like, and everything she taught me. It adds spice to their life." The idea of ethnic traditions adding "a little spice" or "a little special sauce" in their lives illustrates the expressive function of ethnicity for these multiracial adults. In short, practicing ethnic cultural traditions allows Asian-white and Latino-white multiracials to *feel* ethnic without *being* ethnic, just as white ethnics can feel and experience their European ethnicity as a leisure-time activity without cost or consequence (Gans 1979; Waters 1990).

It is striking that some Asian-white multiracials and interracial couples claim that they are practicing and passing on distinctive Asian ethnic cultural traditions to their children by eating Asian ethnic foods and using chopsticks, even though many of them are borrowing cultural elements from other Asian ethnic cultures and adopting them as their own, instead of passing on their own culture. The Chinese husband in a Chinese-white couple explained how he was passing on his ethnic traditions to his children by eating Chinese and Japanese food, and by using chopsticks: "We go out and do sushi once a week, and I think that's important. Eating with chopsticks, we do that." When we asked whether he used chopsticks while growing up, he said, "I didn't grow up using chopsticks, but, yes, a lot of Chinese and Japanese food. So although my folks always ate with forks, they grew up with chopsticks, both sides, so it was important to them that I knew how [to use them]." He believes he is passing down elements of his Asian ethnic culture by teaching his children to use chopsticks. Even though his ethnic background is Chinese, he feels that eating sushi once a week is an ethnic tradition that is important to pass down to his children, even though sushi is Japanese cuisine. Similarly, a Japanese-white man explained that some of the cultural practices he is passing on to his sons include "liking sushi and Chinese food." Again, though Japanese, he considers eating Chinese food—from a local suburban Chinese restaurant—a distinctively ethnic tradition.

These Asian multiracials are adopting and passing on pan-Asian rather than specific ethnic cultural traditions, and are claiming them as part of their own ethnic heritage. These patterns highlight two distinct points. First, multiracials' considering pan-Asian cultural elements as ethnically specific or ethnically authentic indicates just how little they know about their particular Asian ethnic heritages. Second, the adoption of pan-Asian cultural elements may presage the possible emergence of a pan-ethnic and symbolic Asian identity among multiracial Asians in future generations.

Unlike Asian and Latino multiracials, black-white multiracials did not report that they hold or practice particular cultural traditions, apart from the traditional American ones such as Christmas and Thanksgiving. When we asked a black-white woman whether she grew up with particular cultural traditions, she responded, "At home we don't have any culture. I mean, we don't have any traditions-at-home kind of thing. I don't think it's anything we eat, a certain food, or like a certain thing that would put me as being black or anything that had to do with my race or my multiracialness. But I would like to have some."

Unlike the Latino-white and Asian-white multiracials, black-white multiracials feel that they do not have distinct ethnic traditions to base their identities on. As native-born Americans with native-born parents, black-white multiracials are less able to draw on particular ethnic traditions that are distinct from traditional American ones. By contrast, Asian-white and Latino-white multiracials, being only one or two generations removed from their immigrant heritages, more readily identify with and draw on specific immigrant ethnic traditions (even though most are symbolic), and claim them as their own.

Situational Identity

Situational identities are particular social identities that an individual may construct and present as a strategic and adaptive response to a specific context (Saenz and Aguirre 1991). One may choose to highlight, conceal, or even change a certain aspect of one's social identity, depending on one's company, one's location, and the costs and benefits associated with the choice (Okamura 1981; Waters 1990; Yancey, Ericksen, and Juliani 1976). Social identities are not fixed or static; they change depending on the context. All individuals exercise a certain degree of freedom in their choice of identities, but multiracial Americans presumably have even more flexibility, for they can choose to highlight one ethnoracial option over another, depending on the situation.

The extent to which multiracials feel that they can freely choose among various ethnoracial identities attests to the flexibility of group boundaries and to the situational nature of their identities. In order to gauge the situational nature of their identities, we asked the multiracial respondents whether they at times present themselves differently, under what circumstances they choose to do so, and what benefits are associated with the choices they make. We also asked the same questions to the interracial couples regarding their children.

We found that most multiracial Americans choose to identify differently depending on the situation, and most take advantage of the benefits associated with their multiracial backgrounds. Few found this idea problematic. The matter of identity change emerged prominently when we discussed benefits, such as affirmative action, targeted specifically for disadvantaged ethnoracial minorities. A few of the multiracial respondents expressed ambivalence about presenting themselves as ethnoracial minorities in order to take advantage of specific programs, but most felt entitled to do so. They believed they had the option to identify whichever way they chose on a form, even if the category that they marked was not the one they adopted in everyday life. For instance, some Asian-white and Latino-white multiracials may choose to identify as Asian or Latino when they feel that their minority status will beget benefits, even though they identify themselves as white in most other settings.

The interracial couples and multiracial adults were convinced that identifying with their minority racial or ethnic status would help or have helped them gain admission into college, especially into academically elite colleges. A black-white couple whose daughter was accepted into all the academically elite private colleges to which she applied told us that they felt their daughter had been successful because they encouraged her to identify as African American rather than as white on her applications. The wife, who is white, said that she persuaded her daughter to mark African American because she believed that there were concrete benefits associated with an ethnoracial minority status: "On college applications, I present them as anything other than Caucasian because they get special consideration. They definitely get special consideration if they are not Caucasian." When asked what she meant by "special consideration," she said:

> When Bianca was accepted to the University of Chicago, they invited her to come back to look at it, and it was the Students of Color that sponsored her and paid for her way to go back to see Chicago. She is very

bright; she graduated fifth in her class, and she carried a high GPA. But being female and Caucasian with a high GPA wasn't going to get her in, not into any of the schools that she wanted to get into. So I fully felt that she should take advantage of her ethnic background and utilize that. If she had just been Caucasian, she would have just been another kid. They look at that. They really look at that. And she was accepted to a lot of the schools that she was accepted to because of the fact, I believe, that she had African American blood.

When asked directly whether she believed that her daughter's African American background had helped her gain admission into these elite universities, she answered without hesitation, "Absolutely, absolutely. I can guarantee it."

The irony here is that the black-white interracial couples and multiracial adults who earlier claimed that they were upset and offended by teachers and school administrators who identified them and their children as black rather than as multiracial on school forms now voluntarily chose to identify as African American or black and encouraged their children to do the same in order to take advantage of minority-targeted programs. The young woman who was irate because a schoolteacher decided, without her consent, to cross off "white" and mark her as "black" on the school form admitted that she identified as African American on her SAT tests and on her college applications in order to become eligible for minority-based scholarships. Now attending college, she benefits from programs that are designed to assist ethnoracial minorities. Another black-white multiracial female college student explained that because she identified as African American, she can participate in special programs and profit from opportunities that are tailored exclusively for racial and ethnic minorities.

> You get a lot more funding—academically and monetarily—through government funding. Minorities on campus have this program, which is only for minorities, and they offer free tutoring, counseling services. I was in a math and science scholar's program which is also a minority-based program. I'm in this research program right now, and it's a minority-based thing. And I'm going to a research program this summer, and it's a minority-based thing.

Although she is pleased to be in a position to take advantage of opportunities that are available to ethnoracial minorities on this particular college campus, she adds without prompting, "Sometimes I feel bad and feel that I shouldn't be doing it because I'm not African American enough or I'm not minority enough to claim, to get all these special privileges, so to speak, but I don't know." She is ambivalent about being able to take advantage of minority-based programs because she is multiracial and therefore not African American enough to really qualify for the programs.

Interestingly, only the black-white multiracial respondents felt pangs of guilt about applying for and benefiting from programs designed to assist minorities because they felt that they did not fully fit the definition of black or African American, even though they had consistently been identified as such by others. The ambivalence stems from the fact that they have fought hard to clearly assert their white and multiracial backgrounds, yet they now find that by choosing to identify as black or as African American they are entitled to benefits that they would otherwise be denied. The black-white multiracial respondents in our sample were raised in middle-class households, so they felt that they were taking advantage of programs designed to assist economically disadvantaged minorities and this was a further source of guilt. This shows how they often adhere to a narrow definition of blackness—one that couples race with class, and one that leaves little room for middle- and upper-class African Americans or for multiracial blacks.

Multiracial Latinos were more at ease than multiracial blacks with marking their Hispanic, Latino, or Mexican identities in order to qualify for minority-based programs and were often strongly encouraged to do so by their Latino parents. For instance, a Mexican-white woman who identified as white told us that when it came to filling out forms for school, she identified as Mexican. She normally used her father's surname, which was Anglo, but chose to use both her mother's maiden surname as well as her father's surname on application forms whenever she felt that a Hispanic identifier would give her an advantage. Her Mexican mother had planned well in advance so that her daughter could take advantage of minority-based programs.

> For schools and stuff, I think my mom always encouraged me to put Hispanic descent or whatever, and a lot of it has to do with, like, what do you call it, affirmative action kind of things. My mom gave me a Mexican surname so that I would have that name for school loans or whatever. That kind of thing.

Likewise, a Chinese-Mexican woman told us she identified as Hispanic on school applications because she felt that it would be beneficial, which she was able to do so because of her surname: "I would always mark Hispanic, and it was mostly because of my last name. Also, with school programs that look at your ethnic background, I would mark Hispanic because it was more advantageous. It would help me in some situations." She was alluding to the belief that her Asian ethnic ancestry would not work to her advantage when she was applying for admission to college because Asians are not an underrepresented minority, nor are they regarded as a disadvantaged minority group, as are Hispanics.

Ethnic surnames are audible and visible markers of ethnicity, and having an ethnic surname or adopting one in certain situations gives multiracial Americans an avenue to evoke their minority identity when they choose to do so. Although surnames are often inaccurate ethnic identifies, as Mary C. Waters

(1990) has noted in her study of white ethnics, people continue to rely on them to gauge a person's ethnic ancestry. For example, a white woman married to a Mexican man explained that she was happy that their son would carry his father's ethnic surname because she believed his Hispanic surname would lead to "bigger opportunities." She was certain of this because her cousin (who is white but has a Hispanic surname because her mother remarried a Mexican man) received benefits and scholarships targeted for minorities.

> My cousin, she's in college, and her last name is Valdez, but she is the whitest girl in the world. I mean, my aunt married a man from Mexico, and [my cousin] tells me that, you know, because her last name is Valdez, she hasn't paid a dollar for college, and she is going on her second year. She has gotten scholarships—over thirty grand a year in scholarships. She feels that if her last name was Spencer, like my aunt, she probably wouldn't have gotten anything. If you are Hispanic, you have more of a chance of getting help from the state.

Whereas black-white multiracials expressed some ambivalence about exclusively privileging their black identity in particular circumstances, the Latino multiracials we interviewed did not give this a second thought. Regardless of whether others agreed with their decision, they felt they should freely exercise the option of identifying as Hispanic, Latino, or Mexican, especially when they thought that this identity would bring benefits.

Asian multiracials do not feel the way both black and Latino multiracials do about taking advantage of programs by claiming a black or Latino identity. Asians claim that identifying as Asian does not necessarily result in advantages when applying to programs designed to assist ethnoracial minorities, particularly when they are applying for admission to college. A few did, however, mention that it may help to identify as Asian when applying for jobs in which Asians are underrepresented—an example of the situational character of ethnicity for Asian-white multiracials. A Vietnamese-white woman who strongly identified as white in her daily life admitted to choosing to identify with whichever ethnoracial identity would work to her advantage at a particular time. She candidly stated that she identified as Vietnamese when she applied for a position as a flight attendant, since the supervisor who gave her the employment form mentioned that identifying as Vietnamese would be beneficial, as there are few Asians who work in the airline industry. Asked whether there were specific instances when she chose to identify as white, she said that she would do so if she were to return to college and apply to one of the University of California campuses. As a Vietnamese, or an Asian more generally, she would not stand out in the pool of applicants to the University of California campuses: "The UCs have a lot of Asians, and I don't think they want a lot of Asians. I mean, they're trying to look for more than just Asians, right? So I don't think I would put my ethnicity as Vietnamese. I don't think that would help me very much if I were trying to apply there."

When asked how she felt about identifying differently in different contexts, she replied, "I think whatever benefits me is great," and laughed. "I'm all for benefiting because I guess I have the opportunity to use both [ethnicities]. If it gets me into a school or gets me a job, I would put down whatever it was that gets me into the school or gets me the job."

This Vietnamese-white woman's ability to switch ethnoracial categories according to the context highlights the situational character of Asian-white multiracial identities and also helps to explain David R. Harris and Jeremiah J. Sim's (2002) finding that Asian-white multiracial youths are just as likely to choose Asian as white as the one racial designation that best describes them.

Asian-black and Latino-black multiracials closely resemble black-white multiracials when it comes to deciding to leverage their ethnoracial background in order to potentially optimize advantages. For instance, a Korean-black woman explained that she chose to identify as black during high school because teachers told her that doing so would be "more beneficial" in helping her to gain admission to college. Similarly, a Latino-black multi-racial man explained that he now identifies as black because of the benefits of doing so, which he feels he has every right to exploit.

> You know, I just mark African American or black now because you get benefits. See, the whole thing, the whole system feels bad, so now they want to give you benefits. Well, you're a fool if you don't take advantage of the benefits that people are trying to give you. Why not milk the system? Why not, if it's going to allow me to?

Multiracial Americans generally feel that they have the right to highlight the part of their identity that may benefit them the most in particular contexts, but others do not always approve of their decision to choose and switch among various ethnoracial options. When multiracials tell their friends that they have strategically marked African American or Hispanic on an application, some of their friends accuse them of "playing the race card" by unjustly leveraging their minority ethnoracial identity to their advantage, especially when they believe that the multiracials "act white." A multiracial black-white woman who identified as African American on her college application said that her friends feel it is unfair that she receives scholarships targeted for minority students, especially since she grew up in a white neighborhood and even, by her own account, "acts white":

> People get mad because I can get those academic benefits because of it. They are just like, oh, you pulled the race card or whatever to get into school. Or, you know, a lot of times I think people think I got in here because I marked down a minority on my application and, like, getting scholarships or whatever because I can mark a minority on my application. I think they get not mad, but they have some emotion to it because I may look and act and have grown up so much like them, being white with no minorities, and yet I still get the benefits because of it.

Thus, multiracials often have leeway to choose which ethnoracial options to highlight in different contexts, and outsiders often feel that this choice is unfair, especially when multiracials obtain benefits by situationally prioritizing a minority identity that may not define them in everyday life.

The question of who is eligible for race-based programs raises important policy issues regarding these programs (Skrentny 2002). First, they have the unintended consequence of reinforcing nonwhite ethnoracial identities among multiracial adults by privileging these identities. Second, when multiracial Americans are counted as ethnoracial minorities while living their everyday lives as whites, we are essentially placing multiracial Americans on the same plane with racialized minorities, whose experiences with their ethnoracial status may be radically different from those of multiracial Americans and who have genuinely been disadvantaged. We are not arguing that multiracial Americans should not be able to freely choose how they wish to identify, nor are we arguing that multiracial Americans should be excluded from participating in race-based programs. We are saying that we need to recognize that race-based programs may not necessarily benefit the most disadvantaged racialized minorities, whose racial identities are not symbolic or situational and who live each day with racial labels and the negative consequences that go along with them.

Conclusion

Because the multiracial population is growing—it may account for one fifth of the American population by the year 2050 and one third by 2100—it is critical to understand the meaning, content, and consequences that multiraciality holds for this population. Whereas white Americans often enjoy ethnic options as a pleasant addition to their lifestyle, nonwhites often carry the burden and consequences of racial labels. It is unclear at this time where multiracial Americans fit along this continuum of symbolic and constrained identities. Are their identities symbolic, as they are for white ethnics, or are they constrained by racial status?

From our interviews with multiracial adults we found that the nonwhite identities of Asian-white and Latino-white multiracials do not structure their everyday lives, even though they may readily mark their ethnoracial backgrounds on official forms. Most Asian-white and Latino-white multiracials are proud that their ancestry includes Asian Indian, Japanese, Korean, or Mexican heritage—just as white ethnics are proud to claim their ancestry that is part Irish, Italian, German, or French—but their racial status holds little consequence in their daily lives. Instead, they define their ethnoracial ancestry through culture and celebrate their Asian or Latino ethnic heritage through cultural practices, such as eating ethnic foods and enjoying the specific cultural traditions associated with holidays, such as baking tamales, creating piñatas, eating sushi, and using chopsticks. Like white ethnics, these multiracials can feel ethnic without being ethnic, reflecting the voluntary and situational nature of their Asian and Latino cultural connections.

Their Asian and Latino ethnic identities are a source of pride that offers them a feeling of uniqueness that separates them from other white Americans, whom they view as lacking a distinct and unique culture. In many respects, Asian-white and Latino-white multiracials are similar to American Indian multiracials, who exemplify racial fluidity, flux, and choice (Eschbach, Supple, and Snipp 1998), and also resemble white ethnic Americans in the way that they express and celebrate their ethnic identities. These findings suggest that Asian and Latino multiracials are much closer to whites on the U.S. ethnoracial continuum than to blacks at this point in time.

Like many members of the Asian and Latino second generation, born in the United States, multiracial Asians and Latinos feel they have little direct connection to their respective ethnic cultures. And also like the Asian and Latino second generation, Asian-whites and Latino-whites practice their culture only occasionally rather than living it in their everyday lives. What sets the multiracials apart from their monoracial counterparts is that they begin to feel and identify more as whites because they can claim another ethnoracial identity, a white identity, apart from their Asian or Latino ethnicity. This is not the case for second- and later-generation Asians and Latinos: because they do not have another ethnoracial identity that they can claim as their own, their Asian and Latino labels limit their choice of identities in a way that they do not for Asian-white and Latino-white multiracials, even if their ethnic culture plays as marginal a role in their everyday lives as it does in the multiracials' lives.

We also find that the identities for multiracial Americans are highly situational and governed by context. Although many multiracials live their everyday lives as white, they do not hesitate to identify as Asian or Latino if they feel that their minority racial or ethnic identity will work to their advantage. This became clearly evident during discussions about identity choice associated with race-based programs such as affirmative action. As multiracial Americans, our respondents felt that they had the right to choose how they wished to identify, and if marking a minority identity would bring advantages, most would not hesitate to do so. The situational nature of multiracial identification has important implications for programs that are intended to help genuinely disadvantaged ethnoracial minorities. As the multicultural population grows, we will need to reconsider the goal of programs such as affirmative action and carefully reflect on who should be the actual beneficiaries.

~ PART III ~

The Empirical and Policy Significance
of Diversity: Generalization
and Paradox

~ Chapter 9 ~

Ethnoracial Diversity, Minority-Group Threat, and Boundary Dissolution: Clarifying the Diversity Paradox

with James D. Bachmeier

The quantitative findings presented in the preceding chapters based on data from the 1990 and 2000 decennial censuses and the 2007 and 2008 American Community Surveys (ACS) reveal that recent immigration has fueled population growth among Latinos and Asians in the United States, which has led to an increase in ethnoracial diversity and has boosted rates of intermarriage and multiracial reporting. The in-depth interviews about intermarriage and multiracial identification yield qualitative results concerning cultural change expressed as a weakening of the boundaries that separate whites from other groups, especially among Latinos and Asians. To summarize, and perhaps to risk oversimplification, the quantitative findings document boundary-loosening social-structural shifts, and the qualitative results document boundary-dissolving cultural change. In many ways, of course, social structure and culture are two sides of the same coin (Lamont 1992, 2000; Sewell 1992; Skrentny 2008; Van Hook and Bean 2009). Thus, it is not inappropriate to interpret our research results to this point as reflecting complementary aspects of a single process of sociocultural change that has both structural and cultural manifestations.

But the challenge of understanding the origins of ethnoracial-boundary weakening and the reasons why the process of dissolution has proceeded faster for Asians and Latinos than blacks remains partially unmet. In particular, we are interested in shedding light on the extent to which ethnoracial diversity itself—which here is a product of immigration and population change (for example, differential rates of natural increase)—contributes to boundary dissolution. This brings our attention back to intermarriage and multiracial identification, which constitute our indicators of boundary dissolution in both the quantitative and qualitative data. Although they serve as useful markers of boundary weakening because they both involve racial mixing, they must be interpreted with considerable caution, because increases in intermarriage and multiracial reporting could result simply from the greater availability of nonwhites for intermarriage. This would result in concomitantly more multiracial offspring also available for multiracial identification. In other words, the trends and differences we have observed could mostly, or perhaps entirely, reflect demographic shifts and differences in ethnoracial composition rather than processes of ethnoracial-boundary loosening.

However, the findings based on the qualitative interviews with intermarried couples and multiracial adults presented in chapters 5 through 8 reveal experiences with and attitudes about intermarriage and multiracial identification among Asians, Latinos, and blacks in the highly diverse state of California that suggest diversity, at least in that context, has broader implications for boundary loosening. In California, diversity—not just demographic change—seems to have modified cultural attitudes and contributed to the dissolution of boundaries separating ethnoracial groups. Thus, we are inclined to conclude that boundary erosion is a product of both rising nonwhite demographic composition and accompanying social-structural-behavioral and cultural-attitudinal shifts. But because we conducted in-depth interviews only in high-immigration, high-diversity California, this conclusion remains tentative until we can examine connections between diversity and markers of boundary weakening in places with lower levels of diversity, to ascertain whether such places also show boundary dissolution.

Because of recent research implying that diversity carries negative implications for social capital and intergroup relations (Putnam 2007), it is also of considerable interest to gauge the degree to which diversity itself might be initiating boundary dissolution net of shifts in demographic composition. Our qualitative interview results imply this possibility, but they cannot confirm it. As revealing as they are of cultural and attitudinal changes, they nonetheless might be reflecting only cultural and social structural dynamics attendant upon shifts in demographic-ethnoracial composition. Because such a large component of intermarriage derives from opportunity alone—that is, differences and changes in relative group sizes across places and time—shifts in ethnoracial demographic composition, as we noted in chapter 1, could occur without the occurrence of any cultural or attitudinal change that is associated with the increasing sizes of minority groups. And even if such sociocultural changes were occurring hand in hand with shifts in demographic composition, they would not necessarily imply that diversity per se—apart from compositional change—was exerting an effect on boundary dissolution other than that resulting from ethnoracial groups becoming larger. Such social-structural and cultural changes would be important in and of themselves; it is of considerable additional interest to seek evidence that noncompositional elements of diversity, such as greater numbers of groups and more evenness of relative group-size distributions, might also foster boundary dissolution.

Investigating this possibility requires quantitative analyses using nationally representative data to assess diversity's independent effects on boundary dissolution, especially its effects net of compositional effects. Describing and reporting the results of such analyses is the objective of this chapter. We thus turn our attention once more to our examination of census and ACS data across cities, seeking to estimate empirically the multiple aspects of diversity's relationships with intermarriage and multiracial reporting, controlling for the confounding influence of other variables that might affect associations between diversity and these indicators. In chapter 4 we observed that places experiencing more immigration also show growth in the relative sizes of racial and ethnic minority groups, at least in the case of Latinos and Asians, with such increases appearing to loosen ethnoracial boundaries as indicated by higher exogamy and greater multiracial reporting. Now, however, we need to take into consideration in our statistical analyses the possibility that larger minority-group size may not always generate boundary loosening. As we discuss in more detail in a later section, theories that certain ethnoracial groups may be perceived by whites as greater threats than others imply that for these groups, the larger the minority group relative to the majority-group, the stronger will be the boundaries separating that group from the majority group. In that case, group-threat effects involving such groups could lower intermarriage and multiracial identification, offsetting any positive effects of diversity on boundary loosening. Hence, it is important in statistical analyses to examine the independent effects on intermarriage and multiracial reporting of both relative group size and diversity—to assess each, while controlling for the other.

Theoretical Considerations About Diversity Effects

Several theoretical bases exist for the idea that increased racial and ethnic diversity may contribute to the breakdown of barriers between ethnoracial groups and to increased whites' tolerance of both new immigrant groups and African Americans. One such dynamic is that as minority immigrant groups grow relatively larger, the probabilities of contact between the members of such groups and majority natives increase, thus promoting familiarity, respect, and greater liking across the groups. These are the processes that Gordon W. Allport (1954) notes in his long-standing contact hypothesis, which predicts that greater interaction between the members of different groups fosters familiarity and increases affect and liking. A second dynamic is that the presence of a larger number of different groups may tend to diminish the significance of any single group, because multiple minority groups may diffuse the intensity of negative affect and stigmatization. Still a third is that greater diversity may yield other positive psychological and social dividends—such as increased creativity, problem-solving capacities, social resiliencies, and interpersonal skills—that result from learning to cope with the differences, challenges, and opportunities presented by diversity. Such factors have been cited in the context of strengthening workplace and societal communication, cohesion, and effectiveness, especially in technology- and knowledge-based economies (Benkler 2006; Chua 2007; Grewal 2008; Herring 2009; Page 2007). They have also been observed to impart adaptive advantages to second-generation persons growing up in such environments (Kasinitz et al. 2008).

Other social processes are seen to strengthen boundaries between social groups. For example, the group-threat perspective posits that larger minority groups increase the likelihood of negative reactions to diversity because of fear of minorities on the part of majority whites. The latter may perceive some ethnoracial groups—specifically blacks—as more threatening than others. Thus, we would expect stronger negative group-size effects for blacks than for Asians or Latinos. American whites have often seen blacks as threatening, in part because of worries about economic competition and in part because the harsh discriminatory tactics employed against blacks for decades after slavery engendered white fears of reprisal (Blalock 1967; Fossett 2005; Fossett and Seibert 1997). Because the newly arrived largely nonwhite immigrant groups have not experienced similarly crushing discrimination on such a widespread scale for such a long period of time (Zolberg 2006), whites are not likely to perceive the new immigrant groups as so threatening as they do blacks. Thus, negative group-size effects may not emerge at all for Asians and for Latinos falling in between blacks and Asians.

Another reason for a stronger group-threat effect in the case of blacks is that African Americans constitute a less-preferred source of unskilled labor than immigrants (Kasinitz and Rosenberg 1996; Kirschenman and Neckerman 1991; Lee 2002; Waldinger and Lichter 2003; Waters 1999b). Asian immigrants, by contrast, are not as numerous as blacks or Latinos and are much more highly selected for higher levels of education than most Latino immigrants. They thus may be viewed more favorably and be more likely to occupy higher positions in the American stratification system than Latinos and thus be unlikely to generate comparable group-threat effects. Such a hierarchy of group-threat differences is in accord with the tenets of queuing theory (Lieberson 1980; Sakamoto, Liu, and Tzeng 1998) and group-position theory (Bobo 1999, 2004; Bobo and Hutchings 1996; Bobo and Tuan 2005), both of which state that an ordering among groups characterizes the extent to which they face discrimination in the labor market and other kinds of situations in the United States (Dixon 2006; Link and Oldendick 1996).

The possibility of negative white reactions to minority-group threats seems partly to lie behind some of the recent expressions of skepticism about possible benefits that might be associated with greater ethnoracial diversity (Schlesinger 1992; Schuck 2003; Smelser and Alexander 1999; Wood 2003). Indeed, some research has produced results that seem consistent with the idea that diversity strengthens the barriers separating groups (Putnam 2007). However, whether greater diversity leads to rising social tensions remains an open question for two reasons. One is that existing research remains inconclusive. The second is that analysts sometimes assume that new nonwhite groups in America will be treated, and come to see themselves, as more like blacks than whites, thus engendering negative diversity effects. But this possibility has not been adequately demonstrated by prior research, except in the case of blacks. To be sure, skepticism about diversity's positive implications undoubtedly may reflect distaste for the romantic and simplistic terms in which many appeals for increased diversity can often be expressed. But diversity that derives from growing numbers of nonwhites, larger numbers of new ethnoracial groups, and more uniform distributions of ethnoracial groups within locations may indeed foster boundary loosening for the reasons just noted above, even though negative factors, such as group-threat dynamics, may override such tendencies in some instances, especially those deriving from the presence of African Americans.

Additional circumstances suggest that the non-group-size aspects of diversity may foster boundary dissolution. In chapter 4 we noted that at both the state and metropolitan levels, multiracial reporting tends to occur in areas with higher levels of ethnoracial diversity, particularly among Latinos and Asians, which is largely a consequence of the influx of the post-1965 wave of immigrants. But by "ethnoracial diversity," we mean more than the composition of the population; we mean both the presence of multiple ethnoracial groups and the relative absence of statistical predominance on the part of any single group. Thus, the more a single ethnoracial group makes up all of the population of a social, political, economic, or geographic group or area, the less the diversity of that entity. Similarly, the greater the number of groups and the more equally they are distributed within an area, the greater the diversity. In essence, the idea of "diversity," as used here in connection with ethnoracial groups, is akin to the idea of heterogeneity as often more broadly invoked in sociology (Blau 1977; Blau and Schwartz 1984; Laumann 1973). Increased diversity (or, more broadly, heterogeneity) promotes greater tolerance, a tendency often noted by proponents of the contact hypothesis as noted above (Allport 1954; Blalock 1967; Blau 1977; Massey, Hodson, and Sekulic 1999). Diversity thus may contribute to increases in the likelihood of exogamy and multiracial identification because it fosters the loosening of ethnoracial boundaries and thereby promotes more flexibility in marriage and identity options for the members of ethnoracial minorities and their offspring.

Our hypothesis that diversity may be linked with intermarriage and multiracial reporting also resonates with previous research that demonstrates associations between geographic diversity and racial and ethnic identification. For instance, living within a large coethnic community or residing in an area that is greater than 20 percent Asian positively affects the degree to which interracially married Asians and whites identify their multiracial children as Asian (Saenz et al. 1995; Xie and Goyette 1997). Furthermore, comparing patterns of multiracial identification in Hawaii and New Mexico, Cookie White Stephan and Walter G. Stephan (1989) found that the higher rate of multiracial reporting in Hawaii reflected its stronger multicultural environment; while 73 percent of the Japanese in Hawaii identified multiracially, only 44 percent of the

Hispanics in New Mexico chose to do so. Karl Eschbach (1995), too, discovered regional differences in the choice of an American Indian identity for American Indian–white multiracials, ranging from 33 to 73 percent across the country. The results of all these studies support the hypothesis that ethnoracial diversity is positively related to exogamy and multiracial identification.

Thus, opinions differ as to the processes that are driving the evolution of barriers between different ethnic groups. Some analysts and observers suggest that rising diversity will lead to more insularity within groups, increased hostility and prejudice between groups, and a hardening of group boundaries among all whites, blacks, Latinos, and Asians, as each minority group continues to grow in size. Others argue that increased diversity can and will have an opposite effect because increases in the sizes of ethnoracial minority populations create more opportunities for intergroup contact and mixing with majority whites, greater possibilities for reduced prejudice, and, consequently, more favorable intergroup relations. Our overarching goal in this chapter is to assess empirically these contradictory positions by examining the relationship between growing diversity and changing ethnoracial group boundaries across cities. Drawing on theoretical ideas about minority-group size and intergroup relations as expressed in the group-threat and contact hypotheses, we analyze statistically how relative group size and diversity relate to exogamy and multiracial reporting. We also discuss the implications of our findings for how and why the contact and group-threat hypotheses in combination help to explain a pattern of "black exceptionalism," wherein diversity fosters some boundary loosening among African Americans consistent with the predictions of queuing and group-position theory but not enough to compensate for negative group-threat effects in the black case. This illustrates the paradoxical effects of diversity on boundary dissolution in America.

Empirical Findings

To assess these relationships empirically, we relied on data from the 1990 and 2000 censuses and the 2007 and 2008 American Community Surveys, examined across U.S. metropolitan areas. We took metropolitan areas as units of analysis, essentially treating cities as appropriate places within and across which to discern the dynamics of ethnoracial diversity and change and their effects on boundary dissolution. We included 1990 data because some of our analyses look at relationships between 1990 measures of relative group size, ethnoracial diversity, and intermarriage and 2000 measures of multiracial identification. (We present further technical details with respect to data, measures, and statistical analyses in the appendix, "Methodological Approach.")

To begin, we return to our examination of some of the trends first noted in earlier chapters, but we now focus on the period starting in 1990 and on metropolitan areas rather than on the entire country. According to 2007 and 2008 American Community Survey data, vast majorities of the country's foreign-born and nonwhite populations live in metropolitan areas (92.6 percent of the foreign-born and 87.0 percent of nonwhites [Ruggles et al. 2009]), so studying ethnoracial dynamics in metropolitan places captures the important social and demographic processes characterizing relations among ethnoracial groups and changes in boundary dissolution over the past two decades. Metropolitan areas also represent useful approximations of local labor markets and political jurisdictional areas within which intergroup relations play out (Moss and Tilly 2001; Kaufman 2001). They thus provide useful units of analysis for reassessing trends in ethnoracial composition and the effects of diversity on boundary dissolution. And in fact, as we will see, the metropolitan population in the United Sates replicates the dramatic shifts in ethnoracial composition recently occurring in the country.

Starting with recent immigration, from 1990 to 2007–2008, the foreign-born population living in metropolitan areas increased by about half, from 10.1 percent in 1990 to 15.0 percent in 2007–2008 (see table 9.1). The Latino and Asian concentrations and the overall nonwhite population also increased in this time frame. Only the black population remained relatively constant, at around 13.5 percent. Diversity, measured on a scale from zero to 1, rose from 0.41 to 0.47, or nearly 15 percent, from 1990 to 2000, and from 0.47 to 0.50, over 6 percent, from 2000 to 2007–2008. For the present purpose of assessing diversity effects across both high- and low-diversity places, we note that metropolitan areas are characterized by a wide range of diversity values, running in 2007–08 from a low of 0.06, in Altoona, Pennsylvania (where there is hardly any diversity at all), to a high of 0.72 (which is a great deal of diversity), in Oakland, California. Similarly, in 1990 slightly fewer than one in twenty married couples had a spouse of different ethnoracial status, whereas by 2007–2008 almost one in fourteen did. Thus, overall exogamy increased by nearly half in metropolitan areas in less than twenty years. The total multiraciality rate stayed roughly the same, although it increased between 2000 and 2007–2008 for Asians, blacks, and the other census racial groups. Only among Latinos did it apparently drop, but as noted in chapter 3, this occurred because many Latinos who listed "other" as one of their multiracial statuses in 2000 apparently switched to a single race identification by 2007–2008, perhaps because they didn't fully understand or embrace the category "other race" in 2000 or perhaps because they changed their minds about their own identities over the time interval.

In assessing the connection between diversity and indicators of boundary dissolution, intermarriage, and multiracial identification, it is important to control for relative group size. The reason is that if a group-threat dynamic is operating to hinder boundary dissolution, we would expect to see larger group size associated with less intermarriage and lower multiracial reporting, not more, which would mask part of any observed positive relationship between diversity and boundary dissolution. According to the implications of queuing and group-position theory, which suggest a rank order among ethnoracial groups in terms of their access to and accumulation of social and economic resources,

Table 9.1   *Means and Standard Deviations for Indicators of Ethnoracial Diversity and Inequality in U.S. Metropolitan Areas*[a]

	1990 (N = 251)				2000 (N = 297)				2007–2008 (N = 297)			
	Mean	Standard Deviation	Minimum	Maximum	Mean	Standard Deviation	Minimum	Maximum	Mean	Standard Deviation	Minimum	Maximum
Herfindahl Diversity Index	0.41	0.16	0.03	0.67	0.47	0.16	0.06	0.72	0.50	0.15	0.06	0.72
Percentage Black	13.6	9.1	0.0	50.3	13.2	9.3	0.1	50.4	13.4	9.4	0.0	52.5
Percentage Latino	10.9	13.1	0.2	85.1	14.7	14.9	0.5	94.0	17.5	16.0	0.6	94.6
Percentage Asian–Pacific Islander	3.5	5.0	0.1	60.4	4.6	5.4	0.2	53.8	5.6	5.8	0.1	50.6
Percentage Nonwhite	28.6	16.0	1.3	85.7	35.1	17.6	3.2	94.9	38.9	17.9	3.3	95.7

Percentage Foreign-born	10.1	9.3	0.3	45.2	13.5	10.8	0.9	51.3	15.0	10.6	0.6	50.7
White-nonwhite income ratio (median)	1.4	0.2	1.0	2.1	1.5	0.2	1.1	2.1	1.5	0.2	0.8	2.3
Percentage of couples intermarried	4.8	3.5	0.6	20.4	7.7	5.0	1.0	29.0	9.5	5.6	0.8	31.0
Number of multiracials per thousand population	—	—	—	—	29.0	18.0	6.0	200.0	24.0	16.0	3.0	211.0

Source: Tabulations by authors based on data from the 1990 and 2000 U.S. censuses and the 2007–2008 American Community Survey (Ruggles et al. 2009).
a. Means and standard deviations are weighted by total MSA (Metropolitan Statistical Area) population.

the relationships between relative group size and multiracial reporting would be expected to vary appreciably when blacks are compared to Latinos and Asians and when Latinos are compared to Asians. For example, in the case of blacks, we would expect a negative relationship between relative group size and indicators of boundary dissolution (overall exogamy and multiracial reporting). Thus, for blacks, a negative effect from relative group size could offset any positive effects of diversity on intermarriage and multiracial reporting. For Asians, we would expect positive relationships. For Latinos, the situation is less clear. Many Latinos, especially Mexicans, are foreign-born and during the past twenty years have lived in places that have never before experienced much immigration (Hirschman and Massey 2008). These factors may foster negative reactions in such places owing to their native population's unfamiliarity with immigrants. Other places have had Latinos living there for a long time, where they have played essential roles in city workforces and become substantially better integrated. In these cases we would expect positive relationships between relative group size and boundary-dissolution indicators.

It is also important to control for economic inequality in assessing relationships between diversity and intermarriage. Since nonwhite minority groups generally have lower average incomes than whites, places with higher degrees of economic inequality are likely to have lower levels of ethnoracial intermarriage and, because minorities may be more likely to live there, higher levels of diversity (Blau, Blum, and Schwartz 1982; Blau and Schwartz 1997). Thus, we introduce in our regression models statistical controls for inequality of income between whites and nonwhites. For the present purpose of illustrating how relative group size can work differently for various groups and under some conditions operate at least partially to mask the effects of diversity, we first show results for regressions of exogamy and multiracial reporting on diversity and relative group size for blacks, Latinos, and Asians, controlling for inequality (see table 9.2). We present results only for 2007–2008 data (meaning estimates of 2007–2008 outcomes regressed on 2000 independent variables) because we obtain similar findings irrespective of whether we examine relationships between 1990 independent variables and either 1990 or 2000 outcomes, or between 2000 independent variables and either 2000 or 2007–2008 outcomes.

Turning to results, we see that diversity, when examined without any controls, is positively correlated across cities with both exogamy (r = 0.667) and multiracial reporting (r = 0.355). More diverse cities are also places with more exogamy and multiracial reporting. In the case of blacks, the zero-order correlation between group size and exogamy is negative (r = −0.292, a statistically significant association) as predicted (see table 9.3). However, also as expected, when the group-size effect for blacks is examined controlling for diversity, the negative effect increases to −0.678 (see column 4 of table 9.2). Thus, the negative group-threat effect for blacks is suppressed considerably without controlling for diversity because diversity is also associated with some boundary

Table 9.2   *Standardized Coefficients from Regressions of Total Exogamy and Multiracial Reporting on Independent Variables in U.S. Metropolitan Areas, 2007–2008[a] (N = 297)*

	Models for 2007–2008 Exogamy[b]				
	1	2	3	4	5
Diversity, 2000[d]	0.667***	—	0.371***	0.891***	0.308***
Percentage Black, 2000***	—	—	—	−0.678***	−0.229
Percentage Latino, 2000***	—	—	—	—	0.735
Percentage Asian–Pacific Islander, 2000	—	—	—	—	0.352***
Inequality, 2000[e]	—	0.675***	0.401*	−0.062**	−0.416***
R-squared	0.445	0.456	0.519	0.848	0.929

	Models for 2007–2008 Multiracial Reporting[c]				
	1	2	3	4	5
Diversity, 2000[d]	0.355***	—	0.267***	0.856***	0.362***
Percentage Black, 2000	—	—	—	−0.769***	−0.446***
Percentage Latino, 2000	—	—	—	—	0.212
Percentage Asian–Pacific Islander, 2000	—	—	—	—	0.520***
Inequality, 2000[e]	—	0.316	0.119*	−0.407***	−0.493***
R-squared	0.126	0.100	0.132	0.556	0.653

Source: Tabulations by authors based on data from the 2007–2008 American Community Survey (Ruggles et al. 2009).

***p < .001; **p < .01; *p < .05 (one-tailed test).

a. All models are weighted by the total MSA (Metropolitan Statistical Area) population in 2000.

b. Total exogamy is the percentage of all marriages in an MSA involving whites that are interethnic/interracial.

c. Multiracial reporting is measured as the natural log of the rate of multiracial reporting per thousand persons in an MSA.

d. Diversity Index (1 minus the sum of the squared proportion of each group in a given city).

e. Ratio of non-Latino white median income to nonwhite median income.

Table 9.3   *Correlations Among Indicators of Ethnoracial Diversity and Inequality, Multiracial Reporting, and Intermarriage, U.S. Metropolitan Areas, 1990 to 2007–2008*

	1 diversity9	2 diversity0	3 diversity07	4 pblack9	5 pblack0	6 pblack07	7 platino9	8 platino0	9 platino07
1 Diversity 1990 (diversity9)	1								
2 Diversity 2000 (diversity0)	0.963	1							
3 Diversity 2007–2008 (diversity07)	0.919	0.987	1						
4 Percentage black 1990 (pblack9)	0.470	0.420	0.414	1					
5 Percentage black 2000 (pblack0)	0.410	0.365	0.363	0.983	1				
6 Percentage black 2007–2008 (pblack07)	0.362	0.328	0.334	0.968	0.994	1			
7 Percentage Latino 1990 (platino9)	0.613	0.530	0.448	−0.187	−0.228	−0.266	1		
8 Percentage Latino 2000 (platino0)	0.628	0.562	0.495	−0.200	−0.253	−0.287	0.986	1	
9 Percentage Latino 2007–2008 (platino07)	0.623	0.574	0.517	−0.210	−0.262	−0.293	0.968	0.995	1
10 Percentage Asian 1990 (papi9)	0.429	0.449	0.432	−0.128	−0.165	−0.187	0.259	0.255	0.242
11 Percentage Asian 2000 (papi0)	0.475	0.524	0.513	−0.108	−0.169	−0.193	0.272	0.290	0.277
12 Percentage Asian 2007–2008 (papi07)	0.488	0.549	0.544	−0.103	−0.168	−0.192	0.269	0.293	0.283
13 Percentage nonwhite 1990 (pnonwhite9)	0.904	0.816	0.741	0.365	0.311	0.264	0.795	0.776	0.752
14 Percentage nonwhite 2000 (pnonwhite0)	0.908	0.857	0.796	0.283	0.237	0.198	0.810	0.816	0.804
15 Percentage nonwhite 2007–2008 (pnonwhite07)	0.899	0.870	0.821	0.256	0.214	0.182	0.806	0.826	0.824
16 Percentage foreign-born 1990 (pfborn9)	0.718	0.667	0.602	−0.008	−0.064	−0.109	0.766	0.765	0.746

17 Percentage foreign-born 2000 (pfborn0)	0.736	0.719	0.674	−0.007	−0.091	−0.130	0.750	0.774	0.767
18 Percentage foreign-born 2007–2008 (pfbornb07)	0.733	0.736	0.703	−0.003	−0.084	−0.120	0.722	0.755	0.756
19 White-nonwhite income ratio 1990 (incratiomed9)	0.543	0.480	0.430	0.125	0.094	0.068	0.642	0.654	0.648
20 White-nonwhite income ratio 2000 (incratiomed0)	0.633	0.552	0.496	0.080	−0.008	−0.044	0.741	0.742	0.729
21 White-nonwhite income ratio 2007–2008 (incratiomed07)	0.572	0.502	0.450	0.140	0.047	0.009	0.619	0.625	0.613
22 (LN) Multiracial reporting rate 2000 (logpmulti0)	0.593	0.657	0.642	−0.242	−0.291	−0.319	0.588	0.624	0.633
23 (LN) Multiracial reporting rate 2007–2008 (logpmulti07)	0.230	0.322	0.325	−0.386	−0.380	−0.397	0.227	0.258	0.269
24 Percentage of couples intermarried 1990 (pim9)	0.578	0.597	0.554	−0.315	−0.347	−0.381	0.693	0.721	0.726
25 Percentage of couples intermarried 2000 (pim0)	0.626	0.659	0.621	−0.252	−0.293	−0.323	0.701	0.734	0.741
26 Percentage of couples intermarried 2007–2008 (pim07)	0.642	0.688	0.662	−0.250	−0.292	−0.320	0.694	0.731	0.742

(*Table continues on p. 170.*)

Table 9.3   (Continued)

	10 papi9	11 papi0	12 papi07	13 pnonwhite9	14 pnonwhite0	15 pnonwhite07	16 pfborn9	17 pfborn0	18 pfborn07
10 Percentage Asian 1990 (papi9)	1								
11 Percentage Asian 2000 (papi0)	0.971	1							
12 Percentage Asian 2007–2008 (papi07)	0.936	0.991	1						
13 Percentage nonwhite 1990 (pnonwhite9)	0.456	0.469	0.458	1					
14 Percentage nonwhite 2000 (pnonwhite0)	0.490	0.519	0.517	0.978	1				
15 Percentage nonwhite 2007–2008 (pnonwhite07)	0.472	0.508	0.512	0.954	0.993	1			
16 Percentage foreign-born 1990 (pfborn9)	0.494	0.552	0.565	0.776	0.805	0.788	1		
17 Percentage foreign-born 2000 (pfborn0)	0.499	0.595	0.619	0.766	0.815	0.814	0.980	1	
18 Percentage foreign-born 2007–2008 (pfbornb07)	0.489	0.592	0.624	0.742	0.802	0.811	0.959	0.993	1

19 White-nonwhite income ratio 1990 (incratiomed9)	0.110	0.117	0.108	0.630	0.631	0.629	0.566	0.561	0.539
20 White-nonwhite income ratio 2000 (incratiomed0)	0.207	0.265	0.268	0.716	0.707	0.697	0.730	0.720	0.696
21 White-nonwhite income ratio 2007–2008 (incratiomed07)	0.168	0.231	0.231	0.635	0.622	0.609	0.635	0.646	0.626
22 (LN) Multiracial reporting rate 2000 (logpmulti0)	0.636	0.664	0.672	0.558	0.642	0.655	0.688	0.729	0.738
23 (LN) Multiracial reporting rate 2007–2008 (logpmulti07)	0.601	0.578	0.567	0.175	0.265	0.277	0.273	0.300	0.303
24 Percentage of couples intermarried 1990 (pim9)	0.656	0.654	0.644	0.609	0.688	0.699	0.631	0.648	0.638
25 Percentage of couples intermarried 2000 (pim0)	0.656	0.677	0.672	0.648	0.730	0.744	0.694	0.727	0.721
26 Percentage of couples intermarried 2007–2008 (pim07)	0.643	0.678	0.682	0.639	0.727	0.749	0.693	0.739	0.740

(*Table continues on p. 172.*)

Table 9.3   (Continued)

	19 incratiomed9	20 incratiomed0	21 incratiomed07	22 logpmulti0	23 logpmulti07	24 pim9	25 pim0	26 pim07
19 White-nonwhite income ratio 1990 (incratiomed9)	1							
20 White-nonwhite income ratio 2000 (incratiomed0)	0.847	1						
21 White-nonwhite income ratio 2007–2008 (incratiomed07)	0.734	0.843	1					
22 (LN) Multiracial reporting rate 2000 (logpmulti0)	0.265	0.414	0.320	1				
23 (LN) Multiracial reporting rate 2007–2008 (logpmulti07)	−0.064	0.031	−0.022	0.781	1			
24 Percentage of couples intermarried 1990 (pim9)	0.324	0.421	0.322	0.855	0.735	1		
25 Percentage of couples intermarried 2000 (pim0)	0.340	0.446	0.357	0.875	0.711	0.978	1	
26 Percentage of couples intermarried 2007–2008 (pim07)	0.341	0.451	0.354	0.890	0.709	0.963	0.984	1

Source: Tabulations by authors based on data from the 1990 and 2000 U.S. censuses and the 2007–2008 American Community Survey (Ruggles et al. 2009).
Notes: $N = 251$ (1990), $N = 297$ (2000, 2007–2008); correlations are based on pairwise deletion for instances where an MSA (Metropolitan Statistical Area) has a value in 2000 or 2007–2008, but not in 1990.
All correlations are weighted by the 2000 MSA population.

dissolution for blacks. But in the case of blacks, diversity's positive effects are not large enough to make up for the negative group-threat effect. That is, the positive effect of diversity on boundary dissolution is also suppressed considerably in cities where group-threat dynamics are especially strong. Similar patterns emerge when these relationships are examined in the case of multiracial reporting.

Thus, the presence of relatively more blacks in a city drives down intermarriage and multiracial identification, which masks some of the positive effects of diversity on intermarriage and multiracial reporting in such cities. When the relative size of the black population is controlled (compare diversity's coefficients in columns 1 and 3 of table 9.2), diversity's positive relationship with exogamy increases by about half and its relationship with multiracial reporting nearly doubles. Cities with larger black populations appear to undergo less boundary dissolution as a result of higher diversity than do cities with smaller black populations. Overall, when all the independent variables are included in the models—meaning that when differences in ethnoracial composition and economic inequality are held constant across cities—diversity still exerts a strong positive effect on both exogamy and multiracial identification (column 5 of table 9.2). The only minority group that shows a strong and consistent group-threat effect is blacks, with places with larger African American populations showing less exogamy and multiracial reporting.

So far we have not considered that the influence of diversity on multiracial reporting may substantially flow through intermarriage. Thus, our preliminary examinations of diversity and group-size effects have focused on intermarriage and multiracial reporting separately. Now we consider them together, with exogamy included as an independent variable in regression models predicting multiracial reporting. We also add controls for the percentage foreign-born in the metropolitan area and for cities located in the Deep South states of Alabama, Georgia, Louisiana, Mississippi, North Carolina, or South Carolina, or in the so-called new-destination states for Mexican migrants—namely, any states other than the old-destination states for Hispanics of Arizona, California, Illinois, New Mexico, and Texas (Leach and Bean 2008; Massey and Capoferro 2008). Having a high percentage of foreign-born may accentuate any group-threat effects associated with minority-group status, as can location in a new-destination place in the case of Latinos, whereas location in the Deep South may suppress multiracial reporting. Results from these new models show three particularly notable findings, shown in table 9.4. First, as expected, exogamy bears a strong positive relationship to multiracial reporting. Second, a negative group-threat effect appears for Latinos as well as blacks, but a large part of this effect seems attributable to nativity (place of birth) and new-destination dynamics—that is, Mexican-born migrants in new-destination places. The third is that diversity exerts an independent effect (standardized regression coefficient of 0.508) on multiracial reporting, even after controlling for relative group size and exogamy, as well as other control variables.

Table 9.4   *Standardized Coefficients from Regressions of Multiracial Reporting on Exogamy and Independent Variables in U.S. Metropolitan Areas, 2007–2008*[a]

	1	2	3
Diversity, 2000[b]	0.731***	0.201	0.508**
Percentage Black, 2000	−0.592***	−0.269***	−0.386***
Percentage Latino, 2000	0.542**	−0.840***	−0.557***
Percentage Asian and Pacific Islander, 2000	0.629***	0.035	0.116+
Inequality, 2000[c]	−0.219**	0.042	0.265+
Total Exogamy, 2000	—	1.202***	1.200***
Percentage Foreign-born, 2000	−0.803***	—	−0.650***
In the Deep South	−0.108+	—	−0.143**
In a new destination	0.428**	—	0.393**
R-squared	0.707	0.779	0.830

Source: Tabulations by authors based on data from the 2007–2008 American Community Survey (Ruggles et al. 2009).

***p < .001; **p < .01; *p < .05; +p < .10 (one-tailed test).

a. Dependent variable is the natural log of the rate of multiracial reporting per thousand persons in an MSA (Metropolitan Statistical Area). All models are weighted by the total MSA population in 2000.

b. Diversity Index (1 minus the sum of the squared proportion of each group in a given city).

c. Ratio of non-Latino white median income to nonwhite median income.

Another way to illustrate the sometimes countervailing effects of relative group size and diversity on exogamy and multiracial reporting is to make use of analyses that facilitate the depiction of complex pathways of influence among variables. Queuing and group-position theory, which posit a rank order among ethnoracial groups in access to and accumulation of social and economic resources, imply the relationships between relative group size and exogamy and multiracial reporting would be expected to vary among blacks, Latinos, and Asians. For example, for blacks we expect a negative relationship between relative group size and indicators of boundary dissolution (both overall exogamy and multiracial reporting), and this is what we observe in table 9.2. For Asians we expect and find positive relationships between relative group size and indicators of boundary dissolution. For Latinos, the situation is less clear. Many Latinos, especially Mexicans, are foreign-born and during the past twenty years have lived in places that have never before experienced much immigration. It emerges, when we compare tables 9.2 and 9.4, that these complicating circumstances operate to mask some of diversity's positive effects. In table 9.2 we find no effect of relative group size on multiracial reporting for Latinos, but we do find a positive effect of relative group size on exogamy. But in table 9.4 a negative group-threat effect emerges (coefficient = −0.557) when we control for exogamy. These effects, taken together, suggest that for Latinos there are both positive and negative effects, with the positive effect flowing through intermarriage. We turn to "path analysis" (Duncan 1975) to illustrate these kinds of relationships and pathways of influence more clearly.

In the Latino case we expect ambiguous or offsetting relationships between relative group size and boundary dissolution indicators. We think relative group size will positively influence diversity in the case of all three groups because the relative size of a given group constitutes one of the elements in our measure of diversity, the others being the relative sizes of the other minority groups and the similarity of the minority and majority groups' sizes. Thus, we expect the rise in diversity associated with larger ethnoracial groups (which for Latinos and Asians is due substantially to immigration) to show roughly the same magnitude of relationships between diversity and multiracial reporting. To examine group-threat and diversity effects on boundary dissolution operating both directly and indirectly through other factors (such as group size working through exogamy to influence multiracial reporting), we conduct a series of regression analyses and combine their results into a "path diagram," which is used here as a heuristic to illustrate two important patterns of results (see figure 9.1). The first is the differences that emerge among blacks, Latinos, and Asians in pathways of influence affecting boundary dissolution. The second is the positive influence of diversity on boundary dissolution that is operating independent of changes in ethnoracial composition for all groups.

These analyses show that metropolitan areas with more and relatively larger racial and ethnic groups resulting in large part from immigration have higher diversity scores and higher levels of exogamy and multiracial reporting (figure 9.1). Most important for our present purposes, ethnoracial diversity shows an independent and positive relationship with multiracial reporting, as indicated by the significant positive direct effect running from diversity to multiracial reporting. Stated differently, the noncompositional elements of diversity (recall that relative group size for each of the nonwhite groups is controlled) *independently* increase multiracial reporting, our main indicator of boundary dissolution. Also, these same elements work to increase boundary dissolution through exogamy. That is, the arrow running from diversity to exogamy (with an effect magnitude of 0.468) and the arrow running from exogamy to multiracial reporting together represent another independent pathway of influence of diversity on boundary dissolution.

Turning our attention to the left side of figure 9.1, we see that for each group, relative group size indirectly and positively affects intermarriage and multiracial reporting through diversity. But these pathways of influence represent changes in ethnoracial demographic composition, not effects of diversity per se, unlike those noted in the previous paragraph. As expected, they are all positive because increases in relative composition raise scores on the Diversity Index. But it is the net effects noted previously that most reinforce the hypoth-

Figure 9.1   *Metro-Level Standardized Coefficients for Regressions of Diversity, Intermarriage, and Multiraciality on Relative Racial-Ethnic Group Sizes, 2000 and 2007–2008*

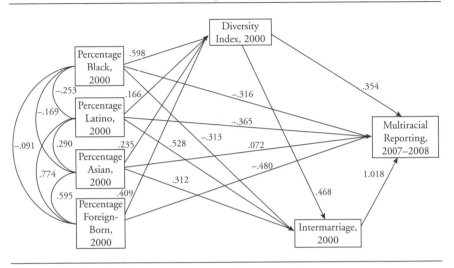

Source: Authors' tabulations from the 2000 U.S. census and the 2007–2008 American Community Survey (Ruggles et al. 2009).

Notes: Weighted by metropolitan population size.
    All models include controls for white-nonwhite inequality, location in Deep South, and location in new Mexican immigrant destination states.
    All coefficients are significant at p < .10 (one-tailed test).

esis emerging from our qualitative in-depth interviews that sociocultural change attendant upon both immigration and changing composition and diversity is helping to dissolve the boundaries separating ethnoracial groups.

Paradoxically, however, this development is undermined by group-threat effects in the case of blacks, and is partially offset by such effects in the case of Latinos. Among blacks, negative direct effects from relative group size emerge on both exogamy and multiracial reporting. For Latinos, a relatively larger number living in metro areas also lead to lower rates of multiracial reporting, but not to greater intermarriage, for which a positive relationship emerges. The latter effect is considerably larger than the negative effect on multiracial reporting, leaving Latinos with an overall balance of positive group-size effects on multiracial identification (see table 9.5). In the case of Asians, group size exerts a positive direct effect on both exogamy and multiracial identification. Moreover, when we sum the direct effect of group size and its indirect effect operating through diversity, we find that relative group size shows a positive overall influence on multiracial identification for both Asians and Latinos, but not for blacks. In other words, for blacks the positive effect of relative group size on

Table 9.5   *Decomposition of Total Relative Group-Size Effects from Path Models of Multiracial Reporting, U.S. Metropolitan Areas, 2007–2008* [a]

	Group-Size Effects			
	Blacks	Latinos	Asians	Foreign-born
Direct effect	−0.316	−0.365	0.072	−0.480
Indirect effects (through diversity and exogamy)	0.178	0.676	0.513	0.390
Other effects (through relative group-size correlations)	−0.091	0.206	0.086	0.628
Total effect	−0.229	0.517	0.671	0.538

Source: Tabulations by authors based on data from the 2007–2008 American Community Survey (Ruggles et al. 2009).
a. Based on the path model presented in figure 9.1

multiracial reporting operating through diversity is not large enough to make up for the negative direct effect deriving from group-threat dynamics.

The positive indirect effect of group size working through diversity can also be viewed as the contribution of differences in demographic composition to higher multiracial reporting. Stated differently, and as previously noted, as relative group size goes up, diversity increases, and then so too does intermarriage and multiracial reporting, in part for the straightforward reason that places with relatively larger proportions of blacks, Latinos, or Asians also have overall higher rates of multiracial reporting on that account alone. Importantly, this composition effect, shown in table 9.6, is not larger than diversity's positive independent effects on multiracial reporting for any of the groups. And if we calculate the influence of immigration separately as represented in the figures for percentage foreign-born at the bottom of table 9.6, compositional elements are again less than diversity's independent effects. Thus, whether we examine diversity's independent effects overall (as indicated by arrows running straight to multiracial reporting and through exogamy to such reporting) or its compositional effects in the case of each of the nonwhite groups, it influences boundary dissolution apart from increases in the relative sizes of the nonwhite groups alone.

Conclusion

These findings thus lend additional weight to the idea that increasing immigration and diversity are working to loosen traditional racial and ethnic group boundaries in the United States, for all the groups examined. Paradoxically, however, for blacks, positive composition and diversity effects are not big

Table 9.6   *Independent and Compositional Elements in the Diversity–Boundary-Loosening Relationship, by Group, 2007–2008*

	Components
Blacks	
Independent diversity	0.830
Compositional	0.364
Latinos	
Independent diversity	0.830
Compositional	0.473
Asians	
Independent diversity	0.830
Compositional	0.446
Foreign-born	
Independent diversity	0.830
Compositional	0.596

Source: Tabulations by authors based on data from the 2007–2008 American Community Survey (Ruggles et al. 2009).

enough to make up for the negative effect stemming from relative group size, an influence that presumably operates through group-threat dynamics. But positive diversity effects emerge even for blacks, implying that increased ethno-racial diversity relates to loosening group boundaries (as reflected in the higher rates of exogamy and multiracial identification), here observed across metropolitan areas with a wide range of diversity levels. It is interesting to contemplate further some of the reasons behind such intergroup differences. Why does an increase in the size of the black population lead to a decrease in multiracial reporting, whereas an increase in the size of the Asian population leads to higher rates of multiracial reporting? The negative direct effects of group size for blacks are considerably offset when we consider the positive indirect effects of group size that operate through diversity. Nevertheless it remains unclear why group size operates differently for blacks, Latinos, and Asians.

The work of Jeffrey C. Dixon (2006) and Michael W. Link and Robert W. Oldendick (1996) provides empirical evidence that minority-group size relates to intergroup dynamics with whites in different ways for Asians, Latinos, and blacks. In the present study, an increase in the size of the black population has a negative relation with multiracial reporting, suggesting that the larger the black presence in a place is, the more blacks are likely to be perceived as cultural and economic threats to whites. This makes it likely that less substantial contact will occur between them and majority-group members. This may in turn reinforce a hardening of group boundaries, making it less likely that individuals will choose to intermarry and identify multiracially. This reflects both a decreased likelihood of earlier interracial unions' occurring and reduced tendencies for people to see themselves as multiracial. The more rigid ethnoracial boundaries in cities with relatively large black groups suggest that whites in those cities may feel more culturally threatened and therefore may be more inclined to defend their sense of group position in these places.

At the same time, relative group size also impinges on multiraciality indirectly through diversity, encouraging ethnoracial boundaries to loosen. Thus, whites may tend to feel somewhat less threatened in areas that exhibit higher levels of diversity, even if these areas also have relatively large black populations. And in the case of Asians, higher relative group size and levels of ethnoracial diversity actually lead to higher levels of exogamy and multiracial reporting through all pathways of influence. Clearly, relative minority-group size affects intergroup relations differently depending on the group in question, with Asians following one pattern, blacks appearing to follow another, and Latinos in the middle. Most important is that racial boundaries appear to be loosening for all groups through diversity. The paradox is that this loosening of racial boundaries can sometimes be offset by negative group-size dynamics, whereby the larger the minority's size relative to the majority group, the greater the potential for a hardening of racial boundaries. This paradox operates primarily to affect the social status of blacks.

~ Chapter 10 ~

Conclusion: The Diversity Paradox and Beyond (Plus Ça Change, Plus C'est la Même Chose)

We opened this book with W. E. B. Du Bois's prediction, "The problem of the twentieth-century will be the problem of the color line—the relation of the darker to the lighter races of men" (Du Bois 1903/1997, 45). Since Du Bois made this forecast, in 1903, the United States has undertaken major national-level legal and legislative initiatives to reduce the harsh effects of the country's black-white color line. These include landmark decisions such as *Brown v. the Topeka Board of Education* in 1954, the Civil Rights Act of 1964, *Loving v. Commonwealth of Virginia* in 1967, and the Fair Housing Act of 1968. The removal of legal barriers to fair and equitable treatment was intended to eliminate the last vestiges of discrimination based on racial status, which would in turn, it was hoped, reduce the black-white gap in education, earnings, wealth accumulation, and residential segregation. In addition, the decriminalization of interracial marriage would, it was assumed, result in a rise in marital unions across the color line. These landmark decisions led to hopes in the late 1960s that old prejudices—as well as the institutional frameworks that supported them—would soon fade away.

During the same era, in 1965, Congress passed the Hart-Celler Act, which opened America's doors to a new wave of non-European immigrants. Well over 80 percent of America's newcomers hail from Latin America, Asia, and the Caribbean, and this influx has forever changed the face of the nation. Latinos and Asians together now make up about a fifth of the U.S. population and may by 2050 constitute one third (Bean and Bell-Rose 1999; U.S. Immigration and Naturalization Service 2002; Waldinger and Lee 2001). Latino and Asian immigrants—neither black nor white—have ushered in a new era of diversity and changed the country from a largely black-white society to one consisting of multiple nonwhite ethnoracial groups.

The rate of intermarriage has increased along with rises in immigration (Bean and Stevens 2003; Jacoby 2001; Lee and Edmonston 2005). In 2008, about 7 percent of marriages—8.8 percent in metropolitan areas—were interracial, a significant increase that cannot be attributed to population growth alone. The rise in intermarriage has resulted in a growing multiracial population whose members were able to mark "one or more races" on the most recent census form, thus acknowledging their multiracial heritage for the first time in the history of the U.S. census. This significant change reflected just how far the United States had come from the days of the legally enforced one-drop rule of hypodescent, which decreed that anyone with a "traceable amount" of black blood was racially black.

All these changes—the legal eradication of discrimination, the new immigration from Latin America and Asia, the way that the U.S. census now measures race, the rising rates of intermarriage, and the growing multiracial population—lead to optimistic conclusions about the breakdown of America's traditional black-white color line. These indicators appear to signal that the boundaries between all ethnoracial groups are loosening, paving the way for a new era of cosmopolitan diversity in the twenty-first century. Racial status seems to be declining in significance and loosening its grip as an organizing principle of opportunity in the United States, and the tenacious black-white color line that has long gripped the country appears to be fading. Moreover, not only is the United States becoming more ethnoracially diverse but the country's new diversity also appears to be contributing to the breakdown of the color line for all groups. Based on the compositional shifts in the U.S. population and sociocultural changes among its people, it seems the country is moving in the postethnic direction that David A. Hollinger envisioned in *Postethnic America* (1995).

Before accepting the validity of this conclusion, it is critical to study differences in the patterns of intermarriage and multiracial reporting, because both rates of intermarriage and levels of multiracial reporting (describing oneself as multiracial) reliably reflect the actual social distance or the lack thereof between groups. For instance, a high rate of intermarriage signifies that individuals of different ethnoracial backgrounds no longer perceive their social, cultural, and ethnoracial differences as significant enough to represent a barrier to a marital union (Alba 1995). As individuals who have chosen to cross group boundaries in their unions, interracial couples represent Americans at the vanguard of social and ethnoracial change. Multiracial Americans—those who choose to claim their multiracial heritage—also embody social change, since the mere acknowledgement of multiraciality means the jettisoning of the long-held idea that racial status is immutable, bounded, and mutually exclusive.

When we examine differences in patterns of intermarriage and multiracial reporting across major ethnoracial groupings, we arrive at less sanguine conclusions about the declining significance of racial status. Not only are the rates of intermarriage with whites much lower for blacks than for Asians and

Latinos, but blacks are also far less likely to identify multiracially than Asians and Latinos (Lee and Bean 2004, 2007). Such findings provide evidence that legal and structural changes alone—while of considerable importance—are insufficient to explain group differences in intermarriage and multiracial identification. It seems that even as the black-white color line weakens, the cultural and behavioral frameworks that sustained it for centuries continue to linger.

In order to understand the nature of these patterns, we turned to the data obtained from the in-depth interviews of interracial couples with children and of multiracial adults. The qualitative data reveals how interracial couples and multiracial adults define themselves and their children, how they view racial divides, and how their perceptions affect their behavior. The data illuminates the social and cultural foundations of intermarriage and multiracial reporting among blacks, Asians, and Latinos, revealing texture and contour that we cannot gleam from compositional change alone. By studying change at both the structural-compositional and cultural-attitudinal levels, we were able to reach some conclusions as to where the color line is being drawn in the twenty-first century and to ascertain which groups are positioned on which side of the divide.

Black Exceptionalism and the Cultural Parameters of Intermarriage and Multiracial Identification

Many Americans believe that falling in love or choosing a spouse is simply an individual choice based on individual preferences, but our research shows that these personal decisions are governed by a set of culturally specific parameters, which can encourage or discourage marriage across the color line. Racial status is a nonissue when it comes to intermarriage between whites and Asians or Latinos, but it becomes a central issue, and often a polarizing one, when it comes to intermarriage with blacks. Most nonblack families object to marriage with a black partner, partly because they assume that black intermarriage connotes downward mobility into a racialized and stigmatized minority status. To them, intermarriage with a black partner is often tantamount to becoming black—the nonblack spouse and the children born of interracial unions will end up being viewed as black and ultimately will adopt a black racial identity. Opposition to black intermarriage is not found only among whites; resistance also emerges from black families and friends, some of whom believe that those who choose to out-marry (especially with whites) are "race traitors" who lack pride in their race.

Most Asians and Latinos, by contrast, do not experience opposition from their families when they choose to marry a white partner. In fact, their families often regard marriage with a white partner as an inevitable step in their children's process of becoming American, "American" to them meaning "white." From the perspective of the Asians, Latinos, and whites in our study, the differences between whites and Asians and whites and Latinos are cultural, stemming from differences in cultural background between native-born whites and immigrant ethnics, rather than racial. This distinction is significant because cultural differences appear more surmountable and fade with time and across generations, whereas racial divides are far more formidable. Thus, in the marriage market the color line that remains the most relevant is the one that defines black. This leaves blacks more maritally isolated than other groups (including other nonwhite groups), and points to a pattern of black exceptionalism in intermarriage.

Black exceptionalism also emerged in patterns of multiracial identification. Whereas Asian-white and Latino-white multiracials exhibited a great deal of fluidity and flexibility in their choice of identification, black-white multiracials experienced the most constraint. In fact, the Asian and Latino backgrounds of Asian-white and Latino-white multiracials are adopting the symbolic, voluntary, and mutable character of white European ethnicity. Multiracial Asians and Latinos are able to exit out of the Asian and Latino categories if they choose. By comparison, black multiracials of any ethnoracial combination feel limited in their identity options; for them, black is neither a choice nor a category from which they can easily exit. In essence, multiraciality involving black ancestry entails a different set of experiences than multiraciality involving Asian or Latino ancestries. So although multiraciality in theory represents the freedom to choose among different ethnoracial options, in practice, cultural and institutional mechanisms continue to constrain black multiracial Americans from feeling free to proclaim and embrace their mixed heritages and—perhaps more important—from having others acknowledge and accept their multiracial background.

One might ask: Why should racial identification and racial status matter? As long as racial status remains an organizing principle of the economic, social, political, and residential life in the United States, racial identification will continue to matter. Racial status affects where one lives, what school one attends, how much education one attains, how much one earns, how much wealth one accumulates, and whom one marries. If Asian-white and Latino-white multiracials feel they have more freedom to choose among various ethnoracial options (including white) while black-white multiracials feel they do not, the latter will perceive themselves as being at a disadvantage. More concretely, if Asian-white and Latino-white multiracials can identify as white and have that identity accepted by others, racial status becomes irrelevant as a barrier to mobility for these multiracial Americans because they are no longer seen as belonging to a separate race. Virtually by definition, black multiracials are constrained from identifying as white. Furthermore, black racial identities—virtually impossible to exit—carry more negative consequences than do Asian and Latino identities.

The flexibility in ethnoracial identification among Asian and Latino multiracials suggests that group boundaries are more porous for Asians and Latinos than for blacks, indicating that Asian and Latino are more malleable categories than black. Given the relative flexibility of boundaries surrounding Asian and

Latino categories, some have speculated that Asians and Latinos may be the next in line to be considered white, with Asian-white and Latino-white multiracials at the head of the queue. This is one possibility. In this scenario, whiteness would expand to encompass Asians and Latinos, eventually leading to the eventual re-creation of a black-white divide.

A second possibility is that Asians and Latinos will not become white, but their ethnoracial status may be as fluid, voluntary, and inconsequential as those of white European ethnics. Rather than becoming white, Asians and Latinos may become like whites, and a new category may emerge that encompasses Asians, Latinos, and whites—one that denotes a separation between these groups and blacks. This nonblack category may not refer to physical appearance but may evolve to connote class or group position. Thus, although Asians and Latinos may be nonblack, this does not necessarily mean that they will become white. This implies that the old black-white divide would not reemerge. The distinction between nonblack and white is significant because nonblack is an even more heterogeneous category than white and encompasses multiple skin-color hues. Shades of nonblack are also different, but they are not similarly inconsequential and costless. Although the social distance between blacks and other groups is decreasing, it is not declining as fast as the social distance between whites and Asians and Latinos is decreasing. Furthermore, the distance separating nonblack groups from one another is far smaller than that separating these groups from blacks. Given the gap between blacks and nonblacks, all that is needed to hasten the creation of a new nonblack identity is for a catchy new term for nonblack to enter the popular vernacular.

At this time, the emergence of a black-nonblack color line seems the most likely scenario, partly because it is strengthened by continued immigration from Latin America and Asia, which replenishes these groups with newcomers. The continuous stream of immigrants serves as a reminder of the differences between Asians and Latinos on the one hand and blacks and whites on the other—the Asians and Latinos arrive under the banner of immigrant heritage, whereas black and white both symbolize native-born status. Immigrant replenishment affects the incorporation pathway of today's Asians and Latinos in a way that it did not for their European predecessors, because mass immigration from Europe came to a halt in the 1920s (Alba and Nee 2003; Foner 2000; Jiménez 2009). Regardless of how the color line ultimately changes, it is hardly likely to disappear, especially for blacks.

Both scenarios—the transformation of Asians and Latinos into white and the reemergence of a black-white color line, or the emergence of a black-nonblack color line—have dangerous implications, for they invite misinterpretation of putative progress in U.S. ethnoracial relations more generally and of progress in black-white relations specifically. Because boundaries are loosening for some nonwhite groups, many Americans could erroneously conclude that "race" is declining in significance for all groups. This is troubling because it could lead to the endorsement of a flawed syllogism: if ethnoracial status seems not to impede appreciably the process of incorporation for Asians and Latinos, then it must not be much of an impediment for blacks, either. But ethnoracial status does continue to matter, and it matters more for blacks than for Asians and Latinos.

By drawing conclusions based on the progress of some nonwhite groups and inferring that these pertain to all nonwhite groups, one can embrace the fallacious assumption about the declining significance of "race" for all groups in the United States. Then, on the basis of such a flawed premise, policymakers and the American public could choose to favor and endorse "color-blind" policies that fail to take into consideration that ethnoracial status still constrains opportunity, most especially for blacks. Our research points to a persistent pattern of black exceptionalism in intermarriage and multiracial identification, one that also emerges in studies of residential segregation, educational attainment, racial attitudes, and friendship networks. Although some blacks are closing the gaps on some of these fronts, our research provides evidence that forebodes the continued existence of barriers to full and complete incorporation of many blacks in the United States.

From a scholarly perspective, our findings suggest that it is critical that the theories we develop to study black-white relations not simply be transposed to Asian-white and Latino-white relations. Asians and Latinos, although considered nonwhite at this point in time, are clearly nonblack. Therefore, theories of intergroup relations and policy prescriptions aimed at improving ethnoracial relations must consider differences among nonwhite groups rather than homogenizing their experiences and uniformly labeling all nonwhites "people of color." In short, whereas the disadvantage that Asians and Latinos experience stems more from their immigrant backgrounds than their ethnoracial ascriptions, the disadvantages that blacks experience stem from the enduring stigma attached to the historical significance of blackness.

The Paradox of Diversity

The United States is more ethnoracially diverse than ever before, yet despite this diversity, we find a consistent pattern of "black exceptionalism" in the marriage market and in multiracial identification. The paradox of diversity is that while the country exhibits a new diversity, and while intermarriage and multiraciality are projected to increase in the foreseeable future, the rates of intermarriage and multiracial reporting are occurring at various speeds for different groups, and the pace for blacks is the slowest. The unevenness of these suggests that boundaries are dissolving more rapidly for new immigrant groups, such as Asians and Latinos, than for blacks.

There is also another dimension to the diversity paradox. Diversity in itself appears to independently foster the dissolution of boundaries, but this effect is differentially offset by the degree to which Asians, Latinos, and blacks appear to be perceived as threatening. For example, the positive effect of diversity for blacks is trumped by a negative group threat effect. Meanwhile, no negative group-threat effect emerges for Asians. Diversity has a positive effect on boundary weakening for Asians and for blacks, but the places where Asians show larger group sizes also have higher rates of multiracial identification, whereas this is not the case for blacks. Latinos fall in between blacks and Asians when it comes to the balance between positive and negative effects of group size. Diversity has a positive independent effect for Latinos, and their increases in group size, though negative, are not large enough to cause group-threat effects to kick in and offset the positive effects of diversity. In sum, although diversity is generally beneficial, its significance for blacks, Asians, and Latinos is unequal because of other differences. It is critical to bear in mind that even among blacks, the relationship between diversity and multiracial reporting is a positive one, revealing that rising diversity alone is helping to break down racial barriers to some extent even for blacks.

A Cleavage Within "Black"

The consistent pattern of black exceptionalism that we found should not blind us to the fact that the notion of "black" is becoming an ever more heterogeneous category, especially along class lines (Lacy 2007; Pattillo-McCoy 1999). For instance, the black middle class has experienced notable earnings gains, a statistic expressing data for black families and households in which the male is working full-time. However, relatively fewer and fewer black families and households contain such a male because of rising black joblessness, due partly to extremely high male incarceration rates (Western 2006; Western and Wildeman 2009). Thus, fewer and fewer black families can justifiably be considered middle-class, and the data on "gains" relates to a relatively narrow band of the black population.

The definition of black is also changing within the black community itself. According to a recent report published by the Pew Research Center (2007), four in ten blacks feel that blacks can no longer be thought of as a single racial category. More than half of blacks (53 percent) believe that the values of middle-class and poor blacks have increasingly diverged over the past ten years, and among the black poor, 37 percent feel that they hold few or no shared values with middle-class blacks. That some middle-class and poor blacks feel they have little or nothing in common with one another underscores the point that although black may appear to be a monolithic category to nonblacks, it is indeed a diverse one, one whose members are increasingly economically unequal (Bean and Bell-Rose 1999).

The heterogeneity among blacks is also evident in patterns of multiracial identification. In 2008, only 8 percent of blacks listed themselves multiracially, but the percentage was 12.1 for those under the age of eighteen. When asked to choose the single best race that describes them, 75 percent of multiracial youths chose black, but 17 percent chose white. (Harris and Sim 2002). In

Kerry Ann Rockquemore and Patricia Arend's (2003) qualitative study of black-white biracial college students, 61 percent identified as mixed race, and in Kathleen O. Korgen's (1998) study of forty black-white multiracial adults, one third of the respondents under the age of thirty did so. That younger and more educated black multiracial Americans are more likely to identify multiracially than their older counterparts provides some optimism that the boundary surrounding black may be fading, albeit more slowly than it is for other nonwhite groups.

This also raises the question of how Americans will define blackness in the future and whether Americans will come to accept black multiraciality as readily as they have come to accept other types of multiraciality. For this to happen, not only must white, Asian, and Latino Americans recognize that black and multiracial are not antithetical categories, but African Americans must also support the idea that one is not exiting the black category when one chooses to identify multiracially. Both black and nonblack Americans must open up a space for multiracial blacks to claim their multiracial heritage. By extension, this means opening up a space for interracial marriage with blacks (Spencer 1997). Similarly, if we want to rid our vernacular of terms such as "acting black" and "acting white," we need to decouple race from class and in particular expand the notion of blackness to include middle- and upper-class blacks. For too many Americans (including African Americans), blackness connotes a disadvantaged class experience (Carter 2005).

If we succeed in expanding our vision of blackness, will black exceptionalism disappear, and will the United States reach a postethnic state in which ethnoracial boundaries are fluid and voluntary for all Americans, as David A. Hollinger (1995) envisions? Making predictions is always a gamble. On the question of the color line, much will depend on the state of the economy—whether there is a strong economy. If the economy is strong, and if blacks participate in the job market, then the color line will probably continue to recede, and the boundary surrounding blackness will continue to crumble, at least for the middle class. Evidence of rising intermarriage and multiracial reporting among blacks suggests that this is a strong possibility. But if economic growth stagnates and more and more blacks find themselves unemployed, the color line may assert itself more strongly, and blacks, especially poor blacks, may continue to find themselves on the other side of the divide.

David Hollinger's (1995) vision of a postethnic America may be overly optimistic, at least at this point in time, and Gunnar Myrdal's (1944) assertion that the black-white color line was erected with a sense of permanency may be overly pessimistic. Signs of black social and economic progress, while slow, are impossible to ignore. As the African American writer John McWhorter noted in 2004, "It is difficult to see 'apartheid' in a country in which the secretary of State, the national security advisor, the CEOs of Time Warner, American Express, and Merrill Lynch, the presidents of the U.S. Conference of Catholic Bishops and the American Bar Association and even the last James Bond and

Austin Powers girls are African American" ("As Racism Recedes, More Blacks Shift to Political Center," *Los Angeles Times,* March 17, 2004). Add to this list the U.S. president, and it becomes even more difficult to argue that black racial status still matters to the same degree that it has in our history. In fact, some journalists claim that Barack Obama is moving our country into a postethnic direction because he appeals to both whites and blacks alike, even while he strongly identifies as African American and also embraces his multiracial and multicultural heritage. Obama's ability to appeal to Americans of all hues gives grounds for optimism, indicating that America may be ready to move "beyond race," as he proclaimed in his campaign. A less optimistic perspective would be that black exceptionalism may continue to persist, as some middle- and upper-class blacks become able to cross over the black-nonblack divide without dismantling it.

Directions for Future Research and Policy Implications

Our research focused on the differences between Asians, Latinos, and blacks that relate to issues of diversity, but in the process of reviewing our results we encountered data that suggests productive avenues of future research relating to the color line in the United States.

Gender

We observed some notable gender patterns that are worthy of further investigation, such as the ways gender differences affect patterns of incorporation and the changing color line. For instance, patterns of intermarriage suggest that the process of incorporation for new immigrants is gendered, with Asian and Latina females experiencing greater facility with incorporation than males. Asian and Latina females are more likely not only to intermarry than their male counterparts but also to marry white males. The children of their unions will then normally adopt Anglo surnames, in accordance with the normative practice of patrilineal passage of names from father to children. Because Asian-white and Latino-white children tend to have white fathers and thus are more likely to have Anglo rather than Asian or Latino surnames, they are more likely to identify and be identified as white, making their Asian and Latino ethnic ancestries more symbolic than instrumental.

Even among multiracial children, there may be gender differences that deserve further investigation. The growing body of research on ethnoracial identity formation in the children of post-1965 immigrants (called the new second generation) provides some insight on this question. Immigration researchers find that females have more leeway in their choice of identity options than males. For instance, second-generation West Indian and Latina females are able to adopt bicultural identities: claiming a racial identity, maintaining a stance of racial solidarity, and straddling two cultures while also exhibiting middle-class behavior and accepting middle-class values (Carter 2005; Waters 1999b). Mary C. Waters (1999b) underscores that being female does not innately promote greater flexibility; rather, black and Latina females are less violently stigmatized in the wider society for their racial status, which gives them more latitude to adopt bicultural identities. By contrast, West Indian and Latino males are more likely to experience overt hostility and instances of interpersonal discrimination than their female counterparts, making them more likely to adopt racial and at times oppositional identities (López 2009; Waters 1999b).

These findings may have implications for gendered patterns of identification among multiracial males and females; ethnoracial status may be more consequential for multiracial males than for multiracial females and especially for multiracial black males. For instance, all the multiracial black males of all ethnic mixtures experienced numerous encounters with the law-enforcement system, such as being stopped by police officers while driving, questioned by security guards, and harassed by the police more generally. None of the black multiracial females mentioned such incidents, signaling that black multiraciality and blackness more generally may be more consequential for males than for females. Yet intermarriage rates among blacks are higher for males than females, so the question of gender, intermarriage, and multiraciality is not so clear-cut. Future research could more closely examine the role of gender in the context of intermarriage, multiracial identification, and the color line.

California Exceptionalism

When we present our research findings to various audiences, a question invariably arises as to whether our conclusions regarding the color line are particular to California or are generalizable beyond the Golden State. Our response is that only the in-depth interviews of the interracial couples and the multiracial adults were with residents of California; the trends in intermarriage and the patterns of multiracial identification that we present are drawn from the entire country. Certainly, California attracts large numbers of the country's newest immigrants from Asia and Latin America, and it also boasts the largest number of multiracial individuals. But California is not unique with respect to its level of racial and ethnic diversity. In fact, the ethnoracial diversity apparent in California is similar to that of other states that attract large numbers of Asian and Latino immigrants, such as Texas, New York, Florida, New Jersey, New Mexico, and Illinois. We have labeled these states the country's "new-diversity states" because their ethnic and racial profiles depart significantly from the earlier pattern characterized by the black-white color line; their populations have significant fractions of at least three major racial and ethnic groups.

The new-diversity states also happen to be the country's most populous states, so the patterns that emerge in these locales affect a sizable portion of the U.S. population. These particular states also tend to be among the country's most prosperous. It is especially troubling that we find evidence of a continuing black-nonblack divide in the country's most ethnoracially diverse, most populous, and most prosperous states because we would expect the most progress in ethnoracial relations to occur in these states. Although diversity exerts an independent effect on the loosening of boundaries, as evidenced by the positive, direct relationship between ethnoracial diversity and multiracial reporting, this effect is overridden for blacks by negative factors, but this is not the case for Asians and Latinos. The fact that black remains a category distinct not only from white but also from other nonwhite groups, such as Asians and Latinos, reflects the persistence of black exceptionalism, which emerges not only in parts of the country in which there are few ethnoracial minorities but also in places where the color line is breaking down fairly rapidly for new nonwhite immigrant groups.

One important caveat regarding the findings about Latinos is that the majority of this group in California are of Mexican origin, and their ethnoracial mixture mainly is Indian and European. Mexicans have relatively little African heritage in their backgrounds, unlike other Latino ethnic groups, such as Dominicans and Puerto Ricans. This is important because the experiences of intermarried Latinos and Latino multiracials with African heritage, such as Dominicans and Puerto Ricans, may be very different from those we interviewed; the non-Mexican Latino groups may exhibit patterns that more closely mirror those of interracial black couples and black multiracials. Conducting a comparative study in New York City, where there is a large Dominican and Puerto Rican population, could shed light on these questions. If such differences emerged from such research, they might reflect a cleavage within the Latino population, with some falling on the black side of the divide.

The Future of Race-Based Policies

In an era when race-based policies, such as affirmative action, have increasingly come under attack and their fundamental relevance has been challenged, the question of whether multiracial individuals with black, Latino, or Asian backgrounds should be eligible for race-based policies is one that we should answer. The question is all the more vexing given our findings that the Asian and Latino identities for Asian-white and Latino-white multiracials are highly situational and symbolic, and that many live their everyday lives as white. For multiracial Americans who identify and are identified by others as white, their taking advantage of race-based programs designed to assist underrepresented or disadvantaged minorities is incongruent with the original goals of such programs. However, as we find in our study, Asian and Latino multiracials feel that they have every right to choose how they wish to identify; most of them feel that if marking a minority ethnoracial identity carries advantages, they will not hesitate to do so. Yet when policymakers count multiracial Americans as minorities, they are essentially placing multiracial Americans on the same plane with racialized minorities whose experiences with racial status may be radically different from those of multiracials. By counting multiracials as minorities, race-based programs may not necessarily benefit the most dis-advantaged racialized minorities, whose ethnoracial identities are not symbolic or situational and who live each day with racial labels and the consequences that accompany them.

Ethnoracial status and disadvantage are experienced differently for nonwhite groups. Black multiraciality is experienced very differently from Asian and Latino multiraciality. As we have clearly demonstrated, black ancestry is not symbolic, as are Asian and Latino ancestries for most Asian-white and Latino-white multiracials. Instead, black remains a much more fixed, consequential, and stigmatizing identity than other nonwhite ethnoracial identities. Whereas black-white multiracials are often identified and treated as black, Asian-white and Latino-white multiracials are often identified as non-Asian and non-Latino and often treated as white.

We are not arguing that multiracial Americans should not be able to freely choose how they wish to identify, nor are we proposing that multiracial Americans should be excluded from participating in race-based programs. We are suggesting that we need to reconsider the purpose of race-based programs, such as affirmative action, in the context of America's new ethnoracial diversity. But before informed recommendations can be made about whether multi-racial Americans should be eligible for race-based programs, policymakers need to tackle a thorny question: What is the main purpose of race-based programs, such as affirmative action? Is the moral vision behind affirmative action to right past racial injustices, or is it to truthfully represent the diversity of contemporary society that is being transformed by the new immigration (Massey et al. 2007; Skrentny 2001b)?

Blacks were intended as the primary beneficiaries of the Civil Rights Act when Congress passed it in 1964. African Americans had endured hundreds of years of slavery, decades of Jim Crow segregation, extreme violence in the South, and severe discrimination in the North (Skrentny 2001a). Blacks had suffered the greatest racial injustice, and they had also protested and lobbied for change more ardently than any other racial or ethnic group. In the words of Senator Hubert Humphrey, the simple purpose of the Civil Rights Act of 1964 was "to give fellow citizens—Negroes—the same rights and opportuni-ties that white people take for granted" (Skrentny 2001b, B7). Civil rights administrators felt that affirmative action was the best way to achieve equal rights and opportunities.

Even today, defenders of affirmative action link the policy to Lyndon Johnson's famous analogy about the need to give an advantage to a runner competing in a race who had previously been shackled and chained. For many pundits commenting on affirmative action, the moral vision is simple: to right past wrongs to African Americans in the United States.

Contemporary opponents of affirmative action question its relevance for today's blacks, not to mention its applicability to new nonwhite immigrants who have arrived after 1965 and their children. The debate on affirmative action reflects the diverging visions regarding its purpose: whether to right past wrongs or to provide assistance to the country's many disadvantaged groups. In the former case, affirmative action benefits would be targeted specifically at African Americans; in the latter case, affirmative action programs would be available to all ethnoracial minorities, including all multiracial Americans, as well as other groups and categories.

What is needed is a clearer, more precise understanding of the intention of race-based programs, such as affirmative action. If the goal of affirmative action has shifted so that the intent is to consider extending compensatory benefits to all new non-European groups as well as other disadvantaged groups, more and more categories of persons are likely to claim that they should be included. For example, interest groups have sprung up during the past fifteen years to lobby for legislation against "reverse discrimination," alleged mistreatment of white males. These new interpretations illustrate the possibility that if all groups are the victims of discrimination, then in effect none are, at least when it comes to finding practical policy solutions.

Be that as it may, our research findings make it clear that despite inroads that diversity has made in helping to erode the color line for all ethnoracial groups, many blacks continue to experience disadvantages not experienced by others, pointing to a pattern of "black exceptionalism," and, by extension, calling for policies aimed to reduce it.

~ Appendix ~

Methodological Approach

We employed multiple research methods to understand the extent to which contemporary immigration to the United States and new ethnoracial diversity may be changing the country's color line and variously eroding the boundaries separating groups. On the basis of patterns of intermarriage and multiracial identification among Asians, Latinos, and African Americans, we gauged where racial divides are disappearing most rapidly and which groups fall on which side of the old black-white color line. We relied on four types of information: comparative-historical data; the results of previous research relevant to the topics under investigation here; in-depth interviews conducted with both multiracial adults and interracial couples with children; and descriptive statistics and quantitative analyses of the 1990 and 2000 census and 2007 and 2008 American Community Survey (ACS) data. Each of these has certain strengths and each also has shortcomings. Combined, they give us a more complete portrait than we could otherwise obtain of the effects of diversity on boundary dissolution and the placement of America's color line in the twenty-first century. In this appendix we seek, first, to explicate more thoroughly than in the book's main text the logic and rationale for employing multiple methods in our research; second, to offer more specific details about the in-depth interviews and the samples they cover; and third, to provide further details about the quantitative analyses presented in the book.

The Use of Multiple Research Methods

In chapters 1 to 3 we draw on the extensive body of comparative-historical research to offer four theoretical possibilities as to where the color line might be drawn in twenty-first-century America. Some scholars maintain that given the historical legacy of U.S. ethnoracial relations, the white-nonwhite divide continues to be the most resilient, with Asians and Latinos falling on the nonwhite side of the color line. Others contend that today's new immigrants are following in the footsteps of their European predecessors, resulting in the birth of a new black-nonblack divide that separates blacks from other ethnoracial groups, including Asians and Latinos.

Still others believe that a dual color line is too simplistic a pattern to capture America's new ethnoracial reality and conjecture that a more complex tri-racial hierarchy is emerging, with an "in-between" category in which most Asians and Latinos fall. Finally, a fourth group envisions a postracial society in which racial boundaries are fading for all groups, and the color line is disappearing altogether. The four theoretical possibilities place our study in the context of comparative-historical research in immigration and ethnoracial relations and provide an indispensable road map to interpret our newly collected and analyzed data as we move forward to the next sections of the book.

In the book's first part, specifically chapter 4, we tentatively gauge the placement of the color line by analyzing descriptive statistics from the 2000 U.S. census and the 2007 and 2008 ACS, focusing specifically on national trends and patterns in immigration, intermarriage, multiracial reporting, and ethnoracial diversity. The ethnoracial landscape of the United States has changed dramatically over the past forty years, and much of this change is due to recent (post-1965) immigration. More than tripling in size since 1970, Hispanic and Asian groups together now account for about one fifth of the country's total population, substantially changing the face of America. Their arrival has ushered in a "new diversity" in some states and metropolitan areas, by the presence of at least three (and in some cases four) sizable ethnoracial groups.

Contemporary immigration, however, is only one factor that is moving the country beyond black and white; the increase in intermarriage and the creation of a new multiracial population is also making the country more diverse than before. Yet this new diversity is not uniformly distributed across the United States; in fact, it is particularly visible in some parts of the country and nearly absent in others. Our task, then, is to determine which states and metropolitan areas are the most diverse and map the geography of the country's new ethnoracial diversity by laying out the changes in the composition of our population brought about by contemporary immigration.

Our analyses indicate that areas with larger proportions of Latinos and Asians exhibit the greatest diversity and also display the highest rates of multiracial reporting. More specifically, we find that California, the most populous state in the country, is also the most diverse, with a nonwhite population exceeding more than half the state's total population, at 57.8 percent (we excluded from our analysis a few small, high-diversity states: Hawaii, the District of Columbia, and New Mexico). California also leads the country with the highest number of multiracial persons and is the only state in the country with a multiracial population of more than one million. Thus, California not only is ethnoracially diverse, but also appears to be in the vanguard of social change, judging by the number of Californians who claim a multiracial ancestry.

The compositional data and descriptive statistics also reveal interesting trends and patterns of intermarriage and multiracial reporting. For instance, we find that Asians and Latinos are more likely to intermarry than blacks and are also more likely to claim a multiracial identity than African American multiracials, indicating that the boundaries for Asians and Latinos appear to be eroding more rapidly than those for blacks. This data alone can tell us little about the underlying mechanisms that generate boundary dissolution and change, but they do provide evidence consistent with the possibility of a black-nonblack color line.

While we have established that Asians and Latinos are intermarrying at higher rates than blacks, as indicated by the compositional data alone, we are unable to determine the driving forces behind their higher rates of exogamy. It may be that because these groups are growing in size, there is simply more opportunity to meet and eventually marry across ethnoracial lines (especially with whites, who are the country's majority group). If this is the case, an increase in the sizes of these groups could produce a shift in marital patterns— not necessarily because of declining prejudice on the part of whites toward Asians and Latinos, and vice versa, but because of increased contact and opportunity. But a rise in intermarriage could indeed be a result of declining group prejudice, reflecting changes in cultural perceptions and orientations on the part of Asians, Latinos, and whites.

A similar logic also applies to multiracial identification. Using the compositional data alone, we are unable to ascertain whether the higher rates of multiracial reporting among Asians and Latinos than among blacks simply indicate an increase in the size of these populations as a result of more intermarriage among the former groups, or whether they reflect substantive changes in the former groups' perceptions about and experiences with ethnoracial boundaries and options.

In order to discern whether the differences are strictly the result of changes in composition in the U.S. population or also reflect changes in perceptions and attitudes, we conducted in-depth interviews with interracial couples with children, and with multiracial adults. In the second part of the book, chapters 5 to 8, we turned to the data collected from qualitative interviews to understand how interracial couples and multiracial adults construct racial boundaries, and how these boundaries in turn affect the way they choose to identify themselves and their children. Incorporating a qualitative component to our study and combining this data with the quantitative analysis was critical, not only because it helped to explain the trends and patterns from the compositional data but also, and perhaps more important, because it provided clearer understandings of the underlying mechanisms that engender boundary change.

The in-depth interviews provided rich and detailed accounts of the meaning and significance of racial divides, marriage across racial boundaries, and multiraciality among those who are at the vanguard of social change. Because our sample included interracial couples with children, we were able to probe how they perceive and construct racial barriers when choosing a suitable marriage partner and how they decide to identify their children born of their unions. And because we also interviewed multiracial adults (not all of whom identify as such), we were able to ask why they had chosen a particular ethnoracial identity, under what conditions they made that choice, whether they felt they had ethnoracial options, and the meaning that multiraciality holds in their lives. By comparing the experiences of black, Asian, and Latino interracial couples and multiracial adults, we were able to examine how different racial statuses affect ethnoracial options.

Focusing on lived experiences rather than attitudes was critical for our study since we were interested in understanding how racial status and racial divides affect cultural orientations behavior, opportunities, and life chances. The disjuncture in attitudes and behavior has been well noted in social science research, especially in polls about intermarriage and residential integration. Americans may support intermarriage and integration in theory, but the relatively low rates of both phenomena reveal an unwillingness on the part of Americans to put theory into practice.

Because our goal was to conduct face-to-face in-depth interviews with interracial couples and multiracial adults, we needed to choose a locale in which they are populous. This task was difficult because we deliberately chose not to recruit respondents from interracial or multiracial organizations, which is how previous researchers have located respondents. For those reasons, we chose to conduct the interviews in California. Also, because California is so diverse, it provided the best example of sociocultural change.

The percentage of marriages in California that are racially mixed is more than twice the national average, and the higher rate undoubtedly stems to some extent from the fact that California overturned its antimiscegenation laws in 1948—nearly two decades before the Supreme Court ruling in *Loving v. Virginia,* in 1967, which ended all race-based legal restrictions on marriage. California also leads the country with the highest number of multiracial individuals and is the only state with a multiracial population that exceeds one million. Because California is the largest state with a sizable proportion of both populations, it was a natural research site to conduct the interviews. An added bonus was that by interviewing respondents in California, we got the most optimistic portrait of where the color line is changing most rapidly in the United States, which could be viewed as a preview of developments in other states.

Some observers might raise the concern that the interviews are conducted only with Californians and, within this group, only with pre-identified individuals with multiracial backgrounds who were willing to talk with us. Perhaps these kinds of selectivities yield a distorted view of the bases and nature of multiraciality in America. There is undoubtedly some truth to this. California is a state that has long been more tolerant of ethnoracial mixing than other states, especially when it comes to intermarriage in particular and marriage and family behavior in general. Moreover, interracial couples and multiracial individuals willing to talk with us probably hold more benign views of intermarriage and multiraciality than those unwilling to talk with us. However, our main interest lay in assessing whether the experiences of Asian, Latino, and black intermarried couples and multiracials seemed to place such persons closer to whites or to blacks, so that we could gauge the direction in which America's color line is moving most rapidly. Any bias of this kind would seem likely to distort things in the same direction for all interracial couples and multiracial adults. The fact that we observed major differences between Asian and Latino interracial couples and multiracial adults as compared to their black counterparts thus would not appear to result from any such biases.

We recognize that we were "sampling on the dependent variable" in our in-depth interviews, meaning that by interviewing only those who had crossed racial boundaries with their unions or were multiracial themselves, we had no basis of generalizing beyond our select cases (Small 2009). We rebalanced our information by combining the in-depth interview data with statistical analyses of census and ACS data for metropolitan areas encompassing a wide range of diversity contexts, and so were better able to pinpoint how boundaries are eroding more quickly for Asians and Latinos than for blacks. The reasons have to do with the different ways group size affects intermarriage and multiracial reporting. Both the interviews and the statistical data showed the workings of deep-seated cultural differences in the ways whites, Asians, and Latinos view one another and the ways the members of these groups view blacks. The differences suggested a pattern of "black exceptionalism" and were evidence of the "diversity paradox" in this country.

In the third part of the book, in particular chapter 9, we completed our investigative circle by studying ethnoracial diversity itself. We learned from the quantitative analyses that diversity per se exerts an independent effect on the dissolution of group boundaries quite apart from changes in demographic composition. It increases rates of multiracial reporting for all groups and helps to break down racial barriers, although other forces offset this in the case of African Americans.

By combining qualitative and quantitative methods, we were able to provide a clearer portrait than we could otherwise offer about America's color line in the twenty-first century, the meanings attached to ethnoracial divides, and the role that diversity plays in the process of boundary change.

The Interview Sample and Methods

The interview sample comprised thirty-six interracial couples with children and forty-six multiracial adults, for a total of eighty-two in-depth interviews. The selection of the sample was complex because it is currently impossible to draw nationally representative random samples of interracial couples and multiracial adults because no national—or even local—lists of such couples or individuals exist. In fact, such a list would be nearly impossible to generate because the history of racial mixing in the country dates back centuries, despite the fact that multiraciality has only recently been officially recognized (Bailey 2008). In fact, virtually all Americans would have some basis to claim a multiracial heritage, yet most do not choose to do so.

Previous qualitative studies have recruited respondents from interracial or multiracial organizations or by placing advertisements in newspapers, newsletters, or magazines geared to this population. We decided not to recruit respondents this way, since most individuals who belong to such organizations join them because of their strong awareness of and identification with their multiracial backgrounds or their status as an interracial couple, which we felt would introduce a bias into our sample. Instead, we recruited respondents through ethnic markets, ethnic restaurants, and ethnic salons near Los Angeles and the San Francisco Bay Area. We contacted the owners of these establishments, and they referred us to some of their regular customers who had mentioned that they had parents of different cultural, racial, or ethnic backgrounds. We recognized that recruiting respondents through ethnic establishments may have biased our sample by excluding those who identify culturally and racially as white; in fact, the inclusion of such a population would have strengthened our findings, particularly since many multiracial Asians and Latinos choose to identify as white or American.

The method of recruiting respondents from ethnic establishments is a marked improvement over previous qualitative studies that recruited respondents from interracial or multiracial organizations. The most important benefit of constructing our initial sample in this way is that although the respondents acknowledged their mixed racial or ethnic backgrounds or their cultural or ethnic differences as a couple, they did not necessarily identify multiracially or view themselves as an interracial couple. This was critical since we were interested in examining the range of ethnoracial options available to interracial couples and multiracial adults. Following the initial interviews, we used snowball sampling to identify multiracial adults and interracial couples who were not customers of these ethnic establishments. By recruiting respondents in these ways, we were able to identify a sample of "potential multiracials" and "potential interracial couples" and create a sample with less bias toward those who clearly identify multiracially or interracially (Waters 2000). Table A.1 lists our respondents by racial and ethnic categories of identification.

Our initial goal was to interview an equal number of respondents in each subgroup, but we found that task difficult for several reasons, especially in the case of black interracial couples and black multiracials. At first glance, this may appear to constitute a weakness in the research, but at another level it is a strength because the likelihood of locating and recruiting various kinds of interracial couples and multiracial individuals itself turns out to yield significant information relevant to the research purposes at hand. This became evident in three ways. First, owners of ethnic establishments referred more Asian and Latino interracial couples and multiracial individuals to us. Second, these

Table A.1 *Respondents by Race-Ethnicity in the Interview Sample*

Interracial Couples	Total
Asian-white	15
Latino-white	11
Black-white	5
Asian-Latino	3
Black-Asian	2
Total	36
Multiracial Individuals	Total
Asian-white	16
Latino-white	8
Black-white	9
Black-Asian	5
Black-Latino	2
Asian-Latino	6
Total	46
Total interviews	82

Source: Authors' compilation.

respondents referred more of their friends, who agreed to participate in the study. Third, when we identified black interracial couples and multiracial black adults, they were more likely to decline our requests for interviews. Some could not understand why we were interested in studying them and were suspicious of our intentions, even after we explained that the study was comparative and did not focus specifically on black interracial couples and black multiracial adults. Others admitted that issues of intermarriage and racial identification had caused a great deal of turmoil in their lives, and they were unwilling to speak about these issues publicly, even when we assured complete confidentiality and anonymity. Still others simply did not return our calls, even after repeated attempts to contact them, making it clear that they were not interested in participating. In the end, more than half of the black interracial couples and multiracial adults who were referred to us declined our request for an interview.

By contrast, none of the Asian and Latino interracial couples or multiracial adults refused our request for an interview. In fact, most were enthusiastic and eager to talk at length about issues of interracial relationships and ethnoracial identification. Thus, the different levels of willingness to participate in the study itself constitute evidence about intermarriage and multiraciality in America, reflecting different histories and experiences among these groups. That Asian and Latino interracial couples and multiracial adults are more willing to discuss issues related to intermarriage and identity indicates that these groups may experience less social stigma than black interracial couples and multiracial adults, an issue that we discuss at length.

Lasting between one and one-half and two hours, the tape-recorded interviews with the interracial couples and multiracial adults were semistructured and open-ended. We took an inductive approach (meaning that we began with specific observations and moved to broader generalizations and theories), asking the respondents questions about their racial-ethnic identities and their cultural practices: how and why they chose to identify themselves and their children in the way they did; whether these identities changed over time or in different contexts; what their identities meant to them; and what cultural and linguistic practices they pursued. The inductive approach in the interviews enabled us to uncover some of the subjective processes that guide the choice of racial and ethnic identification. We transcribed the interviews verbatim, conducting follow-up interviews when responses were unclear or needed further elaboration.

The interviews were then coded by theme, sorted, and analyzed. What emerged from the analyses were distinct themes and consistent patterns among the interracial couples and multiracial adults. Although our sample was not large, it was big enough to generate meaningful and discernible patterns across ethnoracial groups. The findings from the in-depth interviews confirmed the results from the quantitative analyses, so it is quite possible that a larger sample would not have yielded disconfirming evidence.

The Quantitative Data and Analyses

Both the descriptive and analytical quantitative inquiries are based on 1990 and 2000 U.S. Bureau of the Census and 2007 and 2008 ACS data. We use the IPUMS (Integrated Public Use Microdata Series) versions of these data sets (Ruggles et al. 2009). Using all these information sources, we calculated descriptive measures of immigration, ethnoracial diversity, intermarriage, multiracial identification, and other variables, for the country as a whole, for states and the District of Columbia, and for metropolitan areas, including the entire set of metropolitan areas in 1990, 2000, and 2007–2008 (251 areas in 1990 and 297 in 2000 and 2007–2008). When conducting statistical analyses, we estimated regressions using several combinations of these data sets. In the nested regressions, intermarriage was sometimes a dependent variable and sometimes an independent variable. Thus, we ran 1990 independent variables on 1990 dependent variables (multiracial reporting), 1990 independent variables on 2000 dependent variables, 2000 independent variables on 2000 dependent variables, 2007–2008 independent variables on 2007–2008 dependent variables, and 2000 independent variables on 2007–2008 dependent variables. All these analyses yielded similar findings, so we have presented only results for the last set of nested regression models, in part because they include a measure of intermarriage in 2000. This means that the measure of exogamy used is for a time several years before the time multiracial reporting is measured, a useful sequence when treating intermarriage as a predictor of multi-racial identification.

Concerning the indicator of intermarriage, larger numbers of ethnoracially exogamous marriages can occur, especially those involving whites and the members of some other group, even when the nonwhite group, which is almost always a statistical minority, is increasing in size. Although such an increase would lower the probability of minority individuals' out-marrying (because there would be more in-group partners available), it would simultaneously raise the probability of white individuals out-marrying (because there would accordingly be fewer in-group partners available, at least in the two-group case). Thus, it is possible for the relative number of intermarried couples, defined as the percentage of all marriages containing spouses of mixed ethnoracial status (here white and some other group), to increase even as the probability that an individual member of a particular group would out-marry was going down. In our analyses, we use the percentage of all couples that contain spouses of different ethnoracial identifications as our measure of exogamy. This is virtually the same as using the percentage of couples containing a white spouse and a spouse of some other ethnoracial category because 92.2 percent of all intermarried couples involve couples with one white spouse (the correlation between these two measures is 0.842 across metropolitan areas). Also, in constructing our ethnoracial categories, we first put into the Latino category anyone who said he or she was Latino, irrespective of how that person answered the race question on the census. Thus, when we talk of whites, blacks, Asians, and so forth, we are talking about the non-Hispanic members of these categories.

In the diagram presented in figure 9.1, the estimates come from a simple recursive model of effects, focusing on three major racial and ethnic groups: blacks, Latinos, and Asians, examined across metropolitan areas. We focus on relative group size (percentage of the population in the ethnoracial group), percentage foreign-born, diversity, exogamy, and multiracial reporting. To assess the relationships among these variables, we use path analysis, a technique relying on a series of nested multiple regression models. We assume that relationships among these variables can be adequately depicted using a simple recursive set of equations theoretically reflecting a given causal ordering among the variables. We recognize that the nature of the relationships among the variables may not meet these assumptions, so we treat the path-analysis results only as a first-order description of relationships, focusing in particular on the independent relationships between diversity and exogamy and multiracial reporting, on relationships between diversity and multiracial reporting working through exogamy, and on the relationship between relative group size and multiracial reporting operating through diversity and other variables. In the vernacular of path analysis, these include *direct* effects, *indirect* effects, and effects involving common sources of influence and co-variation with exogenous variables. We calculate these using standard path-analytic procedures (Duncan 1975).

~ Notes ~

Chapter 1

1. When we tabulate statistics from the 2007 and 2008 American Community Surveys, we cite Ruggles et al. (2009) in the text because the data come from files made available by the IPUMS project, which Ruggles directs.

Chapter 3

1. We distinguish the concepts of "multiraciality," "multiracial identification," and "multiracial reporting." Multiraciality refers to someone whose parents (or grandparent or other ancestors) were from different racial groups (given current constructions of such groups). Multiracial identification refers to the process and result of seeing oneself as being multiracial. Multiracial reporting refers to the act of reporting oneself as having multiraciality. As we note in various parts of the book, these need not correspond.
2. When we report statistics for 2008, we mean the beginning of 2008, which we infer by combining samples from both the 2007 and the 2008 American Community Surveys (Ruggles et al. 2009).

~ References ~

Alba, Richard D. 1985. *Italian Americans: Into the Twilight of Ethnicity.* Englewood Cliffs, N.J.: Prentice Hall.

———. 1990. *Ethnic Identity: The Transformation of White America.* New Haven: Yale University Press.

———. 1995. "Assimilation's Quiet Tide." *The Public Interest* 119(Spring): 3–18.

———. 1999. "Immigration and the American Realities of Assimilation and Multiculturalism." *Sociological Forum* 14(1): 3–25.

———. 2009. *Blurring the Color Line: The New Chance for a More Integrated America.* Cambridge, Mass.: Harvard University Press.

Alba, Richard D., and Reid Golden. 1986. "Patterns of Ethnic Marriage in the United States." *Social Forces* 65(1): 202–23.

Alba, Richard D., and Victor Nee. 2003. *Remaking the American Mainstream: Assimilation and Contemporary Immigration.* Cambridge, Mass.: Harvard University Press.

Allport, Gordon W. 1954. *The Nature of Prejudice.* Reading, Mass.: Addison-Wesley.

Anderson, Elijah. 1990. *Streetwise: Race, Class, and Change in an Urban Community.* Chicago: University of Chicago Press.

Anderson, Margo J. 2002. "Counting by Race: The Antebellum Legacy." In *The New Race Question: How the Census Counts Multiracial Individuals,* edited by Joel Perlmann and Mary C. Waters. New York: Russell Sage Foundation.

Anderson, Margo J., and Stephen E. Fienberg. 1999. *Who Counts? The Politics of Census-Taking in Contemporary America.* New York: Russell Sage Foundation.

Bailey, Benjamin. 2001. "Dominican-American Ethnic/Racial Identities and United States Social Categories." *International Migration Review* 35(3): 677–708.

Bailey, Stanley R. 2008. "Unmixing for Race Making in Brazil." *American Journal of Sociology* 114(3): 577–614.

————. 2009. *Legacies of Race: Identities, Attitudes, and Politics in Brazil.* Palo Alto: Stanford University Press.

Baldassare, Mark. 1981. *The Growth Dilemma: Residents' Views and Local Population Change in the United States.* Berkeley: University of California Press.

————. 2000. *California in the New Millennium: The Changing Social and Political Landscape.* Berkeley: University of California Press.

Barth, Fredrik. 1969. "Introduction." In *Ethnic Groups and Boundaries: the Social Organization of Culture Difference,* edited by Fredrik Barth. Boston: Little, Brown.

Bean, Frank D., and Stephanie Bell-Rose, eds. 1999. *Immigration and Opportunity: Race, Ethnicity, and Employment in the United States.* New York: Russell Sage Foundation.

Bean, Frank D., Cynthia Feliciano, Jennifer Lee, and Jennifer Van Hook. 2009. "The New U.S. Immigrants: How Do They Affect Our Understanding of the African American Experience?" *Annals of the American Academy of Political and Social Science* 621(January): 202–20.

Bean, Frank D., Jennifer Lee, Jeanne Batalova, and Mark A. Leach. 2004. *Immigration and Fading Color Lines in America.* New York and Washington, D.C.: Russell Sage Foundation and Population Reference Bureau.

Bean, Frank D., and Gillian Stevens. 2003. *America's Newcomers and the Dynamics of Diversity.* New York: Russell Sage Foundation.

Bean, Frank D., and Marta Tienda. 1987. *The Hispanic Population of the United States.* New York: Russell Sage Foundation.

Benkler, Yochai. 2006. *The Wealth of Networks: How Social Production Transforms Markets and Freedom.* New Haven: Yale University Press.

Berlin, Ira. 2003. *Generations of Captivity: A History of African-American Slaves.* Cambridge, Mass.: Harvard University Press.

Blalock, Hubert M. 1967. *Toward a Theory of Minority-Group Relations.* New York: John Wiley.

Blau, Peter M. 1977. *Inequality and Heterogeneity.* New York: Free Press.

Blau, Peter M., Terry C. Blum, and Joseph E. Schwartz. 1982. "Heterogeneity and Intermarriage." *American Sociological Review* 47(1): 45–62.

Blau, Peter M., and Joseph E. Schwartz. 1984/1997. *Crosscutting Social Circles: Testing a Macrostructural Theory of Intergroup Relations.* Orlando, Fla.: Academic Press.

Blight, David W. 2001. *Race and Reunion: The Civil War in American Memory.* Cambridge, Mass.: Harvard University Press.

Bobo, Lawrence D. 1997. "The Color Line, the Dilemma, and the Dream: Race Relations in America at the Close of the Twentieth Century." In *Civil Rights and Social Wrongs: Black-White Relations Since World War II,* edited by John Higham. University Park: Pennsylvania State University Press.

————. 1999. "Prejudice as Group Position: Microfoundations of a Sociological Approach to Racism and Race Relations." *Journal of Social Issues* 55(3): 445–72.

———. 2004. "Inequalities That Endure? Racial Ideology, American Politics, and the Peculiar Role of the Social Sciences." In *The Changing Terrain of Race and Ethnicity,* edited by Maria Krysan and Amanda E. Lewis. New York: Russell Sage Foundation.

Bobo, Lawrence D., and Vincent L. Hutchings. 1996. "Perceptions of Racial Group Competition: Extending Blumer's Theory of Group Position to a Multiracial Social Context." *American Sociological Review* 61(6): 951–72.

Bobo, Lawrence D., and Mia Tuan. 2005. *Prejudice in Politics: Group Position, Public Opinion, and the Wisconsin Treaty Rights Controversy.* Cambridge, Mass.: Harvard University Press.

Bonilla-Silva, Eduardo. 2003. *Racism Without Racists: Color-Blind Racism and the Persistence of Racial Inequality in the United States.* Lanham, Md.: Rowman & Littlefield.

———. 2004a. "From Bi-racial to Tri-racial." *Ethnic and Racial Studies* 27(6): 931–50.

———. 2004b. "We Are All Americans." *Race and Society* 5(1): 3–16.

Borjas, George J. 2001. "Welfare Reform and Immigration." In *The New World of Welfare,* edited by Rebecca Blank and Ron Haskins. Washington, D.C.: Brookings Institution Press.

———, ed. 2007. *Mexican Immigration to the United States.* Chicago: University of Chicago Press.

Brodkin, Karen. 1998. *How Jews Became White Folks & What That Says About Race in America.* New Brunswick, N.J.: Rutgers University Press.

Brown, Susan K., and Frank D. Bean. 2005. "International Migration." In *Handbook of Population,* edited by Dudley L. Poston, Jr., and Michael Micklin. New York: Kluwer Academic Publishers.

Brown, Susan K., Frank D. Bean, and James Bachmeier. 2009. "Aging Societies and the Changing Logic of Immigration." *Generations* 32(4): 11–17.

Bugleski, B. R. 1961. "Assimilation Through Intermarriage." *Social Forces* 40(2): 148–53.

Bumiller, Kristin. 1988. *The Civil Rights Society: The Social Construction of Victims.* Baltimore: Johns Hopkins University Press.

Camarota, Steven A., and Nora McArdle. 2003. "Where Immigrants Live: An Examination of State Residency of the Foreign Born by Country of Origin in 1990 and 2000." Report. Washington, D.C.: Center for Immigration Studies.

Carter, Prudence L. 2005. *Keepin' It Real: School Success Beyond Black and White.* New York: Oxford University Press.

Charles, Camille Zubrinsky. 2001. "Socioeconomic Status and Segregation: African Americans, Hispanics, and Asians in Los Angeles." In *Problem of the Century: Racial Stratification in the United States,* edited by Elijah Anderson and Douglas S. Massey. New York: Russell Sage Foundation.

———. 2003. "The Dynamics of Racial Residential Segregation." *Annual Review of Sociology* 29(1): 167–207.

Choldin, Harvey M. 1986. "Statistics and Politics: The 'Hispanic Issue' in the 1980 Census." *Demography* 23(3): 403–18.

Chua, Amy. 2007. *Day of Empire: How Hyperpowers Rise to Global Dominance—and Why They Fall.* New York: Doubleday.

Conley, Dalton. 1999. *Being Black, Living in the Red: Race, Wealth, and Social Policy in America.* Berkeley: University of California Press.

Cornell, Stephen, and Douglas Hartmann. 1998. *Ethnicity and Race.* Thousand Oaks, Calif.: Pine Forge Press.

————. 2006. *Ethnicity and Race: Making Identities in a Changing World.* Thousand Oaks, Calif.: Pine Forge Press.

DaCosta, Kimberly. 2000. "Remaking the Color Line: Social Bases and Implications of the Multiracial Movement." Ph.D. diss., University of California, Berkeley.

————. 2007. *Making Multiracials: State, Family, and Market in the Redrawing of the Color Line.* Palo Alto: Stanford University Press.

Dalmage, Heather M. 2000. *Tripping on the Color Line: Black-White Multiracial Families in a Racially Divided World.* New Brunswick, N.J.: Rutgers University Press.

Daniels, Roger. 1962. *The Politics of Prejudice.* Berkeley: University of California Press.

Davis, David B. 1998. "A Big Business." *New York Review of Books* 45(10): 50–53.

Davis, F. James. 1991/2001. *Who Is Black? One Nation's Definition.* University Park: Pennsylvania State University Press.

————. 2004. "The One-Drop Rule and Black Identity in the United States." Paper presented at the Race Symposium, sponsored by the Center for Study of Social Inequality, Department of Sociology, University of Iowa. Iowa City (April 22–24).

Dixon, Jeffrey C. 2006. "The Ties That Bind and Those That Don't: Toward Reconciling Group Threat and Contact Theories of Prejudice." *Social Forces* 84(4): 2179–2202.

Du Bois, W. E. B. 1903/1997. *The Souls of Black Folk.* Edited by D. W. Blight and R. Gooding-Williams. Boston: Bedford Books.

————. 1935. *Black Reconstruction in America.* New York: Harcourt, Brace.

Duncan, Otis Dudley. 1975. *Introduction to Structural Equation Models.* New York: Academic Press.

Edmonston, Barry, Joshua Goldstein, and Juanita Tamayo Lott. 1996. *Spotlight on Heterogeneity: The Federal Standards for Racial and Ethnic Classification.* Summary of a workshop. Washington, D.C.: National Academies Press.

Edmonston, Barry, Sharon M. Lee, and Jeffrey S. Passel. 2002. "Recent Trends in Intermarriage and Immigration and Their Effects on the Future Racial Composition of the U.S. Population." In *The New Race Question: How the Census Counts Multiracial Individuals,* edited by Joel Perlmann and Mary C. Waters. New York: Russell Sage Foundation.

Eschbach, Karl. 1995. "The Enduring and Vanishing American Indian: American Indian Population Growth and Intermarriage in 1990." *Ethnic and Racial Studies* 18(1): 89–108.

Eschbach, Karl, and Christina Gomez. 1998. "Choosing Hispanic Identity: Ethnic Identity Switching Among Respondents to High School and Beyond." *Social Science Quarterly* 79(1): 74–90.

Eschbach, Karl, Khalil Supple, and C. Matthew Snipp. 1998. "Changes in Racial Identification and the Educational Attainment of American Indians, 1970–1990." *Demography* 35(1): 35–43.

Espiritu, Yen Le. 2004. "Asian American Panethnicity: Contemporary National and Transnational Possibilities." In *Not Just Black and White: Historical and Contemporary Perspectives on Immigration, Race, and Ethnicity,* edited by Nancy Foner and George M. Fredrickson. New York: Russell Sage Foundation.

Farley, Reynolds. 2002. "Racial Identities in 2000: The Response to the Multiple-Race Response Option." In *The New Race Question: How the Census Counts Multiracial Individuals,* edited by Joel Perlmann and Mary C. Waters. New York: Russell Sage Foundation.

———. 2004. "Identifying with Multiple Races: A Social Movement That Succeeded but Failed?" In *The Changing Terrain of Race and Ethnicity,* edited by Maria Krysan and Amanda E. Lewis. New York: Russell Sage Foundation.

———. 2009. "Residential Segregation in Metropolitan Areas Since 2000." Unpublished paper. Presented at the annual conference of the Population Association of America. Detroit (April 30).

Feagin, Joe R. 1991. "The Continuing Significance of Race: Antiblack Discrimination in Public Places." *American Sociological Review* 56(1): 101–16.

Fields, Barbara J. 1990. "Slavery, Race and Ideology in the United States of America." *New Left Review* 181(May–June): 95–118.

———. 2001. "Whiteness, Racism, and Identity." *International Labor and Working-Class History* 60(October): 48–56.

———. 2003. "Of Rogues and Geldings." *American Historical Review* 108(5): 1397–1495.

Foley, Neil. 1998. "Becoming Hispanic: Mexican Americans and the Faustian Pact with Whiteness." In *Reflexiones 1997: New Directions in Mexican American Studies,* edited by Neil Foley. Austin: University of Texas Press, Center for Mexican American Studies.

Foner, Eric. 2006. *Forever Free: The Story of Emancipation and Reconstruction.* New York: Alfred A. Knopf.

Foner, Nancy. 2000. *From Ellis Island to JFK: New York's Two Great Waves of Immigration.* New Haven and New York: Yale University Press and Russell Sage Foundation.

———. 2005. *In A New Land: A Comparative View of Immigration.* New York: New York University Press.

Foner, Nancy, and George M. Fredrickson, eds. 2004. *Not Just Black and White: Historical and Contemporary Perspectives on Immigration, Race, and Ethnicity in the United States.* New York: Russell Sage Foundation.

Forman, Tyrone A., Carla Goar, and Amanda E. Lewis. 2004. "Neither Black nor White?" *Race and Society* 5(1): 65–84.

Fossett, Mark A. 2005. "Urban and Spatial Demography." In *Handbook of Population,* edited by Dudley L. Poston, Jr., and Michael Micklin. New York: Kluwer Academic Publishers.

Fossett, Mark A., and M. Therese Seibert. 1997. *Long Time Coming: Trends in Racial Inequality in the Nonmetropolitan South Since 1940.* Boulder: Westview Press.

Fredrickson, George M. 2000. *The Comparative Imagination: On the History of Racism, Nationalism, and Social Movements.* Berkeley: University of California Press.

———. 2002. *Racism: A Short History.* Princeton: Princeton University Press.

Fryer, Roland G. 2007. "Guess Who's Been Coming to Dinner? Trends in Interracial Marriage over the 20th Century." *Journal of Economic Perspectives* 21(2): 71–90.

Fu, Vincent Kang. 2001. "Racial Intermarriage Pairings." *Demography* 38(2): 147–60.

Funderburg, Lise. 1994. *Black, White, Other: Biracial Americans Talk About Race and Identity.* New York: William Morrow.

Gallagher, Charles A. 2004. "Racial Redistricting: Expanding the Boundaries of Whiteness." In *The Politics of Multiracialism: Challenging Racial Thinking,* edited by Heather M. Dalmage. Albany: State University of New York Press.

Gans, Herbert J. 1979. "Symbolic Ethnicity: The Future of Ethnic Groups and Cultures in America." *Ethnic and Racial Studies* 2(1): 1–20.

———. 1999. "The Possibility of a New Racial Hierarchy in the Twenty-First-Century United States." In *The Cultural Territories of Race: Black and White Boundaries,* edited by Michèle Lamont. Chicago and New York: University of Chicago Press and Russell Sage Foundation.

———. 2005. "Race as a Class." *Contexts* 4(4): 17–21.

Gerstle, Gary. 1999. "Liberty, Coercion, and the Making of Americans." In *The Handbook of International Migration,* edited by Charles Hirschman, Josh DeWind, and Philip Kasinitz. New York: Russell Sage Foundation.

———. 2001. *American Crucible: Race and Nation in the Twentieth Century.* Princeton: Princeton University Press.

Gilbertson, Greta A., Joseph P. Fitzpatrick, and Lijun Yang. 1996. "Hispanic Intermarriage in New York City: New Evidence from 1991." *International Migration Review* 30(2): 445–59.

Gitlin, Todd. 1995. *The Twilight of Common Dreams.* New York: Metropolitan.

Glazer, Nathan. 1997. *We Are All Multiculturalists Now.* Cambridge, Mass.: Harvard University Press.

Godfrey, Brian J. 1988. *Neighborhoods in Transition: The Making of San Francisco's Ethnic and Nonconformist Communities.* Berkeley: University of California Press.

Goldberg, David T. 1997. *Racial Subjects: Writing on Race in America.* New York: Routledge.

Goldstein, Joshua R. 1999. "Kinship Networks That Cross Racial Lines: The Exception or the Rule?" *Demography* 36(3): 399–407.

Gordon, Milton M. 1964. *Assimilation in American Life: The Role of Race, Religion, and National Origins.* New York: Oxford University Press.

Grant, Madison. 1916. *The Passing of the Great Race.* New York: C. Scribner.

Grewal, David Singh. 2008. *Network Power: The Social Dynamics of Globalization.* New Haven: Yale University Press.

Guglielmo, Thomas. 2003. *White on Arrival: Italians, Race, Color, and Power in Chicago, 1890–1945.* New York: Oxford University Press.

Hacker, Andrew. 1992/1995. *Two Nations: Black and White, Separate, Hostile, Unequal.* New York: Ballantine Books.

Hall, Christine C. Iijima. 1992. "Please Choose One: Ethnic Identity Choices for Biracial Individuals." In *Racially Mixed People in America,* edited by Maria P. P. Root. Newbury Park, Calif.: Sage Publications.

Handlin, Oscar. 1951/1973. *The Uprooted: The Epic Story of the Great Migrations That Made the American People.* Boston: Little, Brown.

Haney-Lopez, Ian. 1996. *White by Law: The Legal Construction of Race.* New York: New York University Press.

Harris, David. 1994. "The 1990 Census Count of American Indians: What Do the Numbers Really Mean?" *Social Science Quarterly* 75(3): 580–93.

Harris, David R., and Jeremiah J. Sim. 2002. "Who is Multiracial? Assessing the Complexity of Lived Race." *American Sociological Review* 67(4): 614–27.

Harrison, Roderick J. 2002. "Inadequacies of Multiple-Response Race Data in the Federal Statistical System." In *The New Race Question: How the Census Counts Multiracial Individuals,* edited by Joel Perlmann and Mary C. Waters. New York: Russell Sage Foundation.

Herring, Cedric. 2009. "Does Diversity Pay? Race, Gender, and the Business Case for Diversity." *American Sociological Review* 74(2): 208–24.

Higham, John. 1963. *Strangers in the Land: Patterns of American Nativism 1860–1925.* New York: Atheneum.

Hirschman, Charles, Richard D. Alba, and Reynolds Farley. 2000. "The Meaning and Measurement of Race in the U.S. Census: Glimpses into the Future." *Demography* 37(3): 381–93.

Hirschman, Charles, and Douglas S. Massey. 2008. "Places and People: The New American Mosaic." In *New Faces in New Places: The Changing Geography of American Immigration,* edited by Douglas S. Massey. New York: Russell Sage Foundation.

Hitlin, Steven, J. Scott Brown, and Glen H. Elder. 2007. "Measuring Latinos: Racial vs. Ethnic Classification and Self-Understandings." *Social Forces* 86(2): 587–611.

Hochschild, Jennifer L. 1996. *Facing Up to the American Dream: Race, Class, and the Soul of the Nation.* Princeton: Princeton University Press.

Hollinger, David A. 1995. *Postethnic America: Beyond Multiculturalism.* New York: Basic Books.

———. 2003. "Amalgamation and Hypodescent: The Question of Ethnoracial Mixture in the History of the United States." *American Historical Review* 108(5): 1363–90.

———. 2008. "Obama, the Instability of Color Lines, and the Promise of a Postethnic Future." *Callaloo* 31(4): 1033–37.

Huntington, Samuel P. 2004. *Who Are We? The Challenges to America's National Identity.* New York: Simon & Schuster.

Hwang, Sean-Shong, Rogelio Saenz, and Benigno E. Aguirre. 1994. "Structural and Individual Determinants of Outmarriage Among Chinese-, Filipino-, and Japanese-Americans in California." *Sociological Inquiry* 64(4): 396–414.

———. 1997. "Structural and Assimilationist Explanations of Asian American Intermarriage." *Journal of Marriage and the Family.* 59(3): 758–72.

Iceland, John. 2009. *Where We Live Now: Immigration and Race in the United States.* Berkeley: University of California Press.

Ignatiev, Noel. 1995. *How the Irish Became White.* New York: Routledge.

Itzigsohn, José. 2004. "The Formation of Latino and Latina Panethnic Identities." In *Not Just Black and White: Historical and Contemporary Perspectives on Immigration, Race, and Ethnicity,* edited by Nancy Foner and George M. Fredrickson. New York: Russell Sage Foundation.

———. 2009. *Encountering American Faultlines: Race, Class, and the Dominican Experience in Providence.* New York: Russell Sage Foundation.

Jacobs, Jerry A., and Teresa G. Labov. 2002. "Gender Differentials in Intermarriage Among Sixteen Race and Ethnic Groups." *Sociological Forum* 17(4): 621–46.

Jacobson, Matthew Frye. 1998. *Whiteness of a Different Color: European Immigrants and the Alchemy of Race.* Cambridge, Mass.: Harvard University Press.

Jacoby, Tamar. 2001. "An End to Counting Race?" *Commentary* 111(6): 37–40.

Jaynes, Gerald D., ed. 2000. *Immigration and Race: New Challenges for American Democracy.* New Haven: Yale University Press.

Jaynes, Gerald D., and Robin M. Williams. 1989. *A Common Destiny: Blacks and American Society.* Washington, D.C.: National Academies Press.

Jiménez, Tomás. 2004. "Negotiating Ethnic Boundaries." *Ethnicities* 4(1): 75–97.

———. 2009. *Replenished Ethnicity: Mexican Americans, Immigration, and Identity.* Berkeley: University of California Press.

Kalmijn, Matthijs. 1991. "Status Homogamy in the United States." *American Journal of Sociology* 97(2): 496–523.

———. 1993. "Trends in Black-White Intermarriage." *Social Forces* 72(1): 119–46.

———. 1998. "Intermarriage and Homogamy—Causes, Patterns, Trends." *Annual Review of Sociology* 23(August): 395–421.

Kashima, Tetsuden. 1997. *Personal Justice Denied: The Report of the Commission on Wartime Relocation and Internment of Civilians.* Seattle: University of Washington Press.

Kasinitz, Philip. 1992. *Caribbean New York.* Ithaca: Cornell University Press.

Kasinitz, Philip, John Mollenkopf, and Mary C. Waters. 2002. "Becoming American/Becoming New Yorkers: Immigrant Incorporation in a Majority Minority City." *International Migration Review* 36(4): 1020–36.

Kasinitz, Philip, John H. Mollenkopf, Mary C. Waters, and Jennifer Holdaway. 2008. *Inheriting the City: The Children of Immigrants Come of Age.* New York: Russell Sage Foundation and Harvard University Press.

Kasinitz, Philip, and Jan Rosenberg. 1996. "Missing the Connection: Social Isolation and Employment on the Brooklyn Waterfront." *Social Problems* 43(2): 180–96.

Katz, Michael B., and Mark J. Stern. 2006. *One Nation Divisible: What America Was and What It Is Becoming.* New York: Russell Sage Foundation.

Kaufman, Robert L. 2001. "Race and Labor Market Segmentation." In *Sourcebook of Labor Markets: Evolving Structures and Processes,* edited by Ivar Berg and Arne L. Kalleberg. New York: Kluwer Academic Publishers.

Kennedy, Randall. 2003a. *Nigger: The Strange Career of a Troublesome Word.* New York: Vintage Books.

———. 2003b. *Interracial Intimacies: Sex, Marriage, Identity, and Adoption.* New York: Pantheon Books.

Kertzer, David I., and Dominique Arel. 2002. "Censuses, Identity, and the Struggle for Political Power." In *Census and Identity: The Politics of Race, Ethnicity, and Language in National Censuses,* edited by David I. Kertzer and Dominique Arel. New York: Cambridge University Press.

Kibria, Nazli. 2002. *Becoming Asian American: Second-Generation Chinese and Korean American Identities.* Baltimore: Johns Hopkins University Press.

Kirschenman, Joleen, and Kathryn M. Neckerman. 1991. " 'We'd Love to Hire Them, But . . .': The Meaning of Race for Employers." In *The Urban Underclass,* edited by Christopher Jencks and Paul E. Peterson. Washington, D.C.: Brookings Institution.

Klein, Kerwin Lee. 1997. *Frontiers of Historical Imagination: Narrating the European Conquest of Native America, 1890–1990.* Berkeley: University of California Press.

Korgen, Kathleen O. 1998. *From Black to Biracial: Transforming Racial Identity Among Americans.* Westport, Conn.: Praeger.

Lacy, Karyn R. 2007. *Blue-Chip Black: Race, Class, and Status in the New Black Middle Class.* Berkeley: University of California Press.

Lamont, Michèle. 1992. *Money, Morals, and Manners: The Culture of the French and the American Upper-Middle Class.* Chicago: University of Chicago Press.

———. 2000. *The Dignity of Working Men.* Cambridge, Mass., and New York: Harvard University Press and Russell Sage Foundation.

Lamont, Michèle, and Virag Molnár. 2002. "The Study of Boundaries in the Social Sciences." *Annual Review of Sociology* 28(August): 167–95.

Laumann, Edward O. 1973. *Bonds of Pluralism: The Form and Substance of Urban Social Networks.* New York: John Wiley.

Laumann, Edward O., John H. Gagnon, Robert T. Michael, and Stuart Michaels. 1994. *The Social Organization of Sexuality: Sexual Practices in the United States.* Chicago: University of Chicago Press.

Leach, Mark A., and Frank D. Bean. 2008. "The Structure and Dynamics of Mexican Migration to New Destinations in the United States." In *New Faces in New Places: The Changing Geography of American Immigration,* edited by Douglas S. Massey. New York: Russell Sage Foundation.

Lee, Jennifer. 2002. *Civility in the City: Blacks, Jews, and Koreans in Urban America.* Cambridge, Mass.: Harvard University Press.

———. 2005. "Who We Are: America Becoming and Becoming American." *Du Bois Review* 2(2): 287–302.

Lee, Jennifer, and Frank D. Bean. 2004. "America's Changing Color Lines: Immigration, Race/Ethnicity, and Multiracial Identification." *Annual Review of Sociology* 30(August): 221–42.

———. 2007. "Reinventing the Color Line: Immigration and America's New Racial/Ethnic Divide." *Social Forces* 86(2): 561–86.

Lee, Jennifer, and Min Zhou. 2004. *Asian American Youth: Culture, Identity, and Ethnicity.* New York: Routledge.

Lee, Sharon M., and Barry Edmonston. 2005. "New Marriages, New Families: U.S. Racial and Hispanic Intermarriage." *Population Bulletin* 60(2): 1–36.

Lee, Sharon M., and Marilyn Fernandez. 1998. "Trends in Asian American Racial/Ethnic Intermarriage: A Comparison of 1980 and 1990 Census Data." *Sociological Perspectives* 41(2): 323–42.

Liang, Zai, and Naomi Ito. 1999. "Intermarriage of Asian Americans in the New York City Region: Contemporary Patterns and Future Prospects." *International Migration Review* 33(4): 876–900.

Lieberson, Stanley. 1980. *A Piece of the Pie: Blacks and White Immigrants Since 1880.* Berkeley: University of California Press.

Lieberson, Stanley, and Mary C. Waters. 1988. *From Many Strands: Ethnic and Racial Groups in Contemporary America.* New York: Russell Sage Foundation.

Link, Michael W., and Robert W. Oldendick. 1996. "Social Construction and White Attitudes Toward Equal Opportunity and Multiculturalism." *Journal of Politics* 58(1): 149–68.

Loewen, James. 1971. *The Mississippi Chinese: Between Black and White.* Cambridge, Mass.: Harvard University Press.

López, David. 2009. "Thither the Flock: The Catholic Church and the Success of Mexicans in America." In *Immigration and Religion in America:*

Comparative and Historical Perspectives, edited by Richard Alba, Albert Raboteau, and Josh DeWind. New York: New York University Press.

Loury, Glenn C. 2002. *The Anatomy of Racial Inequality.* Cambridge, Mass.: Harvard University Press.

Loveman, Mara, and Jeronimo O. Muniz. 2007. "How Puerto Rico Became White: Boundary Dynamics and Inter-Census Reclassification." *American Sociological Review* 72(6): 915–39.

Martin, Elizabeth, Theresa DeMaio, and Pamela C. Campanelli. 1990. "Context Effects for Census Measures of Race and Hispanic Origin." *Public Opinion Quarterly* 54(4): 551–66.

Massey, Douglas S. 2007. *Categorically Unequal: The American Stratification System.* New York: Russell Sage Foundation.

———, ed. 2008. *New Faces in New Places: The Changing Geography of American Immigration.* New York: Russell Sage Foundation.

Massey, Douglas S., and Chiara Capoferro. 2008. "The Geographic Diversification of American Immigration." In *New Faces in New Places: The Changing Geography of American Immigration,* edited by Douglas S. Massey. New York: Russell Sage Foundation.

Massey, Douglas S., and Nancy A. Denton. 1993. *American Apartheid: Segregation and the Making of the Underclass.* Cambridge, Mass.: Harvard University Press.

Massey, Douglas S., Margarita Mooney, Kimberley C. Torres, and Camille Z. Charles. 2007. "Black Immigrants and Black Natives Attending Selective Colleges and Universities in the United States." *American Journal of Education* 113(2): 243–71.

Massey, Garth, Randy Hodson, and Dusko Sekulic. 1999. "Ethnic Enclaves and Intolerance: The Case of Yugoslavia." *Social Forces* 78(2): 669–93.

Moran, Rachel F. 2001. *Interracial Intimacy: The Regulation of Race and Romance.* Chicago: University of Chicago Press.

Morning, Ann. 2000. "Counting on the Color Line." Paper presented at the Annual Meeting of the Population Association of America. Los Angeles (March 23–25).

Morris, Aldon D. 1984. *Origins of the Civil Rights Movement: Black Communities Organizing for Change.* New York: Simon & Schuster.

Moss, Philip, and Chris Tilly. 2001. "Hiring in Urban Labor Markets: Shifting Labor Demands, Persistent Racial Differences." In *Sourcebook of Labor Markets: Evolving Structures and Processes,* edited by Ivar Berg and Arne L. Kalleberg. New York: Kluwer Academic Publishers.

Murguia, Edward, and Rogelio Saenz. 2004. "An Analysis of the Latin-americanization of Race in the United States." *Race and Society* 5(1): 85–101.

Myers, Dowell. 2007. *Immigrants and Boomers: Forging a New Social Contract for the Future of America.* New York: Russell Sage Foundation.

Myrdal, Gunnar. 1944. *An American Dilemma: The Negro Problem and Modern Democracy.* New York: Harper.

Nagel, Joane. 1994. "Constructing Ethnicity: Creating and Recreating Ethnic Identity and Culture." *Social Problems* 41(1): 152–76.

Nakashima, Cynthia L. 1992. "An Invisible Monster: The Creation and Denial of Mixed-Race People in America." In *Racially Mixed People in America,* edited by Maria P. P. Root. Newbury Park, Calif.: Sage Publications.

Nash, Gary B. 1995. "The Hidden History of Mestizo America." *Journal of American History* 83(3): 941–64.

Nevins, Allan. 1962. *The Origins of the Land-Grant Colleges and Universities.* Washington, D.C.: Civil War Centennial Commission.

Ngai, Mae M. 2005. *Impossible Subjects: Illegal Aliens and the Making of Modern America.* Princeton: Princeton University Press.

Nightingale, Carl H. 2008. "Before Race Mattered: Geographies of the Color Line in Early Colonial Madras and New York." *American Historical Review* 113(1): 48–71.

Nobles, Melissa. 2000. *Shades of Citizenship: Race and the Census in Modern Politics.* Palo Alto: Stanford University Press.

———. 2002. "Racial Categorization and Censuses." In *Census and Identity: The Politics of Race, Ethnicity, and Language in National Censuses,* edited by David I. Kertzer and Dominique Arel. New York: Cambridge University Press.

Okamura, Jonathan. 1981. "Situational Ethnicity." *Ethnic and Racial Studies* 4(4): 452–65.

Okihiro, Gary Y. 1994. *Margins and Mainstreams: Asians in American History and Culture.* Seattle: University of Washington Press.

Oliver, Melvin L., and Thomas Shapiro. 1995. *Black Wealth/White Wealth: A New Perspective on Racial Inequality.* New York: Routledge.

Omi, Michael, and Howard Winant. 1994. *Racial Formation in the United States: From the 1960s to the 1980s.* New York: Routledge.

Padilla, Felix M. 1985. *Latino Ethnic Consciousness: The Case of Mexican Americans and Puerto Ricans in Chicago.* Notre Dame, Ind.: University of Notre Dame Press.

Page, Scott E. 2007. *The Difference—How the Power of Diversity Creates Better Groups, Firms, Schools, and Societies.* Princeton: Princeton University Press.

Pagnini, Deanna L., and S. Philip Morgan. 1990. "Intermarriage and Social Distance Among U.S. Immigrants at the Turn of the Century." *American Journal of Sociology* 96(2): 405–32.

Park, Robert E., and Ernest W. Burgess. 1921. *Introduction to the Science of Sociology.* Chicago: University of Chicago Press.

Patterson, Orlando. 1997. *The Ordeal of Integration: Progress and Resentment in America's "Racial" Crises.* Washington, D.C.: Counterpoint.

———. 2009. "A Job Too Big for One Man." *New York Times,* November 4, A25.

Pattillo-McCoy, Mary. 1999. *Black Picket Fences: Privilege and Peril Among the Black Middle Class.* Chicago: University of Chicago Press.

Perlmann, Joel. 2000. "Reflecting the Changing Face of America: Multiracials, Racial Classification, and American Intermarriage." In *Interracialism: Black-White Intermarriage in American History, Literature, and Law,* edited by Werner Sollors. New York: Oxford University Press.

Perlmann, Joel, and Roger Waldinger. 1997. "Second Generation Decline? Children of Immigrants, Past and Present—A Reconsideration." *International Migration Review* 31(4): 893–922.

Perlmann, Joel, and Mary C. Waters. 2004. "Intermarriage Then and Now: Race, Generation, and the Changing Meaning of Marriage." In *Not Just Black and White: Historical and Contemporary Perspectives on Immigration, Race, and Ethnicity in the United States,* edited by Nancy Foner and George M. Fredrickson. New York: Russell Sage Foundation.

Pew Research Center. 2007. "Blacks See Growing Values Gap Between Poor and Middle Class." A Social and Demographic Trends Report. Washington, D.C.: Pew Research Center, November 13.

Porterfield, Ernest. 1978. *Black and White Mixed Marriages.* Chicago: Nelson-Hall.

Portes, Alejandro, Patricia Fernández-Kelly, and William Haller. 2005. "Segmented Assimilation on the Ground: The New Second Generation in Early Adulthood." *Ethnic and Racial Studies* 28(6): 1000–1040.

Portes, Alejandro, and Rubén G. Rumbaut. 2001. *Legacies: The Story of the Immigrant Second Generation.* Berkeley and New York: University of California Press and Russell Sage Foundation.

Prewitt, Kenneth. 2002. "Race in the 2000 Census: A Turning Point." In *The New Race Question: How the Census Counts Multiracial Individuals,* edited by Joel Perlmann and Mary C. Waters. New York: Russell Sage Foundation.

———. 2004. "The Census Counts, the Census Classifies." In *Not Just Black and White: Historical and Contemporary Perspectives on Immigration, Race, and Ethnicity,* edited by Nancy Foner and George M. Fredrickson. New York: Russell Sage Foundation.

Putnam, Robert D. 2007. "*E Pluribus Unum:* Diversity and Community in the Twenty-First Century." The 2006 Johan Skytte Prize Lecture. *Scandinavian Political Studies* 30(2): 137–74.

Qian, Zhenchao. 1997. "Breaking the Racial Barriers: Variations in Interracial Marriage Between 1980 and 1990." *Demography* 34(2): 263–76.

Qian, Zhenchao, and Daniel T. Lichter. 2001. "Measuring Marital Assimilation: Intermarriage Among Natives and Immigrants." *Social Science Research* 30(2): 289–312.

———. 2007. "Social Boundaries and Marital Assimilation: Interpreting Trends in Racial and Ethnic Intermarriage." *American Sociological Review* 72(1): 68–94.

Reimers, David M. 1985/1992. *Still the Golden Door: The Third World Comes to America.* 2nd ed. New York: Columbia University Press.

———. 1998. *Unwelcome Strangers: American Identity and the Turn Against Immigration.* New York: Columbia University Press.

Rockquemore, Kerry Ann, and Patricia Arend. 2003. "Opting for White: Choice, Fluidity, and Black Identity Construction in Post–Civil Rights America." *Race and Society* 5(1): 51–66.

Rodríguez, Clara E. 2000. *Changing Race: Latinos, the Census, and the History of Ethnicity in the United States.* New York: New York University Press.

Rodríguez, Clara E., and Hector Cordero-Guzman. 1992. "Placing Race in Context." *Ethnic and Racial Studies* 15(4): 523–42.

Rodriguez, Gregory. 2007. *Mongrels, Bastards, Orphans, and Vagabonds: Mexican Immigration and the Future of Race in America.* New York: Pantheon Books.

Roediger, David. 1991. *The Wages of Whiteness: Race and the Making of the American Working Class.* New York: Verso.

Romano, Renee C. 2003. *Race Mixing: Black-White Marriage in Postwar America.* Cambridge, Mass.: Harvard University Press.

Root, Maria P. 2001. *Love's Revolution: Interracial Marriage.* Philadelphia: Temple University Press.

Rosenblatt, Paul C., Terri A. Karis, and Richard D. Powell. 1995. *Multiracial Couples: Black and White Voices.* Thousand Oaks, Calif.: Sage.

Rosenfeld, Michael J. 2002. "Measures of Assimilation in the Marriage Market: Mexican Americans 1970–1990." *Journal of Marriage and the Family* 64(1): 152–62.

Roth, Wendy D. 2005. "The End of the One-Drop Rule? Labeling of Multiracial Children in Black Intermarriages." *Sociological Forum* 20(1): 35–67.

Ruggles, Steven, Matthew Sobek, Trent Alexander, Catherine A. Fitch, Ronald Goeken, Patricia Kelly Hall, Miriam King, and Chad Ronnander. 2009. "Integrated Public Use Microdata Series: Version 4.0." Machine-readable database. Produced and distributed by Minnesota Population Center, Minneapolis.

Saenz, Rogelio, and Benigno E. Aguirre. 1991. "The Dynamics of Mexican Ethnic Identity." *Ethnic Groups* 9(1): 17–32.

Saenz, Rogelio, Sean-Shong Hwang, Benigno E. Aguirre, and Robert N. Anderson. 1995. "Persistence and Change in Asian Identity Among Children of Intermarried Couples." *Sociological Perspectives* 38(2): 175–94.

Sakamoto, Arthur, Jen Liu, and Jessie M. Tzeng. 1998. "The Declining Significance of Race Among Chinese and Japanese American Men." *Research in Social Stratification and Mobility* 16: 225–46.

Saldaña-Portillo, María Josefina. 2008. " 'How Many Mexicans Is a Horse Worth?' The League of United Latin American Citizens, Desegregation Cases, and Chicano Historiography." *South Atlantic Quarterly* 107(4): 809–31.

Sampson, Robert J. 2009. "Disparity and Diversity in the Contemporary City: Social (dis)order Revisited." *British Journal of Sociology* 60(1): 1–31.

Sandefur, Gary D., and Trudy McKinnell. 1986. "American Indian Inter-marriage." *Social Science Research* 15(4): 347–71.

Sanjek, Roger. 1994. "Intermarriage and the Future of the Races." In *Race,* edited by Steven Gregory and Roger Sanjek. New Brunswick, N.J.: Rutgers University Press.

Sayler, Lucy E. 1995. *Laws Harsh as Tigers: Chinese Immigrants and the Shaping of Modern Immigration Law.* Chapel Hill: University of North Carolina Press.

Schlesinger, Arthur M., Jr. 1992. *The Disuniting of America: Reflections on a Multicultural Society.* New York: Norton.

Schoen, Robert, and Barbara Thomas. 1989. "Intergroup Marriage in Hawaii, 1969–71 and 1979–81." *Sociological Perspectives* 32(3): 365–82.

Schuck, Peter H. 2003. *Diversity in America: Keeping Government at a Safe Distance.* Cambridge, Mass.: Harvard University Press.

Schwartzman, Luisa Farah. 2007. "Does Money Whiten? Intergenerational Changes in Racial Classification in Brazil." *American Sociological Review* 72(6): 940–63.

Sears, David O., Mingying Fu, P. J. Henry, and Kerra Bui. 2003. "The Origins and Persistence of Ethnic Identity Among the 'New Immigrant' Groups." *Social Psychology Quarterly* 66(4): 419–37.

Sewell, William H., Jr. 1992. "A Theory of Structure: Duality, Agency, and Transformation." *American Journal of Sociology* 98(1): 1–29.

Skerry, Peter. 1993. *Mexican Americans: The Ambivilent Minority.* Cambridge, Mass.: Harvard University Press.

———. 2002. "Multiracialism and the Administrative State." In *The New Race Question: How the Census Counts Multiracial Individuals,* edited by Joel Perlmann and Mary C. Waters. New York: Russell Sage Foundation.

Skrentny, John. 2001a. *Color Lines: Affirmative Action, Immigration, and Civil Rights Options for America.* Chicago: University of Chicago Press.

———. 2001b. "Affirmative Action and New Demographic Realities." *Chronicle of Higher Education,* February 16, B7–B10.

———. 2002. *The Minority Rights Revolution.* Cambridge, Mass.: Harvard University Press.

———. 2008. "Culture and Race/Ethnicity: Bolder, Deeper, and Broader." *The Annals of the American Academy of Political and Social Science* 619(September): 59–77.

Small, Mario Luis. 2009. "How Many Cases Do I Need? On Science and the Logic of Case Selection in Field-Based Research." *Ethnography* 10(5): 5–38.

Smelser, Neil J., and Jeffrey C. Alexander. 1999. *Diversity and Its Discontents: Cultural Conflict and Common Ground in Contemporary American Society.* Princeton: Princeton University Press.

Smelser, Neil J., William Julius Wilson, and Faith Mitchell. 2001. *America Becoming: Racial Patterns and Their Consequences.* Washington, D.C.: National Academies Press.

Smith, James P. 2003. "Assimilation Across Latino Generations." *American Economic Review* 93(2): 315–19.

———. 2006. "Immigrants and the Labor Market." *Journal of Labor Economics* 24(2): 203–33.

Smith, James P., and Barry Edmonston. 1997. *The New Americans: Economic, Demographic, and Fiscal Effects of Immigration.* Washington, D.C.: National Academies Press.

Smith, Sandra, and Mignon R. Moore. 2000. "Intraracial Diversity and Relations Among African Americans: A Case Study of Feelings of Closeness Among Black Students at a Predominantly White University." *American Journal of Sociology* 106(1): 1–39.

Song, Miri. 2009. "Is Intermarriage a Good Indicator of Integration?" *Journal of Ethnic and Migration Studies* 35(2): 331–48.

Spencer, Jon Michael. 1997. *The New Colored People: The Mixed-Race Movement in America.* New York: New York University Press.

Spickard, Paul R. 1989. *Mixed Blood: Intermarriage and Ethnic Identity in Twentieth-Century America.* Madison: University of Wisconsin Press.

Stephan, Cookie White, and Walter G. Stephan. 1989. "After Intermarriage: Ethnic Identity Among Mixed-Heritage Japanese-Americans and Hispanics." *Journal of Marriage and the Family* 51: 507–19.

Tafoya, Sonya M., Hans Johnson, and Laura E. Hill. 2005. "Who Chooses to Choose Two?" In *The American People: Census 2000,* edited by Reynolds Farley and John Haaga. New York: Russell Sage Foundation.

Takaki, Ronald T. 1979. *Iron Cages: Race and Culture in Nineteenth-Century America.* Seattle: University of Washington Press.

———. 1989. *Strangers from a Different Shore: A History of Asian Americans.* Boston: Little, Brown.

Telles, Edward E. 2004. *Race in Another America: The Significance of Skin Color in Brazil.* Princeton: Princeton University Press.

Telles, Edward E., and Vilma Ortiz. 2008. *Generations of Exclusions: Racial Assimilation and Mexican Americans.* New York: Russell Sage Foundation.

Telles, Edward E., and Christina A. Sue. 2009. "Race Mixture: Boundary Crossing in Comparative Perspective." *Annual Review of Sociology* 35: 129–46.

Thernstrom, Stephan, and Abigail Thernstrom. 1997. *America in Black and White: One Nation, Indivisible.* New York: Simon & Schuster.

Tizard, Barbara, and Ann Phoenix. 1993. *Black, White or Mixed Race? Race and Racism in the Lives of Young People of Mixed Parentage.* New York: Routledge.

Tucker, M. Belinda, and Claudia Mitchell-Kernan. 1990. "New Trends in Black American Interracial Marriage: The Social Structural Context." *Journal of Marriage and the Family* 52(February): 209–18.

Turner, Frederick Jackson. 1893. "The Significance of the Frontier in American History." *Annual Report of the American Historical Association.* Washington, D.C.: American Historical Association.

———. 1920. *The Frontier in American History.* New York: Holt, Rinehart & Winston.

Twine, France Winddance. 1996. "Brown-Skinned White Girls." *Gender, Place, and Culture* 3(2): 205–24.

U.S. Bureau of the Census. 2000. "Foreign-Born Population of the United States; Current Population Survey—March 2000; Revised Detailed Tables—Weighted to Census 2000 (PPL-160)." Washington: U.S. Bureau of Census. Available at: www.census.gov/population/www/socdemo/foreign/ppl-160.html.

———. 2001. *United States Census 2000.* Washington.: U.S. Government Printing Office.

U.S. Bureau of the Census, Population Division, Ethnic and Hispanic Statistics Branch. 2002. "Foreign-Born Population of the United States. Current Population Survey—March 2000; Detailed Tables." Vol. 2/2002. Washington: U.S. Government Printing Office.

U.S. Immigration and Naturalization Service. 2002. *Statistical Yearbook of the U.S. Immigration and Naturalization Service, 2001.* Washington: U.S. Government Printing Office.

———. 2003. *Statistical Yearbook of the U.S. Immigration and Naturalization Service, 2002.* Washington: U.S. Government Printing Office.

U.S. Office of Immigration Statistics. 2009. *Statistical Yearbook 2008.* Washington: U.S. Department of Homeland Security.

Van Hook, Jennifer, and Frank D. Bean. 2009. "Explaining Mexican-Immigrant Welfare Behaviors: The Importance of Employment-Related Cultural Repertoires." *American Sociological Review* 74(3): 423–44.

Volpp, Leti. 2003. "American Mestizo: Filipinos and Anti-Miscegenation Laws in California." In *Mixed Race in America and the Law,* edited by Kevin R. Johnson. New York: New York University Press.

Waldinger, Roger. 1996. *Still the Promised City? African-Americans and New Immigrants in Postindustrial New York.* Cambridge, Mass.: Harvard University Press.

———. 1999. "Network, Bureaucracy, and Exclusion: Recruitment and Selection in an Immigrant Metropolis." In *Immigration and Opportunity: Race, Ethnicity, and Employment in the United States,* edited by Frank D. Bean and Stephanie Bell-Rose. New York: Russell Sage Foundation.

Waldinger, Roger, and Jennifer Lee. 2001. "New Immigrants in Urban America." In *Strangers at the Gates: New Immigrants in Urban America,* edited by Roger Waldinger. Berkeley: University of California Press.

Waldinger, Roger, and Michael I. Lichter. 2003. *How the Other Half Works: Immigration and the Social Organization of Labor.* Berkeley: University of California Press.

Warren, Jonathan W., and France Winddance Twine. 1997. "White Americans, the New Minority?" *Journal of Black Studies* 28(2): 200–18.

Waters, Mary C. 1990. *Ethnic Options: Choosing Identities in America.* Berkeley: University of California Press.

———. 1999a. *Black Identities: West Indian Immigrant Dreams and American Realities.* New York and Cambridge, Mass.: Russell Sage Foundation and Harvard University Press.

———. 1999b. "West Indians and African American at Work: Structural Differences and Cultural Stereotypes." In *Immigration and Opportunity: Race, Ethnicity, and Employment in the United States,* edited by Frank D. Bean and Stephanie Bell-Rose. New York: Russell Sage Foundation.

———. 2000. "Multiple Ethnicities and Identity in the United States." In *We Are a People: Narrative and Multiplicity in Constructing Identity,* edited by Paul R. Spickard and W. Jeffrey Burroughs. Philadelphia: Temple University Press.

Western, Bruce. 2006. *Punishment and Inequality in America.* New York: Russell Sage Foundation.

Western, Bruce, and Christopher Wildeman. 2009. "The Black Family and Mass Incarceration." *Annals of the American Academy of Political and Social Science* 621(January): 221–42.

Williams, Kim. 2006. *Mark One or More.* Ann Arbor: University of Michigan Press.

Wilson, Anne. 1981. "In Between: The Mother in the Interracial Family." *New Community* 9(2): 208–15.

Wimmer, Andreas. 2008. "The Making and Unmaking of Ethnic Boundaries: A Multilevel Process Theory." *American Journal of Sociology* 113(4): 970–1022.

Wood, Peter B. 2003. *Diversity: The Invention of a Concept.* San Francisco: Encounter Books.

Xie, Yu, and Kimberly Goyette. 1997. "The Racial Identification of Biracial Children with One Asian Parent: Evidence from the 1990 Census." *Social Forces* 76(2): 547–70.

Yancey, George. 2003. *Who Is White?* Boulder: Lynne Rienner.

———. 2007. "Experiencing Racism: Differences in the Experiences of Whites Married to Blacks and Non-Black Racial Minorities." *Journal of Comparative Family Studies* 38(2): 197–214.

Yancey, William L., Eugene P. Ericksen, and Richard N. Juliani. 1976. "Emergent Ethnicity: A Review and Reformulation." *American Sociological Review* 41(3): 391–402.

Zhou, Min. 2004. "Are Asian Americans Becoming 'White'?" *Contexts* 3(1): 29–37.

Zhou, Min, and Carl L. Bankston. 1998. *Growing Up American: How Vietnamese Children Adapt to Life in the United States.* New York: Russell Sage Foundation.

Zhou, Min, and Jennifer Lee. 2007. "Becoming Ethnic or Becoming American? Reflecting on the Divergent Pathways to Social Mobility and Assimilation Among the New Second Generation." *Du Bois Review* 4(1): 189–205.

Zhou, Min, and John R. Logan. 1991. "In and Out of Chinatown: Residential Mobility and Segregation of New York City's Chinese." *Social Forces* 70(2): 387–407.

Zolberg, Aristide R. 2006. *A Nation by Design: Immigration Policy in the Fashioning of America.* New York: Russell Sage Foundation.

~ Index ~